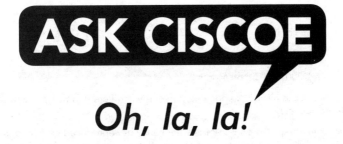

ASK CISCOE

Oh, la, la!

Your Gardening Questions Answered

Ciscoe Morris

SASQUATCH BOOKS
SEATTLE

To DB and Sal, who taught me to love life and to tell a good story, and to my wife, Mary, and my two pups, Fred and Ruby, who've had to listen to way too many of them.

Printed in the United States of America
Published by Sasquatch Books
Distributed by Publishers Group West
15 14 13 12 11 10 09 08   9 8 7

Cover photograph(s): Marco Prozzo (Ciscoe Morris)
                      N joy Neish / Dreamstime.com (Old Watering Can)
                      Kirsty Mosaner / Dreamstime.com (Pink lotus flowers)
Cover design: Kate Basart
Interior photos: Marco Prozzo
Interior composition and design: Bob Suh

Library of Congress Cataloging-in-Publication Data is available.

ISBN 1-57061-432-6

Sasquatch Books
119 South Main Street, Suite 400
Seattle, WA 98104
(206) 467-4300
www.sasquatchbooks.com
custserv@sasquatchbooks.com

Contents

Introduction

The real plant expert is the person who has murdered the most plants.

That makes me uniquely qualified to write this book. Don't get me wrong: I have plenty of credentials. I hold a degree from a horticulture college and a master's degree in public administration, and I've been a longtime Master Gardener, an International Society of Arboriculture Certified Arborist, and a Washington State Nursery & Landscape Association Certified Horticulturist. But my real expertise comes from just doing it. My goal is to have one of every plant on earth in my garden before I die, and I'm only about halfway there. At the moment there isn't room for one more plant in my garden! Well, maybe one, or two, or . . . One thing I can guarantee is that I test everything in my own garden before I tell you that it works.

I've learned lots about gardening by attending many horticultural trainings and lectures, as well as by experiencing successes in the garden, but the truth of the matter is I've learned the most from making mistakes. Even my earliest interest in gardening came from a slight boo-boo. When I was nine years old, we lived next door to the prize peony grower in Wischeescin. It just so happened that I was also a budding baseball star. Two days before the big peony judging at the state fair, I hit every bud off the neighbor's plant for a home run. My punishment was to help my neighbor in her garden, but she burst into tears every time she looked at me. That's when I began to realize there must be something valuable about flowers.

Speaking of Wischeescin, you'll notice that throughout the book I've thrown in a few Ciscoe-isms here and there. All my life I've made up words. One such word is *el kabatski*, the act of placing a harmful insect between thumb and forefinger and proclaiming "El kabatski!" as you squish it. Interestingly, I received an email from someone who ran across the term on my website and wanted to know its origin. His email was signed Bob Kabatski.

My career actually began at age ten, when I harassed the priest at a local church to hire me as the lawn boy. Old Joe the gardener wasn't happy about being stuck with a ten-year-old for an assistant, so he wouldn't even talk to me. One day when old Joe was away, I snuck out with his shears to try my hand at pruning; after that he decided it was safer to teach me how to garden than to risk another plant massacre. I'll always be grateful to old Joe. He hated poisons, and he taught me many of the environmentally friendly techniques I use and recommend today.

During my career, I've worked for many big and small companies, including several of my own. I've done everything from garden design and installation to grounds maintenance and even tree topping (a long time ago, before we knew better). Of course, my favorite job was the twenty-four years I spent directing the gardening at Seattle University. I still remember my anxiety before the job interview. It was to be conducted by a Jesuit, which sounded intimidating; and I was anticipating a difficult interview test that I needed to pass to qualify for the job. To my great surprise, "Father B" sauntered in dressed in a grass-stained sweatshirt and baggy jeans. His only question was whether I talked to plants. I barely managed to choke out an answer. He hired me and we became great friends. Together, with the help of a dedicated staff, we turned the Seattle University campus into one of the most attractive gardens in the Pacific Northwest. Our crowning achievement was establishing the environmental program to care for the campus without using any chemical poisons. The university won the top national EPA environmental award during the last two years that I worked there, and it's still the only campus designated as a Wildlife Sanctuary by the State of Washington.

Of course, I consider myself exceedingly lucky to have the opportunity to answer gardening questions on TV and radio. In fact, my media career happened mostly by luck. About twenty years ago, I received a call one morning from a producer at KIRO Newsradio in Seattle, asking me to sub for a famous gardening personality who was ill. I was to go on air with Jim French and then host the regular garden expert's two-hour question-and-answer show. Although I had become fairly well known locally for giving garden talks, I was a tad bit nervous—I'd never done anything on radio before. As it turned out, I didn't know half the answers to the questions callers hurled at me. I said "I don't know" so many times, it became a comedy routine. To my great surprise, listeners called in to say that they enjoyed my quirky sense of humor and honesty, and asked the radio station to have me on again. The next thing I knew, I was filling in whenever Mariners games ended early, and before the year was up, I was hosting my very own gardening question-and-answer show.

A couple of years later, I landed my first TV role. I received a letter inviting me to audition for the brand-new *Northwest Home and Garden* TV show on KIRO to be hosted by none other than Jeff Probst, better known today for his starring role on the television show *Survivor*. On the letter, I noticed that all the other candidates' names were typed in, but my name had been handwritten as an afterthought. Then, like a total dim-dim, I showed up late for the audition. The producer was patently unimpressed. I was the last one to try out, and he barely allowed me to speak. When I got home, I told my wife I blew it. But that night the phone rang, and I was asked to be on the first show. I couldn't believe it but was determined to do my best. The next day I showed up—all excited and quite nervous—at the garden where we were filming, but no one paid any attention to me. I stood around for about fifteen minutes until I finally caught the producer's attention. When I told him who I was, he shouted, "You aren't Ciscoe, that other guy's Ciscoe." When I finally convinced him that I really was Ciscoe, he told the crew, "We've got to do it with this yahoo now!" Fortunately, I must have done a good job. The show earned great ratings, and I ended up as a regular for the six years it aired. I still wonder what the guy he thought was Ciscoe is doing these days.

After the six-year run of that show, KIRO TV picked me up for their noon news. I went to the studio once a week to do a short gardening segment with the news anchor. I brought in all kinds of show and tell: plants, bug-damaged leaves (along with the bug), and even my little dog Kokie when I talked about protecting plants from squirrels. It was a lot of fun, until the day I was informed that they had to dump the "fluff" on the show to squeeze in the daytime soap *The Bold and the Beautiful.* Such is media.

Throughout the mid-1990s, I occasionally appeared as the garden expert for the local TV stations when there was breaking garden-related news. Then in February 2001, we were hit with a cold front. Meeghan Black from KING5 TV came out to do a story on protecting your plants from the cold. After it aired, Meeghan suggested to the station that they consider asking me to be a regular on their news like I was at the other station. Poor Meeghan: Little did she know that she would get stuck doing gardening tips with me for the next six-plus years. Our partnership is stronger than ever today. Our three-to-four minute gardening tips appear during the morning news on KING5 every Saturday and Sunday, and on the midday news program every Tuesday and Thursday. The half-hour show *Gardening with Ciscoe,* which we co-host, airs on KING5 every Saturday morning and on KONG 6/16 Saturday afternoons. Our gardening tips are also featured on my live question-and-answer show *Gardening with Ciscoe Live* on the weekends throughout Alaska and the Pacific Northwest via the Northwest Cable News network.

All of this has led to the most incredible life anyone could ever ask for. I love everything that I do professionally: gardening, performing, writing, and traveling. When I'm not working, I enjoy spending time with my wife, Mary, walking my two naughty yet adorable puppies, Fred and Ruby, and finally, gardening for the pleasure of it.

Throughout the years I think I've answered every gardening question imaginable. But you won't find a bunch of hard-to-understand scientific explanations and terms in this book. My goal is to keep the answers concise, accurate, simple, and fun. Whatever I do in life, I like to have fun. The quirky humor you'll find in many of the answers is probably my parents' fault. They were performers in the vaudeville days, and they passed on their *joie de vivre* and wild sense of humor to me. Hopefully, you'll learn from my mistakes and keep from murdering plants in your own garden. But to be honest, even if you follow all my advice, you're bound to kill a few. Don't worry about it: It'll give you room for new plants, and it means you're on your way to becoming a better gardener!

By the way . . .

You'll notice many references to the Northwest Flower and Garden Show in this book. For five days every February at the Seattle Convention Center, the premier horticultural event in the Pacific Northwest takes Seattle by storm! It's the third biggest garden show in the nation and attracts well over 50,000 garden enthusiasts each year. The centerpiece is the twenty-plus magnificent display gardens, but the show features much more, including fantastic container gardens and florist displays, a huge orchid show, all sorts of information booths, a children's program, irresistible plant shopping, and everything else on earth related to gardening. The show also offers a record number of seminars and demonstrations presented by well-known regional and internationally-famous gardeners and horticulturists. The show is a must for anyone who has an interest in gardening or who simply wants to gain inspiration and celebrate the coming of spring. I practically live at the show for the whole five days, giving presentations, working booths, signing books, and performing live radio. Best of all, if Meeghan and I can stop hamming it up with the crowds, we shoot our TV shows in the midst of all the excitement.

CHAPTER ONE

Flowering Plants

Earn your credentials by growing a hardy aloe in your rock garden.

Q **I'm known as a plant maniac because I'll try to grow all sorts of succulents and cacti outdoors year round. Now I'm determined to grow aloe. Is there one that can withstand the cold and soggy Northwest winters?**

A Only a certified plant nut would try to grow an aloe outside year round in the Pacific Northwest. But if you can provide the right conditions, *Aloe striatula* will thrive to become a spectacular, long-lived addition to your garden. The highly textural aloe hails from the rocky wilds of South Africa and features rambling, upright green-and-white-striped 3-foot-tall stalks that bow outward under the weight of twisty leaves at the ends of the branches. In early summer, the stalks are spiked with orange-yellow bell-shaped flowers. This aloe is hardy to 10 degrees, but great drainage is absolutely necessary to prevent the roots from rotting during the wet winter months. Plant it in a sunny spot on a mound of gritty soil

1

near heat-absorbing rocks. Even if it doesn't survive, you'll earn accreditation as a bona fide plant maniac just for trying. Do a search on your computer for *Aloe striatula*: It's available from specialty nurseries online.

Overwintering angel trumpets isn't that easy.

Q I grew an **angel's trumpet** (*Brugmansia*) for the first time this summer, and it was spectacular. I really want to keep it. Is this plant hardy, or do I need to bring it inside for the winter?

A Angel's trumpets (*Brugmansia*) have become quite popular. These tropical members of the tomato family can reach 10 feet tall, with huge hanging flowers that are enticingly fragrant from dusk until sunrise. *Brugmansia* can withstand only the lightest touch of frost, so it's best to bring them in by late September. During winter, angel trumpets do best in a cool (50 degrees), brightly lit room, out of direct sunlight. If you don't have those conditions, and you don't have a greenhouse, your best hope is to force your angel into dormancy and store it in an unheated garage. That's a tricky process. First, bring it inside the warm house, and let the soil dry out until the plant begins to wilt. Then cut it back severely, removing about half of the top growth. Immediately store it in the garage in total darkness, and water only enough to keep the soil from turning into dust. Don't worry if the leaves fall off. In March your *Brugmansia* will suddenly begin growing with sickly foliage in the dark garage. To grow healthy leaves, put it out on nice days, but bring it in at night and don't let it get hit by frost. Keep it outside full-time starting around Mother's Day.

Pinch with impunity.

Q Is it better to buy **annuals** when they're in bloom, or before the flowers have opened? I've heard you should pinch them back when you plant, but won't that remove flowers? Finally, what is the secret to keeping the flowers from pooping out in midsummer?

A When you're purchasing annuals at the local nursery, choose stocky young plants that are just beginning to form buds. When you plant them, lightly pinch back the growing points, even if you have to pinch off flower buds to do it. This will delay bloom but will result in bushy plants that will produce more flowers all summer long. Petunias are the exception: A week after you plant them, cut them back by half. It's hard to get yourself to do it, but your petunias will quickly grow back and set gazillions of blooms. Fertilize annual flowers regularly during the season, and deadhead whenever flowers begin to fade. When flowering begins to slow, or the plants become rangy in midsummer, cut the stems back by two-thirds. Encourage new growth with ample fertilizer and water, and you'll be rewarded with new growth and a profusion of late-summer blooms.

Give your annuals a shag haircut.

Q Despite the fact that I deadhead regularly by removing the spent blossoms, every summer in early July my **annual flowers**, such as marigolds, petunias, zinnias, and lobelia, get leggy and thin. The blossoms become fewer and appear only at the end of the branches as the season progresses. Is there anything I can do to keep the plants compact and floriferous?

A Annuals often get leggy after they've been growing for six to eight weeks. The best treatment for most annuals with distinct stems, such as zinnias, petunias, and cosmos, is to cut back about half of the stems two-thirds of the way to the base in early July. Those stems will grow back and begin to bloom in about two weeks. Then you can cut back the other half as soon as the first ones start blooming again. The exception is bushy-stemmed plants such as lobelia and alyssum; shear these back by half. They will look as though you murdered them, but they'll soon grow back and bloom like new. Be sure to keep fertilizing with a high-phosphorus product and provide adequate water. Your annuals should continue to bloom into late October.

Don't freeze your annuals.

 The nurseries carry all sorts of **annual flowers** in early spring. When is it safe to plant them out in the garden?

Every year by mid-April the nursery shelves are full of annuals, but if you bring most varieties home and plant them outdoors that early, you'll soon be memorializing them in a wake. Petunias, zinnias, marigolds, and impatiens are just a few of the annuals that come from the tropics and will melt into frozen goulash if you plant them out before mid-May. These heat lovers must go into an unheated garage or similar protected space during the night until Mother's Day, when they can be planted in the garden or in containers. If you want some early spring annual action, calendulas, English daisies, pansies, snapdragons, stock, sweet alyssum, and violas are hardy enough to go out into the garden or containers as soon as you bring them home.

Deadhead like a banshee.

Some of my **annuals and perennials** that are supposed to bloom all season long quit flowering by midsummer. I fertilized and watered well. Is the problem that I failed to remove the spent blossoms?

A Annual flowers and some perennials must be deadheaded regularly or they will stop blooming. Pelargoniums (Martha Washington geraniums), petunias, and marigolds are just a few of the annuals that will stop blooming if allowed to go to seed. *Armeria* (thrift), *Knautia*, and *Scabiosa* are examples of perennials that will bloom longer and more profusely the more often spent blossoms are removed.

Flowering plants that normally bloom all summer long know they are on earth to reproduce. Deadhead by removing the spent blossoms before they form seed or they will kick back, eat a little fertilizer, get a good suntan, and do nothing for the rest of summer.

Asters like to be pinched.

Q I love **asters** and plant them for fall bloom, but after the first year, most seem to bloom earlier than they did when I first planted them. They are also getting very tall and floppy. Is there anything I can do to delay bloom and keep them compact?

A The botanical name *Aster* means starflower, and the daisy-like blooms are stars of the fall garden. There are all sorts of cool varieties, including some with red foliage. In warm summers, however, the blooming period often begins in midsummer and the show is over by early fall. Also, asters tend to grow tall and by late summer become floppy and require staking. To prevent this and delay bloom, shear them back a third in mid-May, and do it again a month later. Then enjoy watching your aster put on a star performance in the late fall, when the flowers will be most appreciated.

Keep your gift azalea alive.

Q My mother-in-law recently sent me an **azalea** as a holiday gift. I've watered it well, but it's turning brown. I need help fast. My mother-in-law is coming to visit in just a few days!

A Thousands of azaleas are given as holiday gifts, but most end up as compost before Christmas. These plants need to be kept cool (below 65 degrees), bathed in direct sunlight, and in constant high humidity to survive for more than a few days in the home. If yours is still alive, put it outside during the day and bring it in to enjoy in the evening. In spring, plant it outside and hope for the best. Most of them aren't hardy. By the way, if you're expecting a visit from your mother-in-law, you might want to just sneak out and buy a new one right away!

Pot up bare-root plants.

Q I purchased a bunch of **bare-root clematis and perennials** at the Northwest Flower and Garden Show in February. Is it too cold to plant out my new acquisitions right away? How do I store them if I want to wait until it warms up?

A One thing I love about the Northwest Flower and Garden Show is that you can purchase bare-root clematis vines and perennials for about half the price you'd pay if you bought them in containers a month from now. You're right not to plant them out into the garden in February; it's still too cold. Don't leave them sitting in plastic bags, however, or they'll rot. Pot them up in well-drained potting soil as soon as possible and store them an unheated greenhouse, a well-lit, unheated garage, or a cool basement. (Don't try to grow them as houseplants. They won't last long in the warm, dry conditions in the living room.) Wait until early March. Then move the potted plants outside to a protected place. Acclimate them by exposing them to increasing sunlight and to cold each day for about a week before planting them out into the garden.

Divide bearded iris in summer.

Q My beloved **bearded irises** aren't blooming as much as they used to. They're growing in good sunshine and I fertilize them occasionally, but they've been growing in the same spot for years. Do they need dividing?

A Bearded iris flowers are attractive and fragrant, but they need attention to make sure they keep blooming every year. Always remove the flower stalk down to foliage as soon as your bearded iris is finished blooming. If fungus spots mar the leaves, cut the foliage back to 4 to 6 inches from the ground. It's a sure sign that irises need dividing when they stop blooming well. They can be divided any time after they stop flowering through the end of August. Break the rhizomes apart and save only those with healthy leaves. Plant three rhizomes 1 foot apart—two with the leafy ends pointing outward, and one with the leafy end between the other two. Although most of the books tell you to plant the rhizomes right on the soil surface, as long as the soil is well drained it's better to plant them about an inch deep to prevent the plants from falling over.

Don't let your bleeding heart look sad.

Q When I was a kid, my grandmother always grew common **bleeding hearts**. I bought one this year with beautiful golden foliage and pink flowers. Unfortunately, soon after the flower display was over, the plant seemed to die. What did Grandma know about growing these that I don't?

A Common bleeding heart (*Dicentra spectabilis*) is an old-fashioned-looking perennial and a favorite of cottage gardeners. Preferring moist shade, common bleeding heart grows to about 3 feet tall and 3 feet wide. The soft green leaves and arching stems resemble ferns and contrast beautifully with large-leaved hostas and *Ligularia dentata*. The spectacular variety that you found, with glowing golden-yellow leaves and rose-pink, heart-shaped flowers, is called 'Gold Heart'. Despite its appearance, it's not dead; with regular watering, most *Dicentra* foliage lasts into late summer, but without irrigation it begins to deteriorate soon after the flowers fade. Once the foliage begins to decline, nothing can be done to reverse the process. Cut the stems down to about an inch from the ground, and plant something to hide the hole left in the garden. Your bleeding heart won't return to grace your garden with its fine plumage until next spring.

A bloody good plant for dry shade.

Q I saw an interesting plant at the nursery last year, but I didn't buy it because I knew nothing about it. It was called **bloodroot**. What do the flowers look like, and would it survive in dry shade?

A Bloodroot (*Sanguinaria canadensis*) is a native of eastern North America, so named because the rhizomatous roots exude blood-red sap when cut. The pinkish white flowers are lovely when they appear in early spring but are short-lived. The rare double form 'Flore Pleno' has double flowers that last longer than most of the species, but I grow this plant more for the attractive, bluish gray, scalloped 6- to 12-inch single-stemmed leaves, which add a woodsy charm to the shade garden. Books will tell you that bloodroot needs plenty of moisture, but in my garden it readily colonized areas of dry shade where few other plants would grow. Grab these woodland gems if you see them for sale at nurseries and plant sales; they generally sell out quickly.

Don't throw out the baby with the old plant.

Q The flower on my **bromeliad** is fading, and it looks as if the plant is dying as well. Is there any hope for it, or should I throw it on the compost pile?

A Bromeliads are Central and South American plants with spectacular flowers that rival orchids for long-lasting, attractive blooms. Unlike orchids, however, bromeliads die when they finish blooming. Don't be in a hurry to throw out the dying plant, though. You can propagate new plants from offshoots, which often mature to flowering plants within two or three years. Remove offshoots with a sharp knife once they are at least a third the size of the parent and have at least five well-developed leaves. Potted up in good organic potting soil, offshoots generally root quickly. If the new bromeliad won't bloom after a couple of years, try enclosing the plant and pot in a plastic bag with a couple of apples for five to ten days. Then put the plant in a bright spot out of direct sunlight. The one kicker is that the plant won't bloom unless it receives a constant temperature of about 75 degrees. If you can provide all of that, you might win the Golden Brussels Sprout Expert Gardener Award, because in a month or two, you'll see a brand-new bloom appear on the offshoot that your saved from the mother plant.

Cacti are chilly lovers.

Q I have a great **cactus** collection. Some are supposed to have wonderful blooms, but they never seem to flower. How do you make cacti flower?

A Desert cacti have spectacular blooms, but most folks never get to see them, because the cacti need to experience temperatures ranging from 40 to 55 degrees during winter to trigger blooms next summer. The ideal situation is an unheated garage next to a bright window. If the garage lacks windows, grow lights work fine, but the temperature must remain below 55 degrees. Give them just enough water to prevent shriveling. Then don't leave home all summer. Most cactus flowers last only one day, and it's torture to come home and realize you missed the show!

There's nothing common about calla lilies.

Q I don't see why the beautiful **calla lilies** in my garden are known as "common calla lilies." They are my favorite plants. Mine are not looking great, however. A number of the leaves tend to fall over, and the plants aren't blooming as much as they used to. I'm growing them in a wet spot; could that be the problem? Would it help to cut them back?

A *Zantedeschia aethiopica*, known as the common calla lily, is a South African native with 4-foot-tall leaves and exotic 8-inch white spathe flowers that add a tropical flair to the garden. A great plant for wet spots, these evergreen callas love moisture and will thrive in a bog all season long. Normally, common calla lilies die back to the ground only in very cold winters; however, in early winter they often begin to look ratty. The leaves get tattered, and some fall over. Rather than cutting the whole clump to the ground, it's better to cut out individual stalks and let the others remain to produce energy. If you're getting fewer flowers every year, dig and divide in mid- to late September. Discard the middle growth and plant a section from the side of the clump. The flower display you'll enjoy next spring will be anything but common.

Canna no looka so good.

 The winter cold turned the leaves and stems of my canna lily to mush. Do these beautiful plants survive the cold, or do I need to dig mine up and store it in some way? If I do store it, do I just replant it in spring?

Canna foliage burns to a crisp in freezing weather. Fortunately, the temperatures usually must dip at least into the low 20s before root damage occurs. Some cannas are hardy and can be left in the ground, but many of the best varieties won't survive temperatures below 20 degrees. If you leave your plant in the garden, cut off the burned foliage and cover the rhizomes with a thick cover of insulating mulch. The easiest way to make sure they survive is to dig up the root ball and store it in a box full of soil or compost in an unheated garage. Water as needed to keep the soil slightly moist. Heat-loving cannas are notorious for being slow to grow in our cold Northwest springs. Get a head start by potting up divisions in early spring and placing them in the hottest spot you can find, such as against a south wall. Water and fertilize regularly, and you'll have big, tropical-looking cannas to transplant into your garden while your neighbors wait to see if the ones they left in the garden survived the winter.

Gain ten pounds a week: Plant chocolate cosmos.

I recently purchased an incredible plant called chocolate cosmos. The flowers really do smell like chocolate, but I also love their attractive red color. Is this cosmos really a perennial? What conditions does it like, and are there some companion plants that would complement it?

Don't plant chocolate cosmos (*Cosmos atrosanguineus*) if you're on a diet. The flowers give off a delicious chocolate aroma, and no one working near them can be blamed for taking numerous chocolate chip cookie breaks. This Mexican native grows to only about 2 feet tall and, with regular deadheading, is covered with dark red 2-inch-wide flowers all summer long. Chocolate cosmos looks stunning next to the big silver leaves of silver sage (*Salvia argentia*) or paired with the yellow grasslike blades of *Carex elata* 'Bowles Golden' or *C. elata* 'Aurea'. Chocolate cosmos needs full sun and moist soil.

Save your chocolate cosmos.

Q OK, I took your advice and planted **chocolate cosmos.** I love the plant, and I agree that the flowers do smell like chocolate, but I understand it's not reliably hardy in the Pacific Northwest. How can I keep it alive over the winter, so that I can enjoy my "chocolate garden fix" next spring?

A Covered with a thick layer of mulch, chocolate cosmos sometimes survive the winter, but most years if the cold doesn't get them, the soggy, rain-soaked soil does them in. The good news is that the tuberous roots of chocolate cosmos can be stored throughout winter. Carefully lift the tubers, shake off the loose soil, and let the clump dry for several hours. Then store in slightly moistened peat moss in an unheated garage. Replant in spring in early April, and try to resist the urge to make daily excursions to a chocolate shop when you smell the blooms next May.

Don't let clematis quit early.

Q I'm crazy about **clematis**, but some of the varieties that are supposed to flower all season long seem to poop out earlier than advertised. How can I keep them blooming until fall?

A Clematis vines should play a starring role in the summer and fall garden, pumping out showy flowers into autumn. As long as your clematis is one of the kinds that flowers on current-season growth, and the vines keep growing, it should continue to bloom all season long. The minute the root zone is allowed to dry out, however, your clematis will shut down for the season and the show will be over. Water as often as necessary to keep the root zone moist, and fertilize with a healthy shot of alfalfa meal. With a little bit of luck, your clematis will continue to put on an award-winning performance until late September.

Pruning clematis can be confusing!

Q I have several **clematis** vines growing on fences and climbing trees and shrubs throughout my garden. The flowers are spectacular, but the vines are becoming crowded, ugly messes. Is there a way to prune them so I can enjoy the attractive flowers without enduring the dead vines?

A Clematis is one of the most attractive plants in the garden, but if left to grow untended, it can turn into an unmanageable (and horribly ugly) rat's nest. How and when to prune your clematis depends on when it flowers. The easiest kinds to prune are those that bloom on current-season growth, such as the large-flowered *Clematis jackmanii* and the prolific but smaller-flowered viticella hybrids. Cut all of the vines down to the lowest two buds once the vines have become dormant in winter. You won't have to look at dead vines during winter, and your clematis will grow back in spring and flower all summer long. Varieties that bloom in spring with a second lighter blossoming in fall, such as 'Nelly Moser', are more difficult. These clematis flower on vines that grew last season, and then rebloom on current-season growth. Prune by cutting vines to different lengths and thinning out dead or crowded vines after the first flush of blooms fade. Prune clematis that bloom only in spring, such as the evergreen *C. armandii* and deciduous *C. montana*, as soon as flowers fade. Try to maintain a framework of main vines and thin the side branches, cutting out dead or crowded vines. Cut the remaining side branches by half or more. If your repeat- or spring-blooming clematis has become an unmanageable mess, cut all of the vines down to the lowest two buds as soon as the flowers fade. You won't get any flowers for a year or two, but you'll be able to start over and build a manageable framework to work with. Don't know what kind of clematis you have? Cut to two buds in late winter. It will grow back, and if you don't get any flowers for a couple of years, you'll know what to do next time.

Prune spring-blooming evergreen clematis.

 My evergreen **Clematis armandii** is getting out of control. Is there a way to prune it so it doesn't turn into a crowded mess?

Clematis armandii is one of the most attractive of vines, featuring strongly textured dark green leaves and intoxicatingly fragrant porcelain-white flowers. This fast-growing Chinese native can quickly turn into an ugly rat's nest, however, if it's not pruned hard after the flowers fade. To prevent tangling and a buildup of unsightly dead thatch, remove at least a third of the oldest stems by cutting them to the ground or where they attach to a main vine. It's not too difficult to do this if you begin when the plant is young, but if your vine has already become a crowded tangle, you're in for a long day. Begin at the base and cut the stems designated for removal into segments, pulling them out as you work your way out to the end. You'll be exhausted by the time you're finished, but when you see how much more refined and elegant your clematis looks, you'll know it was worth all of the hard work.

Obtain a coleus on steroids.

Q I saw you show a **coleus** with huge leaves on TV. I've never seen them available in nurseries. Where can I find one? Also, can this coleus withstand sunshine? You planted it in full sun, but I was under the impression that coleus require a shaded location.

A New strains of coleus (*Solenostemon*) are now available that feature colossal leaves and can thrive in full sun, making it possible to incorporate these showy mint relatives in borders and sunny containers. 'Giant Exhibition' and 'Oriental Splendor' often grow to more than 3 feet tall and feature brilliantly colored leaves as big as dinner plates. They're available in quality nurseries around Mother's Day, but they sell out quickly, so if you see some, buy them all! These elegant goliaths are too big for all but the largest containers, but they put on an impressive display massed in the summer border. All coleus prefer moist, rich soil and regular applications of a high-nitrogen fertilizer. Pinch off the flowers to maintain an attractive shape and encourage branching. Root cuttings in fall to make sure that you'll have plenty of these refined behemoths to grace your containers and borders the following summer.

Sow columbines.

Q I'd like to grow some of the native **columbines** that I see in fields. Is there a way I can gather the seeds and plant them in my garden?

A Columbine and many other wildflowers are easy to grow in our own gardens from seed collected in the wild. Wait until the seedpods dry, then carefully pull them off the plant and put them in an airtight container. Most wildflower seeds need to experience a cold, rainy winter to break dormancy, so plant them right away in fall. Lightly rough up the soil with a steel rake or weeding tool. Then shake the pods over the area, and step gently on the seeds to plant them about a quarter-inch deep in the soil. Believe me, next spring you'll have plenty of columbine growing in that area of the garden. I should warn you that columbines can become somewhat of a pest, but hey, I'll take this kind of pest any day. Columbines thrive in sun or shade, come in all sorts of colors, and are extremely attractive to hummingbirds. Best of all, they're easy to pull out if they grow where they're unwanted.

Keep your 'Blue Panda' looking chipper.

Q My 'Blue Panda' **corydalis** is spectacular when it's in bloom in spring, but after the bloom fades, the foliage takes on a grayish powdery look and the plant looks ratty for the rest of the season. Overall, the plant does not seem to be thriving. I followed the directions on the tag and planted it in partial shade. Is there anything I can do to help it perform better?

A The many varieties of *Corydalis flexuosa* are attractive low-growing plants with ferny foliage and blue flowers. These members of the poppy family have been extremely popular since the bright blue–flowering 'Blue Panda' was introduced in the 1980s. Now several varieties are available that are easier to grow, with fantastic flower color. 'China Blue' has deep blue blooms, while 'Père David' has bright blue flowers. But the easiest corydalis to grow is 'Purple Leaf'. It has purplish blue flowers and purple-blotched leaves. These Chinese natives do best in moist shade and will bloom from spring into early summer if they are given adequate moisture. Soon after the bloom fades, cut the lacy foliage down to about 1 inch tall. It will grow back looking fresh and lovely. Feed your plant every six weeks with alfalfa meal or an organic fertilizer, and it may reward you with a second set of blooms in fall.

Don't let spider mites ruin your Crocosmia.

Q I planted a **Crocosmia** to attract hummingbirds, but every summer the leaves turn brown and shrivel up before the flowers open. The soil is good, I water adequately, and nearby plants are doing fine. What's wrong with my Crocosmia?

A Crocosmia is a top-rated plant for the mixed border. Every season new cultivars appear, featuring attractive vertical foliage and arching spikes of ever bigger and hotter-colored flowers that hummingbirds can't resist. Unfortunately, Crocosmia is susceptible to spider mites during hot, dry conditions. The first symptom is gray stippling on the leaf, but in severe cases, the leaves quickly turn brown and die, and the flowers may be aborted. Inspect the undersides of the leaves with a magnifying glass and look for tiny spotted mites, eggs, or webbing. Spraying with Superior or Supreme oil at the first sign of trouble is often recommended and may be necessary; but I've found that the best way to control Crocosmia mites is to spray the back of the leaves with a powerful blast of water at least once a week beginning in midsummer. That will not only crush or wash off the mites and eggs, but it will also create a moist atmosphere that mites consider anything but romantic, greatly reducing reproductive rates.

Plant a cutting garden.

Q I enjoy arranging fresh flowers, but I can't bring myself to **cut flowers** that play a key role in my mixed borders. How can I have my bouquets and an attractive garden as well?

A Like you, I love to make fresh bouquets, yet I'm hesitant to remove flowers from my mixed borders. I solved the problem by planting a garden of flowering plants to use exclusively for bouquets. Locate your cutting garden in an out-of-the-way, sunny area with rich, well-drained soil. Unless you're going into the cut flower business, the garden doesn't need to be huge. If you choose the right flowers, a 4-foot-wide by 10-foot-long bed can supply all you need for spectacular bouquets all summer long. Some of my favorite annuals for cut flowers include zinnia, scabiosa, salpiglossis, and salvia. Favorite perennials for cutting are campanula, dahlia, echinops (globe thistle), gerbera daisy, gladiolus, lily, phlox, and calla lily.

Give your fall garden a Turkish treat.

Q I would love to enjoy the butterfly-like flowers of **cyclamen** in my garden, but the kind I see at the store are evidently best grown as houseplants. Are there any kinds that will survive outdoors in the Pacific Northwest?

A Some very attractive varieties of cyclamen are hardy. Boasting colorful flowers and silver-etched leaves, they're cold-season performers that add a warming glow on chilly days in the fall and winter garden. Hardy cyclamen come from the mountains of Turkey. They don't show off with the big flowers exhibited by the florist hybrids, but the long-lasting, whirlybird-like blooms come in a variety of colors that can be counted on to cheer even the gloomiest winter day. The most common varieties available are the fall-blooming *Cyclamen hederifolium* and the midwinter-blooming *C. coum*, but other varieties with fragrant flowers that extend the bloom period well into spring are becoming available, including *C. creticum* and *C. repandum*. Planting them deep increases hardiness. As long as drainage is good, hardy cyclamen can be planted up to 2 feet deep without so much as delaying the bloom.

Move spring-flowering bulbs.

 I need to move a big clump of daffodils. When is the best time to do it? Is there a trick to dividing them?

The easiest time to move spring-flowering bulbs is when they are in full bloom. However, if you want to divide them, wait until the flowers fade, but do it while the foliage is still green. Lift the clump, and then use your hands to separate chunks of bulbs. Replant the sections in well-drained soil. While you're at it, mix a handful of dolomite lime and a tablespoon of bulb food into the planting hole. Water well and voilà, you've started new colonies of spring-blooming bulbs in your garden.

Plant tomorrow's bouquets today.

They saw a sucker coming when I walked up to the dahlia sales booth at the Northwest Flower and Garden Show. How could I resist buying them after seeing the display pictures of the magnificent flowers? Unfortunately, the pictures were better than the sketchy planting instructions that came with the tubers. When and how should I plant the huge collection of dahlias I purchased?

As long as you have lots of sunny space and reasonably well-drained soil, you'll be glad you bought your dahlias. Few perennials can match them when it comes to producing nonstop, long-lasting flowers to add beauty to the mixed border and to supply flowers for bouquets. Plant the tubers after the danger of frost has passed, in early April. The key to growing great dahlias is to mix plenty of organic matter and about a half cup of low-nitrogen organic fertilizer into a wide and deep planting hole. Drive in a stake and place the tuber about 6 inches deep, with the growth bud nearest to the stake. Cover with only 3 inches of soil, and then fill in gradually with additional soil as shoots grow. Don't water until the plants emerge. Soggy soil can rot the tubers, and there's usually adequate moisture at planting time. Don't forget to protect the newly emerging shoots from slugs, or they will have a banquet and you'll get no bouquets. When dahlias reach about 15 inches tall, pinch out the growing point of every branch to encourage side shoots. In future years, don't pinch if you leave the tubers in the ground during the winter, as you'll already have an overabundance of branches. If you want fewer but bigger flowers, allow only six shoots to grow, and remove most of the buds developing below the terminal (top) bud. The more buds you remove, the bigger the flowers you'll get. Once your dahlia is up and growing, keep the soil moist, fertilize with an organic flower food or alfalfa meal every six weeks, and cut flowers before they go to seed. Your dahlia will produce spectacular blooms all summer long.

Seeing red is cool.

Q I just learned about red-leaved **dahlias**. What are some of your favorite varieties and where can I find them?

 I plant a lot of different types of dahlias in my garden, but my hands-down favorites are the varieties attired in red foliage. The deep burgundy stems and leaves, coupled with flashy flowers, look fantastic on their own, yet make exquisite companions for flowering perennials and shrubs. The best known of the red-leaved dahlias is 'Bishop of Llandaff'. Its red flowers feature a dark eye surrounded by bright yellow stamens and are exceptionally stunning foiled against the dark-red, almost-black foliage. 'Ellen Houston' adds a tropical flair, presenting the perfect combination of burnt-orange flowers and coppery black foliage. 'Moonfire' is magnificent, with glistening purple foliage cradling burnt-yellow flowers centered by dark maroon eyes; but it's sensational coupled with the spiky, burnished bronze leaves and golden apricot flowers of *Crocosmia* 'Solfatare'. Finally, wear insulated gloves if you handle 'Roxie': The contrast of reddish-purple foliage and scarlet flowers is so hot, it is subject to spontaneous combustion. Red-leaved dahlias are beginning to show up for sale at local nurseries, but several specialty nurseries carry the best selections online.

A bouquet a day keeps the marriage counselor away.

 I planted some of those **dahlias** with the dinner plate–sized flowers to enable me to make plenty of bouquets to keep me in good standing with my wife. (It's cheaper than marriage counseling.) I followed the directions that came with the tubers and planted them in a sunny location, and worked in plenty of compost, but I'm not getting very many flowers. How do you encourage dahlias to produce more of their romantic blooms?

 If you get in half the trouble I do (how did I fail to notice the clothes drying on the line when I turned on that sprinkler?), then you'll want to grow lots of dahlias. The more flowers you cut, the more that will bloom, so you can make lots of bouquets. To make sure your dahlias keep blooming, remove all spent flowers every day. Use plenty of mulch, and keep the soil moist. Fertilize every six weeks by working a couple of cups of alfalfa meal, or a good organic flower food, into the soil. This should keep your dahlia pumping out flowers and (until the next time you get into trouble) keep you in marital bliss.

Give your dahlias an umbrella.

I grew **dahlias** for the first time this year. The flowers were spectacular. Can I leave them in the ground, or do I have to dig them up and store them?

It's risky to leave dahlias in the ground over the winter, but it's such a royal pain in the kazutski to dig and store them that I rarely go to the effort. An Arctic blast will almost always kill a dahlia, but most would survive our typical mild winter temperatures if it weren't for the constant rain. Usually what does them in is rot caused by our soggy soil. Cover the ground above the tubers with a thick layer of evergreen fern fronds. Fronds are great insulators, but more important, they repel water. Don't forget to put a rock on top to keep them from blowing away. Remove the fronds in early April and, with a wee bit of luck, your dahlia stems will reemerge dry and happy.

If you wait to stake your flowering plants such as lilies, delphiniums, dahlias, and Crocosmia until after they fall down, they end up looking like hostages in the front yard.

Daylilies need attention.

Q I love **daylilies**, but either mine have a short bloom period, or I'm doing something wrong. Are there varieties that bloom longer than others, or do I need to talk to them nicer?

A Daylilies have attractive flowers that stand out like jewels in the mixed border. Each flower lasts only one day, but each morning new ones take their place. Most daylilies produce flowers for only a month or so, but the plant experts have developed recurrent flowering hybrids capable of blooming from late spring until fall. The golden-flowered 'Stella de Oro' is the most famous, but other long-blooming hybrids include 'Happy Returns' (pale yellow), 'Black Eyed Stella' (yellow with red eye), and 'Pardon Me' (dark red). Even recurrent varieties will poop out early and stop blooming if they're neglected, however. Keep them blooming by watering regularly and feeding every six weeks with alfalfa meal.

By the way, be careful where you situate daylilies in your garden. The flowers turn to follow the sun, and it's a big disappointment if all you see is the backs of the flowers.

Keep delphiniums alive and blooming.

 I'm so jealous when I visit famous gardens and see lovely delphiniums in full bloom. When I plant them, I enjoy one spectacular flower display and then the plants die back, never to return. Is there a trick to growing these plants, or do the famous gardens replace them every year the way I do?

The brilliantly colored flower spikes of delphiniums make glorious additions to the mixed border, but a few key requirements must be satisfied to make sure that they return to put on another show the following year. The trick to keeping delphiniums alive, not to mention getting them to rebloom in the same season, is to incorporate large amounts of organic compost before you plant. Mulch with compost to slow evaporation, and never allow the soil to dry out. Delphiniums are big feeders. Fertilize heavily with alfalfa meal or an organic perennial food by working it into the soil just outside the root zone every six weeks. Chances are that your delphiniums will become a permanent attraction in your garden. If things don't work out, don't forget to incorporate large amounts of compost before you plant a replacement next spring.

Divide fall-blooming perennials.

When is the best time to divide perennials that bloom in the fall? What is the easiest way to divide them?

A The best time to divide established fall- and summer-blooming perennials is in spring, when the emerging plant growth is 2 or 3 inches high. Dividing is a good way to get new plants, and often necessary to keep perennials blooming and vigorous. I use a good digging spade and slice the plant into sections. The center is usually worn out and best tossed into the compost bin. Warn worms of the impending disaster by shouting "Hyaku!" before you slice in with your digging spade.

Don't try to divide all perennials.

Q I know that it's important to **divide perennials** from time to time to keep them growing and blooming well. Most of the time I can successfully divide them, but some seem to resent my efforts. Are some perennials difficult to divide—and better off left alone?

A In general, perennials should be divided to keep them vigorous and floriferous, but some are almost impossible to divide and are better left undisturbed. *Cimicifuga* (bugbane), *Aruncus* (goatsbeard), *Gypsophila* (baby's breath), *Eryngium* (sea holly), and *Platycodon* (balloon flower) have woody, ropelike roots that tend to break easily, causing severe dieback when dividing is attempted. Others—such as *Aconitum* (monkshood), *Aquilegia* (columbine), some euphorbias, and *Pulsatilla* (pasque flower)—simply resent root disturbance and show their displeasure by going into major decline. Fortunately, these perennials are not aggressive spreaders, and they rarely die out in the center or stop blooming, so the only reason for trying to divide them is to attempt to make new plants. Give them room, resist the urge to try to make free plants, and enjoy the fact that these perennials will thrive with little or no effort on your part.

Hellebores need help.

Q Last year I paid a bundle for one of those **double Oriental hellebores.** Now, a year later, I'm seeing sticky stuff all over it, and it doesn't look healthy. Am I going to lose my expensive plant?

A Check under the leaves. What you'll find is a huge population of aphids. These sucking insects are especially attracted to hellebores that are under water stress, and quickly build up to numbers capable of doing serious harm if nothing is done. Give these nasty sucking insects the liquid equivalent of *el kabatski* by blasting them off with the hose. Be prepared to do it a few more times in the next few days. By the end of the week, your plants will be both free of aphids and well watered.

Don't treat echeverias like succulents.

Q I couldn't resist buying some **echeverias** this spring. Unfortunately, they haven't grown as big and colorful as I expected. Do they require special care? Will they overwinter outside?

A Echeverias come in a variety of brilliant colors and resemble a hen and chickens plant on steroids. The colorful echeverias are hard to find, so anytime you see a spectacular one at a nursery, snap it up. Grow these tender Mexican and Central American sun lovers in a pot so that you can bring them into a brightly lit spot in the house or into a greenhouse for the winter. Unlike most other succulents, echeverias need plenty of water to get big and colorful. During summer, water every few days and fertilize with a good 20-20-20 soluble fertilizer at least once every two weeks, soaking the leaves in the process. In winter, water as often as necessary to keep the soil surface moist, but hold off on fertilizer until spring. Keep them well hydrated, and echeverias will be the crown jewels of your plant collection.

Behead your echeveria.

Q Last year I grew a gem of a plant called **echeveria.** The succulent leaves got huge and colorful. I knew it wasn't hardy so I kept it alive during winter by placing it in a bright window in an unheated garage. It survived and the top looks fine, but the stem grew tall and thin, and is too weak to hold the rosette of leaves at the top without bending. If I cut off the head of leaves, will it form new roots?

A No matter how much light and warmth you give echeveria, the stems always seem to grow thin and long during the winter. Solve the problem by beheading your echeveria in early spring. Cut the stem about 4 inches below the leaves. Encourage the remaining stem to root by inserting and firming it upright in a pot filled with moist cactus soil (available in the potting soil department at most quality nurseries and garden centers). Put your echeveria outside in a sunny location on nice days, but remember to bring it in during the evening until temperatures warm up in April. Make sure the soil remains moist, but not soggy, at all times. Roots will quickly form all along the stem. Once you see the top begin to grow, fertilize and water regularly, and before you know it, your echeveria will once again become a well-proportioned jewel of a plant.

Cut back epimedium.

Q I'm delighted with the way **Epimedium** (*bishop's cap*) has thrived in an area of dry shade in my garden. The leaves turned red and looked great all winter, but in spring the foliage began drying up and turning brown. How far, and when, should I cut it back?

A Although it resembles a perennial, epimedium is a shrub in the barberry family. One of its many attributes is its ability to adapt, and indeed thrive, in dry shade. As you mentioned, the leaves of many varieties turn a lovely red during winter. The spurred early-spring flowers are small but colorful and unique. Cut the foliage back to about 2 inches from the ground in February, before the flowers begin to grow. The fresh new foliage will emerge bronzy pink before turning green in summer. Cutting the old leaves back will also enable the unusual spring flowers to show up much better.

Give euphorbias a makeover.

Q My **Euphorbia wulfenii** was magnificent last spring, covered with huge chartreuse flowers. This spring some of the stems are flowering, but others look as if they're dying back. Should I cut the dying stems off? If I cut all of the bad ones off, there may not be many left to enjoy.

A Euphorbias (spurge) are relatively short-lived plants. When they reach a few years old, they often look pretty ragged after a long, cold winter. It's best to remove the dying branches immediately after the blooms fade. Even when in bloom, however, your euphorbia will have a greatly improved appearance if you cut out the unsightly branches. If the whole plant looks bad, cut down all of the branches to allow emerging shoots to grow and fill in. Wear protective glasses, and use the utmost caution to make sure that none of the sap gets into your eyes. It's highly caustic and can cause serious eye damage. If most of the branches are dying back and no new growth is evident, visit your local nursery for a replacement.

Grow an evergreen hydrangea relative.

Q Do you know anything about a new **evergreen hydrangea**? It's supposed to look just like a lace-cap hydrangea but it doesn't drop its leaves.

A *Dichroa febrifuga* is an extremely close relative of the hydrangea, and if you see one, you'll be convinced it is a hydrangea until winter comes and it hangs on to its leaves. Many of its evergreen leaves take on gorgeous tints of red during the cold season. *Dichroa* means "two colors" and refers to the two-toned look caused by color variation in the lace-capped flowers. In acid soil the petals vary from lavender to bright blue, while in alkaline conditions flowers tend to edge toward lavender and pink. The flowers occur in early summer and are followed by attractive blue berries that remain throughout winter. Size can vary, but most dichroas remain small shrubs, rarely growing more than 4 feet tall and wide. Hardy to about 10 degrees, dichroa does best in partial shade. Plant it where you can stump the tweetle out of visitors when they see your "hydrangea" covered in leaves and berries in the middle of winter.

Cut back evergreen penstemons.

Q I love **evergreen penstemons** because the blooms keep coming all summer long, but my plants are getting so big that they're smothering everything growing next to them. Can I cut them back without killing them? When is the best time to do it, and when is the best time to divide them?

A Evergreen penstemons are wonderful plants for the sunny border. Most varieties bloom all summer long. The showy, tubular flowers are supposed to be attractive to hummingbirds, but I've noticed that the birds usually avoid them. I suspect it's because you rarely find a blossom without a chubby bumblebee butt blocking the entrance. Evergreen penstemons often get so big that they grow over, and snuff out, neighboring plants. Cut them back to the emerging new growth at the base in mid- to late April. The foliage will look better, and the plant will be a more manageable size. The first blooms will be delayed by a couple of weeks, but once the flowering begins in mid-May, your penstemons will continue to flower all summer long. Evergreen penstemons are difficult, if not impossible, to divide. Fortunately, low-growing stems often layer themselves. In spring, rooted stems can easily be dug up and moved to start new plants in sunny areas of the border.

Plant a trumpet vine, even if you don't have an outhouse.

Q I need a **fast-growing vine** that will cover an ugly structure in the garden at my cabin. The vine must be drought tolerant, take hot sun, and have clinging tendrils so it can climb wooden walls. It can be deciduous because I only use the cabin during summer months. I'd prefer something that blooms. Any suggestions?

A Trumpet vine (*Campsis radicans*), also known as trumpet creeper, is your plant. In the southeast United States, where this plant is native, it is still known as the outhouse vine because it was commonly used to cover the outdoor privy. The vine spruces up everything it climbs because from mid-May until fall, it blooms steadily with radiant orange or red 3-inch-long trumpet flowers that attract hummingbirds. The only requirement for fast growth and profuse blooming is a dry, sunny location. Prune back vines to keep them from becoming top-heavy and pulling off the wall, or worse yet, toppling over your outhouse.

Be brutal to leggy fatsias.

Q I'm looking for a low-maintenance plant to add a tropical look to a shady entryway. Will **fatsia** survive in shade or does it require sun? My one concern is that I heard it has bug problems. Are they serious? Can I prune it to keep it from getting too big?

A Aralia (*Fatsia japonica*) is the perfect plant to lend a tropical look to a shady entryway, or any low-light area where bold texture is desired. This plant features evergreen, deeply lobed 16-inch-wide leaves and is hardy to about 10 degrees. The dark green leaves make the perfect foil for umbels of creamy white flowers that occur in fall and shiny black fruits that hang on through winter. Fatsia looks its best when planted in a shady location. Too much sun results in ugly yellow leaves. Fatsia is susceptible to psyllas and other sucking insects. Little harm occurs to the plant, but an ugly, sooty mold grows on the honeydew excreted by the bugs. Control the insects by regularly blasting them off with sprays from the hose. If constant insect attacks have made your fatsia look unsightly, or if it has simply become leggy and spindly over time, cut it back to about a foot from the ground in April: This tough, fast-growing plant will grow back looking fresh and attractive in no time.

Add an exotic flair with ginger relatives.

Q I saw a plant that I assumed was canna lily, but the flowers were wonderfully fragrant. The garden owner told me it was a **flowering ginger**. Is flowering ginger difficult to grow, and is it available at nurseries, or do you have to order it from specialty catalogs?

A *Hedychium* or flowering ginger resembles a cross between a banana and a canna, with stems that rise to 6 feet tall covered with lance-shaped 20-inch-long leaves. The showstopper comes in late summer when the torchlike heads of tubular fragrant flowers burst into bloom. Flowering ginger is easy to grow as long as you plant it in moist, rich, well-drained soil. It wants full sun (don't we all?) and wind protection. Feed regularly with a good organic flower fertilizer, or work alfalfa meal into the soil around the clump every six weeks. The easiest flowering ginger to find and grow in the Northwest is *H. coccineum* 'Tara'. It features orange, slightly fragrant flowers. You can purchase many other varieties with much more fragrant flowers from mail-order catalogs or online nurseries. It's worth a try to grow them. Even marginally hardy flowering ginger will usually survive and bloom if planted against a south-facing wall and mulched deeply with water-repelling fern fronds in winter.

Discover the delights of *Abutilon.*

Q I've grown a **flowering maple** indoors for years, but the other day I was amazed to see one growing outdoors. Will they survive year round as a garden plant? What conditions do they require?

A They are called Chinese lanterns or flowering maples, but no matter what you call them, abutilons are becoming popular for use in container gardens and mixed borders. These South American members of the hibiscus family sport vividly colored bell-shaped blooms all summer long. The red-flowering varieties are not only attractive to human eyes but also magnets to hummingbirds. The leaves of *Abutilon* are also attractive. They resemble maples in shape, but a number of hybrids feature showy variegated leaves. Abutilons bloom best in fertile, well-drained soil basking in a hot, sunny location. Mulch heavily and water regularly. Give them extra moisture in hot, baking sun. Beginning in April, fertilize every six weeks with alfalfa meal or an organic bloom fertilizer. Although abutilons can reach 6 feet, you can keep them compact and bushy by pruning out upright shoots in late winter. They tend to bloom more prolifically, however, if you allow them to form long, arching branches. Most abutilons aren't reliably hardy in our area, but they often survive if they're planted against a heat sink such as a south wall or a large outcropping rock. To be safe, dig them up in fall and grow them as houseplants, or if they are in pots, leave them out in winter and move them into an unheated garage only during freezing weather. *Abutilon megapotamicum* is a relatively hardy species that usually survives outdoors in all but the coldest winters. Once it gets through the winter, your flowering maple will reward you in summer with nonstop exotic red-and-yellow blooms that are irresistible to hummingbirds.

Cut back hardy geraniums.

 My perennial garden contains several lovely hardy geraniums that knit the garden together and add attractive flowers, but after the flowers fade, the foliage gets ratty-looking and the leaves are covered with a powdery fungus. How can I keep the foliage looking good?

 Hardy geraniums are the workhorses of the perennial garden. They come in a staggering array of flower color, sizes, and growth habits, and can fulfill the role of everything from groundcover to midborder accent plant. The foliage of many spring-blooming geraniums disintegrates once the flowers fade, however. Remove ratty-looking foliage by cutting it to within a couple of inches of the ground. Provide adequate water and a shot of fertilizer, and your geranium will rebound with fresh foliage and a second bloom. Some varieties, such as 'Claridge Druce' and 'Mourning Widow', can often be coaxed to produce a third flowering if you cut them back again after the second bloom fades.

Lift or leave them—what to do with garden-variety gladiolus.

 Are gladiolus hardy in the Pacific Northwest? If they aren't, when should I dig them up, and what's the best way to store them through the winter?

 Although there are hardy varieties of gladiolus, most of the garden varieties are not hardy, so they must be lifted and stored to guarantee that they'll survive to bloom next summer. Normally it's best to wait until all the leaves turn yellow. Unfortunately, wet fall weather can encourage botrytis, a fungus that can infect the corm (underground bulblike structure). If the leaves have brown spots, dig your gladiolus in early October. You'll find that the old corm has shriveled up and been replaced by new ones. Remove and dispose of the old corm, and break off any small offsets that have formed on the new one. Offsets take a few years (and a bit of luck) to bloom, so it's questionable whether it's worth storing and replanting them. Dry the corms in a dark, dry area for a couple of weeks, then store throughout winter at 40 to 50 degrees in a single layer in flats.

Plant a florist's dream.

Q I love cutting **gladiolus** flowers for arrangements, but they all bloom at once. Is there a way to make them bloom at different times? Also, how deep should I plant the bulbs, and when should I cut the flowers for the prettiest display?

A The big hybrid gladiolus make impressive cut flowers. Plant them at one- to two-week intervals, from the first week of April through mid-June, to extend the bloom period. Gladiolus prefer rich, well-drained soil in full sun. Plant about four times deeper than the height of the bulb, and mix in a tablespoon of bulb food under each bulb. Cut flower spikes when the lowest buds begin to open, but leave at least four leaves on the stem to enable the plant to store the needed energy to produce a bloom the following year.

Plant a gem.

 Where I come from in southern Australia, we grew a spectacular plant called **Grevillea**. They usually had red flowers. Do you know if these lovely plants from Down Under will survive in the Pacific Northwest?

A While traveling in southern Australia last winter, I was thrilled to see *Grevillea* blooming in its natural setting. It's one of the few Australian plants that will thrive in the Pacific Northwest. We're lucky that it does, because grevilleas are exceptional shrubs that bloom in winter and look spectacular in Northwest gardens. My favorite grevillea is 'Canberra Gem', which I found at Jungle Fever Nursery in Tacoma, Washington. The attractive evergreen foliage resembles rosemary, but the pièce de résistance of this 6-foot-tall (and 6-foot-wide) shrub are the sparkling cerise spiderlike flower clusters that appear in great profusion throughout winter and spring. My 'Canberra Gem' began blooming just after New Year's Day and continued blossoming well into May. The biggest surprise of all is that it's extremely attractive to the Anna's hummingbirds that remain in the Pacific Northwest during winter. Several varieties of grevillea have proven to be rock-hardy here, but they must have sharp drainage and a sunny location. They rarely need fertilizer and are harmed by phosphorus (as is true of all members of the family Proteaceae), so if you feed, use a low-phosphorus product such as alfalfa meal.

Move Oriental hellebores while they are in bloom.

Q I recently purchased a number of the new **hybrid Oriental hellebores**—at great expense, I might add. They seem to be thriving, but they're planted in the middle of the garden and it's hard to see the flowers. Can I move them to a better location while they're in bloom?

A Hybrid Oriental hellebores are one of the loveliest additions to the winter garden, but their colorful charm is wasted if the shy, nodding flowers are located in the back of the garden, where no one will see them. Fortunately, these pricey perennials are easy to move while in full bloom. Plant them along a sidewalk or near the entrance to your house, preferably in a spot that receives morning sun. Just make sure the location has well-drained soil, and add lots of moisture-holding compost. Visitors and passersby will be so awestruck by the lovely flowers that it'll be worth your having fasted for the last two months in order to pay for them.

Cut back hellebores in winter.

Q I got a little carried away with the **hybrid Oriental hellebores**. The winter blooms are so enchanting and colorful that I couldn't resist buying a truckload of them. What conditions do they prefer?

A Oriental hellebore flowers are seductively beautiful, with new introductions of even more exotic-looking flowers showing up every year. Give these forest natives moist, well-drained soil and partial shade, and they'll perform admirably for years. Blooms often open in January and sometimes last into early summer. The new leaves emerge around Christmastime. As soon as you see the new leaves beginning to grow, remove the old ones by cutting the stems right to the ground.

Cut last season's leaves off hybrid Oriental hellebores.

Q I adore the beautiful flowers on my **hybrid Oriental hellebore**, but by early summer the leaves always seem to get ugly brown dry spots that detract from the appearance of the plant. What's causing this, and is there something I can spray to stop it from happening?

A Those crinkly brown spots on the old leaves are caused by botrytis, a fungus disease. Keep it from spreading to the new leaves and flowers by cutting the old leaves to the ground in December as soon as you notice flower buds appearing at the crown. Don't try to compost the old leaves, as the disease spores might survive; it's better to send them off to a composting facility that's equipped to deal with disease problems such as botrytis. Bonus: When you cut off the ugly old leaves, the emerging flowers show up better. If botrytis continues to be a problem, consider spreading a quarter-inch layer of either lime or marble chips over the ground around the plant. The object is to prevent the spores from being splashed up onto the leaves. I use lime chips because hellebores love alkaline soil. The problem is that the only place I know of to find lime chips is Manufacturing Minerals on Monster Road in Renton, Washington. They sell the chips only in 100-pound bags. It cost me just $2.97 for the 100-pound bag, but it cost me $60 for the trip to the chiropractor after I lifted it!

Keep an eye out for hellebore seedlings.

Q Is it possible that the seedlings I'm finding near my expensive **hybrid Oriental hellebore** are its offspring? If so, will they look like the parent plant? When can I move them?

A As expensive as they are when you buy one, many varieties of *Helleborus* reseed in the garden. This year I found hundreds of seedlings under one of my Oriental hybrids. Because the parent is a hybrid, the offspring will be somewhat different depending on what it crossed with, and there's no way to know what the flowers will look like. Most of the time they resemble a hellebore that's already growing in your garden, but sometimes you come up with a real treasure. Although it's rare, other varieties of *Helleborus* also reseed. I've found a few *H. argutifolius* over the years, and species *H. foetidus* are known to come up from seed, but I've yet to find one, probably because I grow only hybrids that may not easily reproduce from seed. Move the seedlings to a desired location as soon as you spot them. They're much easier to move when they're small. Lightly fertilize your transplants with organic flower food and keep them well watered. Who knows, you might discover the newest horticultural star.

Change the color of your hydrangea.

Q Is it true that you can change the color of **hydrangea** flowers by changing the pH of the soil? What's the best way to do it?

A Contrary to what most gardeners believe, the color of hydrangea flowers is not entirely dependent on the pH (measure of alkalinity) of the soil. Color is actually determined by the amount of aluminum available to the plant. The pH makes a difference because the uptake of aluminum is increased in acid soils and decreased if the pH is raised to 6 or above. Therefore, to encourage pink or red flowers, before the end of November incorporate about a pound of agricultural lime into the soil around the drip line to give the limestone time to break down and change pH by the time growth begins next spring. To keep the flowers on the red side, yearly applications of lime are usually required. Feeding with a fertilizer high in phosphorus has also been shown to reduce aluminum uptake, so for red flowers, feed only with organic fertilizers that contain more phosphorus (second number on the bag) than nitrogen (first number on the bag). To turn flowers blue, wait until early March, and then apply a solution of a tablespoon of aluminum sulfate per gallon of water. Warning: Apply aluminum sulfate only to plants that are at least two years old. Generally, one application per year is sufficient. Water your hydrangea well about an hour before you apply the aluminum sulfate, and don't exceed the application rate. Too much aluminum can burn the roots.

Dry the flowers of your favorite hydrangeas.

Q I'm wondering if there's a better way to dry **hydrangea** flowers. I was told to hang the flowers upside down in a dark room, but it doesn't always work very well. Is there a better way to do it?

A I never knew how to dry hydrangea flowers until, as head gardener at Seattle University, I caught a woman from the local women's club swiping a bunch of the flowers, which the club dried and then sold to support good causes. When I went over to give them a "talking to," they sat me down with a cup of coffee and a plate of homemade cookies, and before I knew it, they had carte blanche to take any of my flowers they wanted! They taught me the foolproof way to dry hydrangeas, however. Cut them at the desired length when the blooms look best, and put each stem in a shot glass half-full of water. Only fill the shot glass one time. Also, don't try putting a bunch in a vase with the equivalent amount of water; they'll act like cut flowers and rot after a while. Instead, prop each stem in its own shot glass. Leave them in a dark, well-ventilated room for a couple of weeks, and they'll dry perfectly. The only question I have is this: Why do they have five hundred shot glasses at that women's club?

Hydrangeas are not all the same.

Q My **hydrangea** is getting too tall and wide, but the last time I pruned it down, I didn't get any flowers for the next two years. How and when do you prune them to keep them a reasonable size without sacrificing the flowers?

A Late February or early March is the time to prune hydrangeas. Most hydrangeas, such as *H. macrophylla* (both the pom-pom and the lace-cap varieties), *H. quercifolia* (oakleaf hydrangea), and *H. aspera* (Asian hydrangea), bloom on last year's growth. Resist the urge to cut them back hard; they'll sprout everywhere you cut, and you'll end up with a crowded, ugly mess that won't flower for at least a year. Instead, symmetrically thin out about one-third of the older branches. Cut any remaining branches with last year's flowers to the first healthy bud immediately below the spent bloom. The result will be an attractive, slightly taller shrub that will produce outstanding flowers in midsummer. *Hydrangea paniculata* 'Grandiflora' (Peegee hydrangea) and *H. arborescens* (smooth hydrangea) are different. The flowers occur on current-season growth. These hydrangeas can be cut back hard annually to control height without sacrificing the current summer's flower display.

Thin rather than whacking back hydrangeas.

Q I'm ready to yank out my pom-pom **hydrangea** bush. It gets too tall, but when I whack it back down, I don't get any flowers. Is there a way to cut it down without losing all of my blooms?

A *Hydrangea macrophylla* (both the pom-pom and the lacecap varieties) blooms off last year's growth. If you whack it back hard, you're most likely removing last year's growth, so you'll get no flowers. Instead, your hydrangea gets revenge by growing zillions of sprouts right where you made the cuts, creating an ugly, crowded shrub. Rather than pruning all of the branches down, symmetrically remove a third of the older canes by cutting them off at the ground, or where they connect to a branch near the ground. Your hydrangea will be taller but will have an elegant, open appearance. You'll get fewer, but bigger and better, flowers. When removing last season's spent blossoms, cut to the first healthy bud just below the flowers for sturdy uniform growth.

Jack-in-the-pulpits cast magic spells.

Q While visiting a friend, I spotted an exotic plant with a mottled stem and a hooded flower. My friend called it a **jack-in-the-pulpit**. Where can I get some, and what conditions do they need? I've got to have this plant!

A Jack-in-the-pulpits (*Arisaema*) are sometimes available at nurseries that specialize in unusual plants, or you can order them from specialty nursery catalogs. These are mysterious-looking plants that you'd expect to see in a sorcerer's garden. Close relatives of calla lilies, they have ornate hooded callalike spathe flowers that resemble snake heads. *A. urashima* has a long, tonguelike spadix (fleshy flower spike) that reminds me of a cobra about to strike, while the gigantic spathe of *A. wilsonii* rises to a menacing 3 feet tall, nestled in a covering of black-purple mottled leaves. *A. kelung-insularis* is a less threatening specimen that should be planted where light will shine through the spathe, to illuminate the dazzling purple and white striping. *A. sikokianum* is absolutely bewitching. Its black-and-silver spathe will enchant total strangers, who will knock on your door begging to know what it is and how to find and grow one. Plant it in bright shade where your neighbors can see it, and keep it moist and well fertilized. It will cast a spell that will win you new friends in your neighborhood.

They're not all fragrant.

Q I've finally moved into my own home with a garden, and I've got to plant some heavenly scented **jasmine**. Which kinds are the most fragrant? When is the best time to prune them so they don't climb into my other plants?

A Jasmines can be some of the most fragrant of vines, but choose carefully. Many varieties are odorless, others are shrubby and won't climb, and some aren't reliably hardy. The fragrant climbers must live in a sunny location and be near something they can twine around. The most fragrant and long-blooming climbing jasmine comes from the Himalayas. *Jasminum officinale* (poet's jasmine) is semievergreen, is hardy to about zero degrees, and can rapidly twine its way to 30 feet. It blooms profusely all summer long with staggeringly fragrant inch-long white flowers. The variety *J. officinale affine* from Spain shares similar attributes, but only climbs to 15 feet. *Jasminum polyanthum* is another, similarly hardy evergreen climber that reaches 20 feet, but its highly fragrant white and rose-colored flowers occur only in late winter and early spring. A wonderfully fragrant deciduous hybrid is *J. × stephanense*, which quickly climbs to 20 feet and is blanketed with pink flowers from late spring into midsummer. This one is slightly less hardy, surviving only dips to about 10 degrees. Jasmine is best pruned in summer to keep it in bounds. If it becomes a tangled mess, cut the entire plant to within inches of the ground in spring. It will quickly grow back to set fragrant blooms in summer.

Lilies are a must.

Q I've always wanted to grow **lilies**, but there seem to be many kinds. What's the difference between the various types? Do they come only as bulbs, and are some kinds easier than others to care for?

A Lilies can be easily planted at almost any time of the year. They're available as bulbs in fall, or as potted plants in spring and summer. These tall, stately plants add color, fragrance, and elegance to the garden. There are quite a few varieties (some are rarer than others), but they're usually divided into three main categories. The easiest to grow are Asiatic lilies. These are generally the first lilies to bloom, and although most are unscented, they make up for that shortcoming with some of the hottest colors in the garden. Aurelian hybrids (trumpet lilies) bloom in midsummer. Some reach 9 feet tall, carrying as many as twenty incredibly fragrant flowers. The Oriental hybrids are the last to bloom, but their huge, fragrant flowers are well worth waiting for. 'Stargazer' is the most popular, but there are many incredible varieties and all sorts of colors to choose from. Most lilies are relatively easy to grow and do best with full sun in the Pacific Northwest. Keep the soil moist at all times, and feed regularly with high-phosphorus organic fertilizer. Cut off the flowering portion as soon as the blooms fade, to prevent energy from being wasted in seed production, but wait to cut the plants back until the leaves and stems turn yellow in the fall.

Give lilies an energy boost.

Q I love **lilies** for their superb fragrance and magnificent flowers. I've been growing trumpet and Oriental lilies for a few years now, but this year I was surprised to find that they didn't get as large and showy as they did in past years. They look healthy, just smaller. What can I do to make them strong and big again?

A The trick to growing huge lilies is to feed them right after they're done blooming. Food manufactured in the leaves is sent down to be stored as energy in the bulb. The more energy that's stored, the bigger the bulb, and the more spectacular your lily display next year. Give your lilies a shot of organic bulb food, and you'll be rewarded with huge flowering stalks next summer. Just don't ask me how in the world to stake these monsters. . . .

Overwinter your tender geraniums and fuchsias.

Q Will my **Martha Washington geraniums and hanging fuchsias** survive if I leave them outside over the winter? I've got some unusual varieties, and I'd like to keep them going. How should I store them if they aren't hardy?

A Although they sometimes survive outdoors in mild winters, Martha Washington geraniums (pelargoniums) and hanging fuchsias need to be protected from the ravages of winter cold. The easiest method is to put your tender perennials in an unheated garage for the winter. Some folks put them in a crawl space, but if there's a really hard freeze, that might mean "goodbye Charlie." Leave them in their pots or, if you dig them out of the garden, put them in a box and cover the roots with compost. Water just enough to keep the root balls from going totally dry. Cut the branches to about 8 inches tall. That will remove most of the leaves and prevent you from having to do a cleanup job in the garage. Transplant and cut back further in spring, and with a little luck, you'll have healthy geraniums and fuchsias to give you a head start on next year's garden.

What's in a name?

Q I found a plant called **Miss Willmott's Ghost** at a nearby nursery, and it looks like a magnificent plant. Yet, something about the name makes me hesitant to plant it. Am I just being superstitious?

A Anyone who has tried to rid the garden of *Myosotis sylvatica* knows how forget-me-not earned its common name. So, you'd think I'd have known better than to plant *Eryngium giganteum*, known as Miss Willmott's Ghost, in my garden. This irresistible behemoth perennial grows to over 4 feet tall and 2 ½ feet wide and sports milky white, spiny leaves that reach 10 inches long. When it blooms in midsummer, the sheer number of sharply spined 4-inch silver-blue flowers is truly impressive. Unfortunately, so is the number of deeply rooted seedlings that come back to haunt you for years to come. The plant earned its common name because Miss Ellen Willmott, a famous English gardener, secretly scattered the seeds of it whenever she'd visit a garden, leaving a haunting memory of her presence. Don't invite Miss Willmott's Ghost into your garden; or, if you can't resist tempting the supernatural, cut off the faded flowers before they go to seed.

Rid your garden of embarrassments in fall.

Q I'm new at this **mixed-border** thing, and mine didn't quite work out the way I planned it. I've created some color clashes that make me cringe. When is the best time to make some badly needed changes?

A Fall is one of the best times to move perennials in your mixed border, with the goal of fixing those little disasters that embarrassed the tweetle out of you earlier in the season. Believe me, even the experts make infamous boo-boos. One of my biggest mistakes, for instance, was planting a *Codonopsis pilosula* where it spills over a pathway. The flowers are spectacular, but whenever anyone brushes against the foliage, it gives off a skunk-like odor that makes Pepe Le Pew smell like a perfume salesperson at Macy's! Fall is also a great time to try something new. The nurseries don't want to nurse perennials through the winter, so they sell them dirt-cheap. Look for the half-price table, and don't worry if the plants don't look great. Loosen the roots when you plant them, and they'll come back like gangbusters in the spring. Of course, half-price plants won't be in flower at the fall sales, so you can't be sure that you aren't creating even worse color clashes, but that's the fun of perennial gardening. It's always a surprise.

Plant a beastly beautiful plant.

Q I planted some bulbs of the spectacular **Mexican tiger flower,** but they didn't come back the following year. What did I do wrong?

A Don't give up trying to grow Mexican tiger flower (*Tigridia pavonia*). The flowers are so beautiful that people who don't even know me knock on my door and ask if it's an orchid. The exotic, red or yellow, 4-inch-wide flowers consist of a central cup crisscrossed with boldly colored tiger stripes, surrounded by three large, dark-colored petals and three shorter, highly colorful ones. Each exquisite flower lasts only one day, but the plants produce a succession of replacements throughout most of the summer. These iris relatives are bulbous perennials and, despite coming from Mexico, can flourish here in the Northwest. The books say they are only hardy to 20 degrees, but at my house they've survived dips to below 10 degrees. The key is planting them in well-drained soil. Plant them 4 inches deep in a sunny location and in the fall cover them about a foot deep with fern fronds to repel winter rains. If you live in a colder area, dig up the bulbs in October, store them in dry peat moss during winter, and replant in early March. Don't plant Mexican tiger flower if you don't like meeting your neighbors, because I guarantee they'll be knocking on your door after they catch a glimpse of this wild tiger.

Don't let nasty aphids take the zing out of your nasturtiums.

Q Is it true that **nasturtiums** are edible? Which parts can you eat? Also, what killed a few of my nasturtium plants? They looked fine one day, but they were dead the next. I turned the leaves over and saw millions of black bugs.

A The fiery red and orange flowers of the annual nasturtium (*Tropaeolum majus*) will not only spice up your garden but add pizzazz to your salad too. The new leaves, flowers, and unripe seedpods have a delicious peppery taste. Cooks actually used the flower buds in place of capers during the world wars, when capers were unavailable. Unfortunately, there's a black aphid that also appreciates the savory qualities of your nasturtiums. These bugs seem to descend by the gazillions to suck the life right out of your nasturtiums overnight. Actually, they hang out in small numbers for at least a week before the population suddenly explodes into devastating numbers. If you catch them early, a timely *el kabatski* will eliminate them before it's too late. Every morning, turn over a few leaves and squish the early intruders. A few timely treatments will ensure that you'll be the one enjoying the zingy qualities of your nasturtiums rather than the aphids.

Add an exotic touch in the garden by planting hardy orchids.

Q I grow several attractive orchids in my home. Are there any **orchids** hardy enough to grow outside year round in the garden?

A There are several kinds of orchids that are easy to grow outside in the garden year round. One of the most attractive is *Bletilla striata* (Chinese ground orchid). Hardy to –10 degrees, this orchid has pinkish purple blossoms that resemble cattleya (a spectacular nonhardy orchid). They bloom from spring to summer, with each plant producing up to twelve 2-inch-long blossoms on a foot-and-a-half-tall stem. Bletillas spread readily forming large clumps, but don't be in a hurry to divide them: They bloom best when crowded. Another easy-to-grow orchid is *Dactylorhiza* (spotted orchid). Also hardy to –10 degrees, this Chinese orchid displays spotted leopardlike foliage that is almost as showy as the flowers. In May, an upright, lance-shaped, 4- to 6-inch raceme is densely covered with lilac-purple blossoms. Another truly spectacular hardy orchid is *Cypripedium calceolus*. I was amazed to see this orchid, covered with cheery yellow lady's-slipper blossoms, growing wild in upper New York and Massachusetts. And I was equally surprised to find it at a local nursery. Be sure to ask if the cypripedium is seed grown, and don't buy this endangered plant if it was dug from the forest. Cypripediums require the same conditions as other hardy orchids: rich, moist soil and light shade. Cypripediums prefer a sweeter soil, however, and need regular additions of lime.

Keep your puppy away from hellebore.

Q Someone recently told me that **Oriental hellebores** are poisonous. Is that true? I have a young puppy that chews plants.

A Don't allow Fido to play among the hellebores until he grows out of the chewing stage. All through the Middle Ages, anyone suffering from mental anxiety was treated with a potion made of hellebore. We now know that hellebore is one of the most poisonous plants around. Aren't you glad you didn't live in the Middle Ages?

Get your paperwhite narcissus a little tipsy.

Q When I force **paperwhite narcissus** bulbs for the holidays, the flower stalks inevitably grow tall and then fall over. Is there a way to keep that from happening?

A Paperwhites are powerfully fragrant narcissus that you can easily force to bloom in the house for the holidays. Place the bulbs in an attractive container on top of glass balls or some other decorative material. Fill with just enough water to touch the base of the bulbs and watch them take off. Just as you described, the problem is that in our warm homes, the flower stalks often grow too tall and fall over. Prevent this by keeping the bulbs in a cool, bright location until they bloom. If that's not possible, add a tablespoon of vodka when the stalks reach 5 inches tall. The vodka burns the roots and slows the growth. Your paperwhites may stagger a bit and make fools of themselves at your party, but the blooms will remain standing.

It's easy to be passionate about passionflower.

Q I'm in love. I recently discovered a blue **passionflower** at my local nursery. According to the tag, the plant comes from South America. Will it really grow well in the Northwest? I love the blue one, but I'd like to try other colors as well. Are there varieties of passionflower that can withstand Northwest winters?

A It's hard to imagine a vine with more spectacular blooms than *Passiflora caerulea* (blue passionflower). The evergreen vine comes from tropical South America, but it's hardy to about zero degrees and easy to grow here. It loves heat, so give it a sunny exposure with something for the tendrils to grip and climb. Passionflower features unusual 4-inch blooms containing a complex structure of creamy white petals, crowned with numerous narrow filaments beginning dark purple, turning white, and ending in lavender. Each flower lasts only one day, but new ones open every day. Evergreen in mild winters, blue passionflower will drop its leaves in cold winters and even freeze to the ground if temperatures reach below 20 degrees. Fortunately, it will grow back in spring to produce a plethora of blossoms in summer. Although rarely available at local nurseries, there are other hardy varieties of passionflower that feature multicolored, sometimes fragrant flowers. If you decide to buy an unusual species from a catalog, first make inquiries: A friend ordered *P. jorullensis*. The flowers were beautiful, but they gave off an unusual fragrance. We nicknamed it "eau de monkey pee" and it didn't enjoy a long stay in his garden.

Save money on peonies.

Q **Peonies** are so expensive to buy at the nursery. I grow several spectacular ones that I'd like to divide, but I've heard that you're never supposed to do that. Is that true, or can I make new ones for free?

A Herbaceous peonies are long-lived perennials that never need dividing. That being said, there's no truth to the old myth that says you should never divide them. New ones really do cost a mint, so it's worth the effort to occasionally divide your peony to make new plants. Once the foliage dies back, dig up the clump and use a hose to gently wash the soil off the roots. Divide into sections using a sharp knife or a bow saw, making sure that each section has at least three eyes. The eyes can be found on the roots, just below where the stems attach, and are easy to see once the soil has been removed. Replant the sections immediately to prevent the roots from drying out. Add lots of compost; then plant the eyes right at the soil surface in a sunny location with good air circulation. Be patient. It will take the plant a couple of years to regain enough energy to bloom again, but it's worth the wait. Soon you'll be enjoying many more of your favorite peony blooms without taking out a second mortgage to pay for them.

Keep the floriferous display going.

Q What's going on? All of my **perennials** are blooming much earlier than ever before. The show is fantastic, but at the rate it's going, I'm afraid there'll be nothing left in bloom by fall. Is there anything I can do to slow down the process?

A Our warm spring weather creates spectacular flower displays by causing perennials to flower earlier than ever with huge, vibrant blooms. Even perennials that normally flower in fall, such as asters, lobelias, and phlox, burst into blossom by midsummer. Not surprisingly, many perennials tend to bloom themselves out early. Deadheading in early summer is critical, or there will be few flowers left to enjoy by the end of August. Remove the spent flowers of *Kniphofia* (torch lily), evergreen penstemon, *Nepeta* (catmint), herbaceous salvia, *Scabiosa*, *Knautia*, Spanish lavender, dahlias, hardy fuchsias, and roses before they go to seed. Early bloomers that are beginning to fade and flop, such as delphiniums, hardy geraniums, and tradescantia, should be cut back hard to induce them to grow back and bloom a second time. Coax vigorous growth and flowering by applying a generous shot of alfalfa meal every six weeks, and make sure perennials receive adequate water and never go dry. You'll be rewarded for all of the hard work with a floriferous, colorful garden in fall. Better yet, plant a bunch of cool hebes. Unless we get an Arctic express, these New Zealand shrubs will be covered with dazzling purple, pink, or white flowers from now until well after Christmas. Most hebes aren't reliably hardy, but a good-sized plant costs only about $10, so even if a few die, it's worth planting lots.

The good thing about perennial gardening is that you can move plants anytime you want. The bad thing about perennial gardening is that every time you bring home a new plant, you have to move 540 plants in order to put the newest in that perfect spot.

Stake perennials before they fall over.

Q My delphiniums, lilies, and a host of other **perennials** are getting so tall! I'm worried that if I don't stake them soon, they might fall over. I don't like that look of heavy rebar stakes in my garden, though. Is there something a bit more subtle that will do the job?

A Delphiniums, crocosmias, lilies, and a host of other perennials should be staked as soon as they grow tall, before they fall over. Once a flower stalk tumbles, you might as well cut it for a bouquet, as it generally ends its career as a garden attraction for the season. English Y stakes, available at most good nurseries, consist of a thin metal bar that's inserted in the ground. The bar is topped with two metal wires that can be bent to support the plant. Connecting wires can be inserted into eyes at the end of the bendable wires to help hold the plant if necessary. Y stakes come in different sizes and can be used to stake almost any kind of plant, even English roses and peonies. Best of all, the stakes are unobtrusive and barely noticeable in the garden.

Fertilize perennials.

Q I'm confused about whether I should fertilize my perennials. Some experts seem to say that you don't need to fertilize at all, while others advise fertilizing regularly. Who's right?

A Just as my puppy Fred needs adequate nutrition to make sure he grows up healthy and strong, flowering perennials need feeding to make sure they will get big and bloom with showy flowers. Begin feeding in March and apply an organic perennial fertilizer at the recommended rate, or work alfalfa meal into the soil (a couple of handfuls per average-size perennial). Perennials that bloom only once per season, such as peonies, generally require only one application of fertilizer. To keep repeat-bloomers such as clematis, dahlias, and delphiniums flowering away, fertilize about once every six weeks until September.

Cut back phlox in early summer for a better display in fall.

Q It seems as though all the perennials in my garden bloom earlier in the season every year. In particular, the perennial garden **phlox** that used to bloom in September has been blooming in July. Is there anything I can do to delay the bloom? Also, is there anything I can do to prevent the powdery mildew that always seems to attack phlox in late summer?

A I don't know if it's global warming or just a change in our climate, but I agree that everything's blooming earlier than it used to these days. To save a bit of the show for late summer, pinch the new growth on your border phlox (*Phlox paniculata*) in May. Then, in June, cut the stems back by half. You can cut back by a third in July, as long as you do it before the flower buds form. This will produce shorter plants and delay flowering by two to four weeks. Be sure to water your phlox well to help prevent powdery mildew, which tends to run rampant in plants suffering from drought stress. Better yet, replace disease-ridden types with resistant forms. Check the plant tag to find one of the many resistant varieties, including some with colorful foliage, that aren't bothered by powdery mildew.

Create an abundance of a popular plant.

Q I bought one of those **pineapple lilies,** and it's a winner. I love the interesting flowers, and even the leaves are attractive. It's getting almost too large for the spot I planted it in, though. Plus I'd like to have more of these exotic-looking lilies to plant in other places. Can you divide pineapple lilies?

A Every year, new varieties of pineapple lily (*Eucomis*) are becoming available, and it's not surprising that gardeners find them irresistible. They're interesting African plants with strappy leaves and spotted flowers that resemble pineapple tops. New varieties are coming out, such as 'Oakhurst', with 2-foot-tall leaves that remain dark red all summer and attractive dark-spotted burgundy flowers. The green-leaved variety 'Pole-Evansii' is purported to grow 6 feet tall! *Eucomis* are easy to divide in spring. Just use your digging spade to remove one of the outside leaf clusters, making sure to dig up the bulb, or dig up the whole clump and use your spade to make lots of new plants.

Flowers you'll love to cut.

Q I'm looking for something interesting to plant in my sunny blue border. I love to make flower arrangements, so I was hoping to find an architecturally interesting **plant with blue flowers** that would look nice in the garden and add interest in bouquets. Any suggestions?

A Globe thistle (*Echinops*) is a rugged-looking, prickly-leaved, structural perennial that can reach 6 feet tall. Given rich, moisture-retentive soil in full sun, *Echinops* will repay the favor with a plethora of metallic blue flowers that resemble bristly, oversized golf balls. Depending on the variety, the flowers come in several shades of shimmering blue or white. You'll love the look of each and every bloom. Despite this, you'll want to cut them off because they look fantastic in flower arrangements. The cool blue flowers add an icy glow, especially when contrasted with the hot-colored blooms of hibiscus, gerbera, and daisy, or spiky favorites such as gladiolus and crocosmias. By the way, the pollen-rich flowers are irresistible to pollinating insects, so don't use them in table displays at outdoor parties, unless your guests like bees!

Keep your plumeria happy.

Q I managed to get the **plumeria** cutting I bought at a flower and garden show to root. Now how do I get it to bloom so I can enjoy the incredible fragrance?

A Congratulations on rooting your *Plumeria* (frangipani) cutting. Here's how to keep it happy in order to win a big payoff in fragrant flowers. Frangipanis grow 1 or 2 feet per year. Transplant yours into a pot an inch bigger every other spring. Pot it up in cactus mix. These fragrant small trees aren't from Hawaii; they actually come from barren desert conditions in South America and require extremely well-drained potting soil. In spring and summer, water deeply and wait to water again until the surface of the soil is dry. In mid-October, begin cutting back on the watering and move the plant into an unheated garage or basement. Stop watering completely as soon as the leaves fall off, usually by mid-November. Your plumeria will remain dormant until conditions begin to warm up in mid-March. Then it's time to move your plumeria inside near a bright window and begin watering again. Place it outdoors on nice sunny days, but be sure to bring it back inside at night. By Mother's Day, leave your plumeria outdoors in full sun for the duration of summer. Beginning in April, fertilize every two weeks with a high-nitrogen soluble houseplant food to promote growth; but in May, switch to a high-phosphorus fertilizer to encourage blooming. Visitors just might break into the Hukilau, a hula dance that I recently mastered in Hawaii, when they fall under the spell of the fragrance.

Give your plumeria cutting a fighting chance.

Q At a local garden show, I came home with a cutting of a **plumeria**, but my dreams of sweet Hawaiian fragrance were dashed when the cutting rotted before setting roots. I followed the directions that came with the cutting. What went wrong?

A Hundreds of garden show visitors buy *Plumeria* (frangipani) cuttings in the hopes of enjoying the sweet scent reminiscent of Hawaii. Unfortunately, most of the cuttings rot before they ever root. If you've kept the cutting, don't throw it in the compost bin just yet. Cut off the rotten part and try rooting what remains the way the professionals do it: Fill all but 1 inch of a one-gallon pot with a mix of two-thirds perlite and one-third potting soil. Dip the bottom of the cutting in rooting hormone, then insert it 3 inches deep into the rooting medium and firm the soil enough to hold it straight. Fill the top inch of the pot with pea gravel. Water thoroughly, and remove any excess water from the saucer. Place the cutting in a warm, sunny window inside your house and water only when the soil is dry enough that the pot feels light when lifted. Even if you do everything right, the part of the cutting in the soil medium may rot. If that happens, cut off the rotten part and try again. It's kind of a hassle, but you'll know it was worth it when your entire patio smells like a luau.

Protect primrose from slugs.

Q I recently moved to the Pacific Northwest, and I love those bright **primroses** that bloom in late winter and early spring. I assume they are easy to grow. Are there any varieties that are especially attractive?

A The Pacific Northwest is one of the best areas in the world for growing primroses. All they require is a moist location in bright shade and protection from slugs and snails. Apply the new, much-safer brands of slug bait containing iron phosphate (such as Sluggo, WorryFree, or EscarGo) to keep these midnight marauders at bay. There are hundreds of primrose varieties to choose from, but for a little extra pizzazz, try some unusual species: *Primula florindae* (cowslip) has glossy leaves and spectacularly fragrant umbels of as many as forty sulfur-yellow flowers per stem in mid-summer. Another interesting one is *P. japonica*, with whorls of candelabra blooms that build on top of each other, forming as many as six levels of flowers on a 2-foot-tall stem in midspring. Perhaps the most unusual of all, *P. vialii*, shoots up 6-inch-long lance-shaped stems that open to become dense pointed spikes of tubular blue-violet flowers topped with crimson.

Russian sage isn't Russian, but it's cool.

Q A couple of summers ago, I discovered a great plant from Russia called **Russian sage**. It thrives in a hot, dry corner of my garden and puts on a magnificent flower display. It's developing bare, woody stems at the base, however. Will it harm my Russian sage if I cut the woody stems back to near the base to try to get it to branch out?

A *Perovskia atriplicifolia* (Russian sage) is native from India to Iran. So why do they call it Russian sage? Evidently because it was named after a Russian guy named Perovski, plus it's fun to say! This drought-tolerant, sun-loving perennial is a wonderful addition to the dry, sunny border. The lacy, silver foliage reaches 3 to 4 feet tall before disappearing behind a smoky blue cloud made up of hundreds of flowers in late spring and summer. Left to grow naturally, the stems become woody and unsightly. To prevent this, every year in early March, cut back each stem to a strong pair of buds as close to the ground as possible. If the framework has become woody and congested, remove a few of the oldest canes by cutting them to the ground.

It's not ugly!

Q I'm always looking for plants that will bloom in fall to make my late-season garden more interesting. I recently found a fall bloomer called **Salvia uliginosa** for sale at my local nursery. I understand that it's from Mexico, and I noticed that its common name is bog sage. Will it do OK in my drought-tolerant garden?

A *Salvia uliginosa* once caused a great deal of levity in a group of plant experts (and a whole lot of embarrassment for me) when I accidentally pronounced it *Salvia* "ug-ly-no-sa" while leading a tour at Seattle University. The species name of this Mexican salvia actually means "of marshes," and this is one of the few salvias that prefers damp soil conditions. Fortunately, as long as you live where temperatures rarely drop below 15 degrees, this stunningly beautiful perennial will thrive in moderately dry conditions. *Salvia uliginosa* is a must for the fall garden. It grows 4 to 6 feet tall and is topped by swarms of airy, sky-blue flowers, beginning in late summer and continuing well into autumn. Besides its difficult name, *Salvia uliginosa* has one other undesirable attribute: In moist soil conditions, it spreads aggressively from rhizomes. Fortunately, it's easy to curb this salvia's rampageous nature. It won't run as long as you plant it in well-drained soil and water only moderately. Then "uglynosa" will be a well-behaved, *beautiful* addition to your fall garden.

Plant a whiff of spring.

Q I'm looking for a fragrant plant that will grow in the shade. Someone told me about a plant called **Sarcococca** that is supposed to smell great. Is it easy to grow here, and is it really fragrant?

A To say that *Sarcococca* is fragrant is like saying that I like brussels sprouts (a severe understatement)! We're talking big-time fragrance here. The flowers are small, but they pack a wallop. Bring a sprig into the house, and visitors will be convinced that someone is getting married in a back room. Sarcococca blooms in late winter, and its only drawback is that the intense fragrance always leads to a severe attack of spring fever. Native to China, this easy-to-grow member of the boxwood family sports dark green leaves and attractive berries. Grow it only in shade; the foliage turns an ugly yellow if it gets too much sun. *Sarcococca ruscifolia* can reach 4 or 5 feet tall, while *S. hookeriana humilis* seldom exceeds 1½ feet tall, spreads by underground runners and, once established, will make a wonderful groundcover even in relatively dry shade.

Would I lie to you?

Q I saw you on TV showing how to cut **sedum** back by two-thirds in the first week of June. Are you sure you know what you're doing?

A What is it about my suggestion to cut back sedum that has home gardeners so up in arms? One spring I recommended over the airwaves to cut back sedums by two-thirds. A day later, while I was walking my puppies Fred and Ruby, all three of us ended up jumping for cover after being startled by the sound of screeching tires. An elderly lady had slammed on her brakes in the middle of the road upon seeing me. She rolled down the window and shouted, "Are you sure you're right about cutting sedums back?" When I answered in the affirmative, she said, "You'd better be right!" and tore off, never to be seen again. Trust me: You can cut your sedums back up to two-thirds in the first week of June. They'll bloom a little later, you'll get more flowers, and they won't get floppy and need staking.

Cut back browning *Tradescantia*.

Q My **spiderwort** looked great for most of the spring, but in early summer it stopped blooming. Is there anything I can do to make it bloom again?

A *Tradescantia* × *andersoniana* (spiderwort), an East Coast native, sports clumps of grassy leaves and attractive three-petaled flowers that come in purple, blue, white, or pink. Each flower lasts only a day, but new flowers usually bloom every day. Eventually all of the buds in the clusters bloom themselves out. If your plant is vigorous, cut to lateral bud clusters that you'll find forming lower on the stems. If, on the other hand, the foliage begins to brown and flop over, cut all of the stems to within an inch of the ground. Keep the soil moist and fertilize with alfalfa meal or an organic flower food. New lush foliage will emerge within about three weeks, and hopefully your plant will rebloom for the rest of summer. By the way, unless you like looking like a hippie, don't make the mistake I did and wear a new white T-shirt while pruning. The purple flowers leave stains, and to this day my T-shirt looks like it was tie-dyed.

Combine bulbs for showy spring displays.

Q While on a walk, I noticed a colorful display of **spring-blooming bulbs**. What caught my eye was a bunch of daffodils coming up right through a different type of blue-flowering bulbs. Can you plant different bulbs in the same hole together?

A You can create sensational color combinations by placing different types of spring-flowering bulbs together in the same planting hole. Place bulbs that bloom at the same time in the same hole by planting the bigger bulbs deeper, covering them with a couple of inches of soil, and planting the smaller ones right on top of them. My all-time favorite combination is a mix of 10-inch-tall, bright orange and yellow 'Jetfire' daffodils with 6-inch-tall, gentian blue *Chionodoxa* (glory-of-the-snow). Different-colored bulbs in the same genus can look stunning together as well. Imagine glacier-white *Iris reticulata* 'Natasha' mixed in with the dark-blue *I. reticulata* 'Harmony'. Squirrels a problem? They don't eat daffodils, but they devour most kinds of crocus. For a winning rodent-proof combination, combine the cheery yellow miniature daffodil 'Tête-à-Tête' with the showy, squirrel-resistant *Crocus tommasinianus* 'Ruby Giant'. Then your only problem will be the need to wait till spring to see the results of your artistic endeavors.

Spring-blooming bulbs add color to stepping-stone walkways.

Q I planted my parking strip and installed a stepping-stone walkway through the garden. It's in full sun, and the space between the stepping-stones varies from 6 inches to a foot or more. I've considered planting **spring-blooming bulbs** between the stones to add color. Is that a good idea?

A Planting spring-blooming bulbs between stepping-stones in a walkway is a great way to add colorful flowers. You can plant the bulbs in fall; if you don't get a chance, most nurseries carry a wide variety of flowering bulbs in containers in spring, and you can mix and match to create sparkling combinations. Pick a spot with full sun and good drainage, and don't forget to work bulb food into the planting hole. Bulbs probably won't survive in a thoroughfare, but in less-used walkways, folks notice the colorful bulbs and avoid stepping on them. Plant bulbs with delicate tall flowers, such as *Iris reticulata* and miniature daffodils, near the outer edges of the walkway, where they're less likely to be stepped on. Fill the center of the walkway with miniature crocus. These sturdy little bulbs are better able to withstand an occasional encounter with a size 9.

It might not be too late to plant spring-blooming bulbs.

Q How late in the fall can I plant **spring bulbs**?

A Spring-blooming bulbs generally need a cold period of eight to ten weeks to set their blooms. As long as you plant them by the end of November, they'll experience enough winter weather to ensure a great display in spring. The longer you wait, the later they'll bloom. If you find a bag of blooms in the garage in spring, try planting them anyway. They definitely won't grow in the garage, and with a little luck, once planted they might still bloom. They probably won't come back the following year, but if you get one season of blooms out of them, it's better than nothing.

Spring-blooming bulbs need companions.

Q What's the trick to creating a terrific **spring bulb display**? My neighbor plants about the same number of bulbs that I do, but her display is so attractive that all the neighbors come by to see it, while mine is so boring even the squirrels won't stop by for a visit.

A There's nothing worse than having a neighbor whose showy spring-flowering bulb display makes yours look like a desert scene. Spring bulbs add cheer and are attractive on their own, but unless you plant them en masse, small clumps here and there have limited impact. Blow your neighbor's display out of the water by companioning your spring bulbs with other bright flowering bulbs, perennials, and shrubs. Most of the nurseries carry spring-blooming bulbs potted up in flower. A lonely clump of yellow daffodils becomes a fireworks display when you surround it with a few pots of dark-blue giant crocus. Or start with the gorgeous 'Apricot

Beauty' tulips, but add a background of the heavily tinted purple foliage and bright green inflorescences of *Euphorbia amygdaloides* 'Purpurea' and the effect is absolutely seductive. Species tulips tend to be long lasting in the landscape, and one of the most exotic is *Tulipa acuminata*, with gray-green, undulating foliage topped by 18-inch-tall, narrow 3- to 5-inch-long scarlet-and-yellow twisty flowers. It is absolutely sensational teamed with the dusky, sword-shaped leaves of *Phormium tenax* 'Bronze' or planted next to the caramel-red and yellow emerging leaves of *Spiraea japonica* 'Magic Carpet'. If squirrels, mice, or deer are eating the flowers off your tulips, add a few clusters of the flaming orange *Fritillaria imperialis* 'Rubra Maxima' to the mix. It looks spectacular with yellow, red, or purple tulips, and this fritillaria emits an odor guaranteed to chase away pests. Make sure to be nice to your neighbor when he or she comes over asking for design tips.

Star jasmine is (usually) hardy in the Pacific Northwest.

Q On a garden tour, I saw—or should I say, smelled— a fragrant vine called **star jasmine**. I'd like to try planting it. Will it withstand winter cold, and how big does it get?

A According to most garden encyclopedias, *Trachelospermum jasminoides* (star jasmine) is hardy only to about 20 degrees, yet one of these attractive vines has graced my garden for years and has survived dips to below 12 degrees. Although the white, inch-wide flowers smell like those of true jasmine (*Jasminum officinale*), the two plants are totally unrelated. In its native China, star jasmine can reach 20 to 30 feet, but it rarely gets that tall in our area. To grow it as a 2-foot-tall by 4-foot-wide shrub, give it nothing to climb and cut it back regularly during the growing season. Star jasmine can be planted in sun or shade and will reward you with beaucoup clusters of fragrant flowers during early summer. If you live in an especially cold area, pot it up and bring it into the house during the winter. You might not want to put it back into the garden. Star jasmine makes an unbelievably fragrant houseplant.

It's not stinky.

Q While visiting the nursery I discovered an attractive hellebore, but I didn't buy it because the common name was **stinking hellebore**. I wanted to try it, but I don't want to plant something that's going to smell bad. Does it really stink?

A Don't let the malodorous moniker scare you off. The leaves of stinking hellebore (*Helleborus foetidus*) give off a bad smell only if you crush them. Stinking hellebore is a distinctive, long-lived evergreen that will provide color and interest year-round. Unlike those of other hellebores, the 8-inch-long, leathery leaves are narrowly dissected, producing an almost fernlike appearance. An added benefit is the nodding, pale greenish flowers that appear in late winter. Exciting new introductions have been developed. One that has taken the gardening world by storm is 'Wester Flisk'. An enchanting infusion of purplish red in the stems, leaves, and flowers makes this shade lover a must-have plant. 'Red Silver' is even more elegant, with exquisite silvery gray leaves blushed with pink. Unlike most strains of *H. foetidus*, which prefer moist soil and require protection from afternoon sun, 'Red Silver' requires sharp drainage and full sun to perform at its best. 'Gold Bullion' is a spanking-new introduction. This one thrives in morning sun or semishade and lives up to its name, lighting up the winter garden with finely dissected golden leaves. Plant it among a mass of midnight black *Heuchera* 'Obsidian' for a breathtaking combination.

Enjoy a fragrant moon garden.

Q We frequently entertain in the evening. Are there plants that we could use in our garden or containers that would add a **sweet scent** at our dinner parties?

A Add a sensory treat to your evening garden parties by planting night-fragrant members of the tomato (nightshade) family. *Brugmansia, Nicotiana,* and petunias originated in South America. Although they're wonderful, the exotic scents they release into the evening air are not meant for us. These plants open their fragrant nectaries at night to seduce night-flying moths for pollination. *Brugmansia* (angel's trumpet) is the queen of the nightshade family. Simple to grow in a container, this tropical-looking, semi-hardy perennial can easily top 10 feet tall. The astonishing 8- to 10-inch hanging tubular flowers come in a variety of colors and flavor summer nights with delicious fragrance all season long. *Nicotiana* (flowering tobacco) also boasts wonderful evening fragrance. Most types of nicotiana flowers are scented, but the crown prince is *Nicotiana sylvestris.* This statuesque annual can reach 5 feet tall and will bloom with intoxicatingly fragrant, white tubular flowers that glow in the moonlight. Many varieties of petunias are also fragrant at night, but not all share the gift. Choose a single variety with dark blue or purple blooms, and with a little luck, your evenings will be filled with tantalizing scents. By the way, the pollinators that the fragrance is meant to attract remain south of the border, so your guests will be able to enjoy the delicious aromas without being bombarded by amorous moths.

Leave spent torch lily flowers for fall birds.

Q I'm delighted with the **torch lily** I planted this spring. It's been pumping out flowers nonstop all summer long. Winter's coming, however, and few new blooms are coming up to take the place of spent ones. I'm not crazy about the look of the dead flowers. Is there any reason to leave the spent flowers in fall, or should I cut them off?

A *Kniphofia* (red hot poker or torch lily) is an incredibly attractive plant that can add color and spiky form to the garden. The orange-flowered hybrids look stunning with red laceleaf maples. Best of all, the flowers are magnets for hummingbirds. New hybrids, such as 'Primrose Beauty' (bright yellow flowers), 'Bee's Sunset' (yellow and orange), and 'Sunset' (orange to red), will bloom all season long if you deadhead regularly by cutting the spent blossoms to the ground, and keep them well fertilized and watered. In fall, though, don't be in a hurry to cut off the flower spikes; the spent blossoms may not be attractive to you, but Nicolas and Nelly Nuthatch can't resist the seeds and will put on quite a show as they walk upside down, munching away.

Wake up the robins.

Q Why are **trilliums** called wake-robins? I've always wanted to plant a native trillium, but I'd also like to try some unusual varieties. Are they easy enough to grow to make it worth spending the undoubtedly high price to buy one?

A Trilliums earned the common name wake-robins because their early blooms are said to wake up the robins in spring. No woodland garden is complete without trilliums, and one of the loveliest of all is our West Coast native *Trillium ovatum*, with the characteristic three-petal flowers emerging white and fading to pink above attractive leaves that are also in whorls of three. Once you hear about some of the other incredible species out there, however, you might as well get ready to spend some big bucks, because they're so beautiful you won't be able to live without them. Absolutely irresistible is the Northern California native *T. chloropetalum*, featuring sessile (stemless), glistening burgundy-red 4-inch flowers that crown dinner plate–sized whorls of lightly mottled leaves on a 4-foot-high by 3-foot-wide plant. Another knockout from California and Oregon is *T. kurabayashii*. This woodland gem is similar to *T. chloropetalum*, except that it forms a 10-inch-tall clump of spectacularly mottled leaves supporting 4-inch blood-red flowers. These trilliums are just a few of the spectacular yet easy-to-grow rarities available online from specialty nurseries, such as www.heronswood.com. Plant them in partial to full shade in moist, well-drained soil; feed with alfalfa meal in spring; and protect them from the occasional mollusk invader. Plant a bunch of these magnificent trilliums, then listen to the robins sing at 5 a.m. while you contemplate another broke, but happy, day at the office.

Bergenias add a tropical touch.

Q I'm into **tropical-looking plants**, but I can't figure out what to plant as a groundcover that will look good with my bananas and other big-leaved plants. What will add to the tropical look?

A Bergenias are evergreen perennials in the Saxifrage family, originating from Afghanistan to Mongolia. The large, leathery heart-shaped leaves evoke a tropical flair and are especially effective companioned with bananas, cannas, and palm trees. The attractive spring flowers come in a variety of colors including white, red, pink, and magenta. As a bonus, the foliage of many varieties turns a beautiful red or bronze in winter. Bergenias prefer humus-rich soil and a sunny location, slightly shaded from the hottest afternoon sunshine. Cut off any tattered or unsightly leaves. Deadheading will promote longer blooming and make the plants look better. After three or four years bergenias usually become overcrowded and flowering often declines. Divide as soon as flowering is over by transplanting divisions taken from the vigorous corners of the clump.

Lily bulbs don't want to rest.

Q I brought home three golden-orange, incredibly fragrant 'African Queen' **trumpet lilies** from the Northwest Flower and Garden Show. Can I store them like tulips until I'm ready to plant them? Do you plant them the same way as you do tulip bulbs?

A Unlike most bulbs, lilies never go dormant, so they need to be planted as soon as possible after you bring them home. (If you must wait, store them in moist sand, compost, or peat moss.) Dig a deep, wide planting hole, and mix half a handful of bulb food into the soil. Planting depth depends on the size of the bulb. Generally, small bulbs should be covered with 2 inches of soil, medium with 4 inches, and big bulbs with 6 inches. It's better to plant too shallow than too deep, because lilies have special roots that pull the bulb down in the soil to the proper depth. In our region, lilies prefer full sun, but they do best if planted among low-growing perennials to keep their roots shaded.

Store your tuberous begonias for next summer's containers.

Q I love **tuberous begonias**. The flowers are so big and colorful, but the plants are so expensive. Is there a way to store them through the winter so I can plant them again next spring?

A Tuberous begonias make fabulous container and bedding plants for shade. Like you, I love the attractive foliage and large colorful flowers. Most folks grow them as expensive annuals, but it's easy to store the tubers through the winter and replant them in spring. In late October, move the plants under cover and stop watering them. When the leaves fall off, cut off the shoots and gently wash the dirt from the roots. Dry the tubers and store them in peat moss in an unheated garage or basement. In spring, plant the tubers hollow side up in moist peat moss, and when shoots are a couple of inches high, transplant into pots. Every year the tubers will get bigger and result in a larger, more spectacular display. Don't wait too long to get them out of the garden in fall. Tuberous begonias come from South America, and they won't survive the first light freeze.

Avoid the spring surprise.

 If I plant tulips that I forgot to plant in fall, and found in the garage in spring, will they still flower?

 How many times have you been surprised in spring to find a big bag of tulip or daffodil bulbs ruined because they were forgotten in the back corner of the garage? I'm sorry to tell you that most spring-blooming bulbs need at least eight weeks in the ground during cold weather to survive and bloom. You can still give 'em a try, though. Usually it's best to plant your spring-blooming bulbs between mid-September and the end of December. If you're like me and can't remember where you've planted them over the years, avoid the shovel and use one of those little cup-shaped bulb planters. You're less likely to skewer the bulbs that are already in the ground.

Plant deep or plant species.

 My tulips bloom beautifully during the spring following planting, but after that, I never see a bloom again. Won't tulips bloom for more than one season here?

 You're one of the many gardeners befuddled by tulips that won't come back. Tulips are indigenous to the mountains of Kazakhstan, Uzbekistan, and Tajikistan, where they rest comfortably under a blanket of snow all winter long. Here, if the tulips don't rot in the cold, wet ground, they tend to try to divide. The mother bulb wipes herself out making babies, but the new bulbs never mature to bloom in our less-than-perfect conditions. One trick you can try is to plant the tulips deeper than normally recommended. This works only with Darwin and Empress hybrid tulips, and you have to have very well drained soil. The normal recommendation is to plant the bulbs three times as deep as the diameter is wide. Instead, plant the bases 12 inches deep. For some reason, this prevents the bulbs from dividing. I've had great success using this technique; bulbs I planted 10 years ago still return to bloom each spring. Another method that definitely works is to plant species tulips. The flowers are smaller, but they make up for their small stature with vibrant colors and a tough constitution. They often naturalize and come back year after year, where the hybrids fail. A few favorites are *Tulipa bakeri* 'Lilac Wonder' (lilac flowers with a yellow center), the unpronounceable *T. kolpakowskiana* (yellow flowers streaked with red), and the even-harder-to-pronounce *T. vvedenskyi* 'Tangerine Beauty' (red flowers streaked with orange). Of course squirrels still eat tulip bulbs, so you might have to buy yourself a Jack Russell terrier as well.

Cut unsightly tulip foliage to prevent disease.

Q I know that we're supposed to wait until the foliage dies down before cutting off the foliage on **tulips**, but it looks horrible in the spring garden. Will it cause that much harm if I cut the leaves off before they wither?

A We've all heard that you shouldn't cut down your tulip foliage until it withers. According to Jeannette DeGoede, who with her husband, Tom, owns one of the biggest tulip farms in the Skagit Valley, that's a bunch of bull-tweetle. To keep your tulips healthy and strong, pull off the flower as soon as it begins to fade, but leave the stem. That helps send energy down to the roots to be stored in the bulb. Then wait only three weeks before cutting the foliage right to the ground. The bulb will have stored all of the energy it needs, and removing the foliage at this time helps reduce fungus disease problems. If your tulips are growing in a location that can be left dry during summer, they can be left in the ground. Otherwise, dig and store the bulbs in a rodent-proof container in an unheated garage until you replant them in the fall. With a little luck, you can rid your garden of unsightly tulip leaves before they die back, and you'll enjoy profuse blooms next spring as well.

Landscape location affects tulip and daffodil digging.

Q My **tulips and daffodils** have finished blooming. What can I do to make sure they bloom again next year? Is it better to leave them in the ground or to dig them up after they die back?

A Fertilize with bulb food and pick off the faded blossoms from spring-blooming bulbs before they put energy into growing seeds instead of storing carbohydrates. With all spring bulbs except tulips, wait until the foliage dies down before you cut the leaves off. That will give the bulbs time to store the energy they need to remain strong and bloom again next spring. Spring bulbs resent summer watering once the foliage has withered. If it's impossible to avoid watering their area of the landscape, it's best to dig them up after the foliage dies down and store them in ventilated trays in a cool place.

Sow a colorful groundcover.

Q Help! I've got a big area of open ground, and I know that weeds are going to run rampant there by spring. Are there any pretty **wildflowers** I can plant in fall that will fill these spots and outcompete the weeds?

A Fill up that empty area before it becomes a weed patch by sowing the seeds of hardy annual flowers. Alyssum, California poppy, godetia, lupine, bachelor's button, forget-me-not, and larkspur are just a few of the flowers that can be sowed in fall and will sprout in spring to quickly form an attractive, weed-smothering groundcover. Be forewarned, though: These are all rampant self-sowers. Don't put them in a spot near dainty perennials or vegetables unless you're willing to deadhead like a banshee.

Pick the right wisteria for your garden.

Q I visited my local nursery to purchase a **wisteria** vine, but I was surprised to find a number of different types to choose from. Please explain the differences between them.

A Wisteria is a member of the pea family, with six species, including a North American native. Generally, only varieties from China and Japan, and a few hybrids, are readily available at local nurseries. *Wisteria sinensis* is the Chinese wisteria. It's the most popular species, perhaps because the showy, foot-long, fragrant flowers open all at once, before the leaves emerge, putting on quite a show. It's the only wisteria that will bloom well in shade. The vines twist in a counterclockwise direction. My personal favorite is *W. floribunda*, commonly called Japanese wisteria, which twines in a clockwise direction. The strongly fragrant flowers are not as showy because they appear with the leaves and open in succession, beginning with the base onward, but the long flower stalks, known as racemes, are considerably longer than those of Chinese wisteria. (The record length of a raceme on Japanese wisteria is almost 6 feet!) Japanese wisteria looks best grown on an overhead structure to allow the long, hanging flowers to drop unimpeded. *Wisteria venusta* is a fast-growing climber, more commonly known as silky wisteria, that has attractive downy leaves. Each slightly fragrant flower is quite large, but the racemes are about half as long as those of Chinese wisteria and open all at once, when the leaves emerge. *Wisteria × formosa* is a hybrid that has attractive downy shoots as well, but little fragrance. The pale pink flowers are about the same length as those of Chinese wisteria and open all at once. Armed with this knowledge, you'll be twice as confused the next time you're wisteria shopping at your local nursery!

Wisterias need well-drained soil.

Q My **wisteria** suddenly died this spring. It seemed to be doing fine, although it wasn't putting out much new growth for the last couple of years. Do you have any idea what could have killed it? I thought these vines were supposed to be invincible.

A Wisteria vines are pretty much invincible and long-lived, if they are in the right conditions (some wisterias in Asia are centuries old). Although they can be bothered by scale, they have relatively few pests or disease problems. Wisteria must have adequate drainage to thrive, however, and are known to succumb to root rot in poorly drained soil. It can often take years before the plants die, but a sure sign of problems is dieback at the end of tendrils and vines, and lack of growth. Dig around the plant after a rainy day and see if the roots are sitting in water. If you decide to replace your departed friend with another wisteria, choose a location with better drainage, or plant on a raised bed to provide adequate drainage.

Think twice before you plant wisteria.

Q I'm thinking about planting a **wisteria** vine on a pergola in my back garden, but I've been warned that it's an aggressive grower. I don't mind garden work, but I don't want to plant something that will mean endless travail. How aggressive is wisteria, and is it worth the effort to grow it?

A Wisteria is a beautiful vine, but it takes a heck of a lot of work to keep it in bounds. I found out about its wicked disposition when I was in the market for a house some years ago. My wife and I went to check out a three-story house that was for sale cheap. It didn't take long to find out why it was priced so low. There were two wisterias, each about a hundred years old, growing up two sides of the house. They had picked up the three-story house and pulled it off its foundation! We're talking serious vine here. Those little tendrils that begin so small are capable of growing more than 25 feet per year. Wisteria has been known to rip siding and roofing from houses, and even strangle tall trees. The attractive, twisting vines often destroy the structures built to support them. They become extremely heavy and exert the pressure of a python, crushing all but the strongest beams. That said, I would not trade the wisteria that's growing over my patio for anything. No other vine can match the beauty and fragrance of the flowers, provide such great fall color, and look so magnificent in winter. The key is to train the wisteria correctly when you plant it, and then constantly prune it to keep it from becoming a "kudzudian" monster. Wisteria is not a plant for the lazy gardener; it requires an enormous amount of work to keep it beautiful and, more important, manageable.

Get your wisteria off to a good start.

Q I've heard you lament ever having planted your **wisteria**, but despite all of your nasty comments, I can tell you love it, so I'm trying one as well. How should I train it so that it doesn't take over the neighborhood?

A When it comes to wisteria, correct training from the beginning is the key to success. Select three vigorous stems, and twist them around the support that the vines will climb. These vines will form the framework and must be tied in to hold them in place as they climb. Be ruthless in removing all other growth. Never fight Mama Nature by trying to force the vines to twist in a direction other than the one in which they naturally grow; the vines will revert to their natural direction, and they'll uproot the trellis and tie you to it! Cut off the top of the vines as soon as they reach the top of the trellis. That will promote the development of strong laterals. Again, be ruthless: Allow no more than three lateral vines to grow on each horizontal support. Twist the laterals around the beams, and then tie them in. As the vine grows and matures, sublateral vines in the form of tendrils will continually grow out of the vines that were selected to form the framework. A few of these sublaterals can be allowed to remain if they fit in with the overall design; however, most of the tendrils should be removed to keep them from taking over your garden and ruining your house. Rather than totally removing unwanted tendrils, cut them back to 4 inches long, a method called spur pruning. It causes flower-bearing buds to form on the shortened branches. Spur pruning will enable your wisteria to bloom earlier in life (usually within four to five years), and you'll be amazed at the number of flowers. Prune back the tendrils at least three times per year. If you can stand all of that work, you'll get an impressive number of blooms. Our wisteria covers a trellis that measures 15 by 25 feet, and we never get less than a thousand blooms in spring.

Gain the upper hand over an out-of-control wisteria.

Q My **wisteria** is 15 years old and has never bloomed! It has, on the other hand, ripped the siding off the house, broken the structure it's growing on, and entangled itself in the top of the neighbor's 60-foot tree! What can I do to get it to bloom and to keep it in bounds?

 When growth begins in spring, cut all of the vines, even the huge ones, right to the ground. It sounds brutal, but you'll never get the plant under control without taking drastic action. When it grows back (and it will, with a vengeance), select three strong vines, and remove all of the others by cutting them to the ground. Then follow the advice I gave on the preceding question regarding how to train a new vine. Remember to cut the tendrils growing out of the structural vines to 4 inches long whenever they begin to grow. That will initiate flower-bud formation, improve the appearance of the twisted, gnarly vines, and give you at least a fighting chance of preventing the nasty old beast from ripping the roof off the garage next spring!

Do the sniff test.

Q I bought a **yellow-flowering deciduous azalea** that the nursery told me would have wonderful fragrance, but when it bloomed, to my surprise it smelled like a skunk. Did they give me the wrong plant?

A Few plants are more fragrant than yellow-flowering deciduous azaleas (*Rhododendron luteum*). To me the flowers smell like sweet butter. All supposedly fragrant yellow azaleas are not scented equally, however. While some waft tantalizing odors, others turn out to be duds or even smell unpleasant. Buy your *Rhododendron luteum* while it is in full bloom, and let your nose do the shopping for you. Plant it with the deep purple–blooming *Clematis* 'Rooguchi' to create a feast for the eyes as well as the nose.

Take cuttings, just in case.

Q I want to wring your neck! Last year I followed your advice regarding how to overwinter my **zonal geraniums,** but in spring they were dead as doornails. What should I do differently next year, so I won't be mad at you again?

A Hard to believe as it is, occasionally folks follow my advice regarding overwintering their pelargoniums and fuchsias, but the plants don't make it. Just in case, take a few cuttings of your prize plants. That way, if a plant dies, you'll have new ones on the way, and you won't want to strangle me! The easiest way to do this is to root the cuttings in water. This method almost always works, but some unusual varieties may not take root. A more foolproof method involves perlite. Put the perlite in a strainer, moisten, and shake out the excess water before using it to fill a clean zip-lock bag one-third full. Take a 6-inch cutting, remove the leaves on the bottom 3 inches, and dip the bare part in a rooting hormone such as Dip 'N Grow before inserting it into the perlite and sealing the bag. Make sure no leaves touch the rooting medium. Leave in a warm, bright location and wait until you see roots in the bag before potting up your new plants. If your plants in the garage survive *and* your cuttings root, you'll be in pelargonium heaven.

CHAPTER TWO

Edible Plants

It's apple pie time.

Q I planted apple trees a few years ago, and this year I have my first bumper crop. How do I know when the **apples are ripe** and ready for harvest?

A The easiest way to tell if apples are ripe is to taste them. If you grow an unfamiliar variety, however, and don't know what they're supposed to taste like, cut one or two open. If the seeds are brown, it's time to get out the pie plate.

Outwit apple pests.

Q I'm beginning to lose my appetite for the **apples** on my tree. Every time I bite in, I'm greeted by a half worm! I've tried putting sticky apples in the tree and even spraying the fruit with clay. The sticky trap caught lots of fruit flies, but there still were worms in the apples, and spraying every week with the clay product was too much bother. Is there anything that really works or should I simply develop a taste for worms?

A When you bite into an apple and a worm smiles back at you, the extra protein is compliments of a codling moth. If, on the other hand, you're greeted by the smiles of several half worms, you've just snacked on apple maggots. My best efforts to control these pests using environmentally friendly methods—from sticky traps to spraying clay—have failed miserably, and every year most of my apples end up as a gourmet treat for my neighbor's horse. Now there's a new, natural way to control these pests, and according to members of the Seattle Fruit Society who have tried it, the method is 100 percent effective. You simply place a pantyhose footie around each apple when you thin your fruit in early spring. You don't need to tie a knot: Simply stretch the footie over the fruit, making sure the apple ends up in the middle. Footies won't harm your apples. They breathe, don't absorb water, and expand with the apple as it grows. Buy them by the box from the Seattle Tree Fruit Society. They'll ship anywhere in the Pacific Northwest. Call 206-782-7352 for information and prices, or order them by emailing applesandmore@hotmail.com.

Prevent apple scab.

Q The leaves of my apple trees are plagued with black spots, and they fall off the tree in midsummer. The apples usually hang on, but by the time the fruit matures, the **apples have unappetizing scabby-looking bumps** all over them. Help!

A Although your apples are edible, who wants to eat fruit covered with scabby, yucky bumps? Your apple trees are suffering from a fungus disease known as apple scab. There are many fungicides that will control it, available at your local garden center. You need to spray the minute you see color in the bud, and then you'll have to do it again at full bloom, and then about 10 days after that. Unfortunately, apple scab is a chronic problem, so you'll need to spray every spring. Consider replacing your disease-prone trees with resistant varieties. Akane, Liberty, Chehalis, and Spartan (my favorite) taste great and rarely get scab at my house. Plant semi-dwarf trees, and you'll never climb a ladder to harvest fruit again.

A good cleanup now will help fight apple scab next year.

 Can I control apple scab without resorting to poisons?

Apple scab is caused by a fungus that survives the winter in the leaves and fruit that fall from the tree. The following spring, those leaves and fruit produce spores that quickly reinfect the tree. Theoretically, if you rid your garden of every infected leaf and piece of fruit (and all your neighbors do the same thing), your tree would be scab free. Naturally, you can't get rid of every leaf, but removing most of them will greatly reduce the disease pressure next season. Don't compost the diseased leaves at home; rather, send them out to a commercial composting facility whose process is designed to destroy disease spores.

Mini-dwarf apple trees are great for containers.

I love apples, but I live in a condo and can grow only plants in containers on my deck. Are there apple trees that grow well in containers?

If you want an apple tree that's ideal for a container, mini-dwarf is what you're looking for. These trees are grafted on EMLA 27 rootstock (specialized roots that restrict top growth) and can easily be kept at 4 feet tall. Most of the popular, disease-resistant apples such as Akane, Liberty, MacFree, Dayton, Enterprise, and Chehalis are available on mini-dwarf rootstock. It's lucky that dwarf trees are so small, because you're going to need two of them: As is true of most apples, mini-dwarf varieties must have a different variety nearby for cross-pollination. Bare-root grafted apple trees are available in December and February. One outstanding source is Raintree Nursery in Morton, Washington. You can order online at www.raintreenursery.com.

Start artichoke seeds early.

Q I've always wanted to grow **artichokes from seed**, and this year I'm going to try it. When should I start the seeds indoors? Should I do anything special to make sure I'll have plenty of these delicious gourmet treats to harvest the first season?

A Nothing—not even brussels sprouts—makes me drool as much as thinking about chowing down on artichokes! Artichoke seeds should be started indoors by mid-February. Sow each seed a quarter-inch deep in an individual 4-inch pot. Sow lots of them: Artichoke seeds don't tend to germinate in high numbers. Of the seedlings that come up, approximately 20 percent will be albino or lack vigor and should be culled out. Fertilize the remaining seedlings with a diluted transplant fertilizer and transplant out into the garden in about mid-April. But don't wait too long to transplant. Although a freeze could kill the seedlings, they must receive ten to twelve days of temperatures below 50 degrees to induce strong growth and budding. Plant the seedlings 24 inches apart in rows 3 feet apart. Artichokes are big feeders, so work in a cup of organic vegetable food under each plant. Make sure you harvest the flower buds before they open. Most important, when you serve them, obey the late Julia Child, who said, "Don't skimp on the melted butter!"

Harvest Asian pears before someone else beats you to it.

Q I understand that most European pears must be stored for a period before you can eat them. Is that also true of **Asian pears?** How do I know when to pick them? What are some good varieties?

A Unlike European pears, Asian pears can be eaten right off the tree. When they change from green to their mature color, taste one to determine if it is ripe. Birds and raccoons love Asian pears, as do marauding teens, so harvest as soon as the fruit tastes sweet. Fall is a good time to plant Asian pears, and some good ones include Shinseiki (yellow skin), Ichiban (brown skin), and the new huge-fruited Mishirasu (brown skin). Pears need cross-pollinators, so plant more than one. Don't forget to wear a bib when you bite into one of these juicy delights!

Asparagus is a big eater.

Q How often and how much should I feed my **asparagus?**

A Asparagus is a heavy feeder. A few years ago I would have recommended a good top-dressing of washed cow manure in the first week of March, followed by an application of organic all-purpose vegetable food. Since the fears of *E. coli* came along, many gardeners now prefer using organic fertilizers. There are good vegetarian fertilizers available at garden centers that do not contain bone or blood meal from cows. Apply about 2 cups per 10-foot row, in early March and again after harvest.

Plant asparagus crowns in February and March.

Q I'm crazy about **asparagus**, but it's so expensive at the store that I've decided to grow my own. When is the best time to plant, can I plant from seed, and are there any special conditions or considerations I need to know about?

A Only brussels sprouts can compete with the flavor of steamed asparagus smothered in garlic butter or hollandaise sauce! It's best to plant asparagus crowns rather than seeds. Choose mostly male varieties such as the commonly available 'Jersey Giant' or 'Jersey King'. Look for the bare-root crowns at good nurseries in February and early March. Asparagus is a long-lived perennial, so a well-prepared, deeply dug bed, amended with plenty of organic matter, is the key to getting abundant harvests for many years to come. Find a sunny location with well-drained soil where the plants will be able to grow undisturbed for years. After working in plenty of compost, plant the crowns in a trench 4 inches deep. Gradually fill in the trench as the asparagus grows. Now for the bad news: You won't be able to harvest for two or three years, or until half-inch-thick spears reach at least 5 to 8 inches long. During the first year of harvest, cut for only four to six weeks. Stop cutting when newly emerging spears reduce in size to the diameter of a pencil. (Cut at a 45-degree angle to avoid injuring emerging spears.) By the fourth year, you should be able to harvest them for at least ten weeks. Until then, you'll just have to console yourself with those yummy little brussels sprouts.

Don't prune the tweetle out of your new tree.

Q I recently planted a **bare-root fruit tree**, but I'm not sure how to prune it. My instinct is to cut the ends off the branches to force it to branch. Am I on the right track?

A Resist the urge to prune the living beetle hopper out of your new tree when you plant it. Bare-root fruit trees generally come prepruned. The worst thing you can do is to lop off the end of every branch. Tip pruning, as the process is called, will stimulate a great deal of branching and side growth, diverting energy needed for strong root growth. Instead, prune only to remove parallel branches and twigs that are growing into the center of the plant. Wait to tip prune until the second season, and then only do it if side branching hasn't begun. By the way, don't allow any fruit to ripen the first year, as fruit production also uses up energy needed to establish a healthy root system. Pull the fruit off as soon as it forms. Don't wait until it begins to look big and juicy or you'll never be able to part with it.

Pick disease-free fruit trees.

Q I am considering planting apple trees and maybe some other type of fruit trees in my yard in winter or early spring. Is it better to plant **bare-root or container-grown trees**? Also, is there anyone I can talk to about choosing the best fruit trees for areas with rainy springs?

A Bare-root fruit trees are less expensive and generally establish healthy root systems faster than those in containers, but you're wise to take time to learn which are the best fruit trees to grow in your area. Not all fruit trees do well in areas that experience rainy springs, and some varieties fare much better than others. For instance, the tasty apple varieties Liberty, Chehalis, Akane, and Spartan are resistant to scab and rarely, if ever, need to be sprayed. To discuss what variety of fruit might work best for you, call your local cooperative extension agency or Master Gardener program. These experts will help you solve any garden problem you have in an environmentally friendly way. There may be a fruit society organization in your community as well.

Don't murder your basil.

Q I'm crazy about **basil**, but trying to grow it is driving me crazy! Every year I plant it around Mother's Day, and it dies. What am I doing wrong?

A Like you, I'm obsessed with basil. The word comes from *basileus*, the Greek word for king, and I feel like a king when I'm eating pesto made from homegrown basil. Unfortunately, just like you, I feel more like a court jester every spring when I plant basil too early and it promptly gets killed by the cold. It's best to wait until at least June 1 to plant out basil starts. Basil can be sowed in the garden, but again, patience is the key. Wait until soil temperatures are consistently above 50 degrees. You'll be enjoying a regal treat by mid-July.

Try African blue basil (if you dare).

Q I saw a spectacular-looking **basil with purple leaves and flower spikes** at my local nursery. It was unlike any I've ever seen before. Can you eat this kind of basil, or is it only an ornamental? It is so romantic-looking.

A The romantic-looking basil you spotted at the nursery is known as African blue basil. Interestingly, most of us associate basil with romance and fine dining, but it hasn't always been that way. Joseph Pitton de Tournefort, a seventeenth-century botanist, wrote the following about basil: "A gentleman of Siena was wont very frequently to dry the herb and snuff it up his nose, but he soon turn'd mad and died; and his head being opened by surgeons, there was found a nest of scorpions in his brain." Oh, la, la! If you still dare, try African blue basil. This unique hybrid is hardy to at least 40 degrees and can be planted much earlier than the other types of basil. Unlike all other basil, which must be harvested before bloom for spicy flavor, the taste of African blue is not affected by flowering; you can enjoy the blooms and eat it too. The flowers are edible and attractive in salads and other dishes, but the flavor is stronger than, and different from, "normal" basil. If you're afraid of getting scorpions in your brain, grow African blue basil as an ornamental. The leaf veins and flower spikes are purple, giving the plant a striking purple-blue cast.

Leaf miners aren't appetizing.

Q What is causing the whitish brown blotches on the leaves of my **beets, chard, and spinach**? Is there anything I can do, or are these plants goners?

A A leaf-mining insect causes the whitish brown blotches on the leaves of beet-family vegetables. Tiny black-and-yellow flies lay their eggs inside the leaves of beets, chard, and spinach, and these eggs hatch into pale green maggots. The maggots then feed inside the leaves, leaving wandering tunnels of frass (polite word for bug poop) behind. The mining won't kill your plant, but you obviously won't want to eat any blotched leaves. It's too late to spray once the insects are in the leaves, but pulling off and destroying the infested ones will help keep the problem from spreading. Next year, rotate the location where you grow your beet-family crops and cover the plants with row cover as soon as seedlings emerge, or apply Bioneem, available at local nurseries or at Ace and True Value hardware stores. Don't confuse Bioneem with the often-recommended neem oil. Bioneem is an organic plant-based spray that effectively repels leaf miners and is totally safe to use on vegetables. Begin spraying when the first leaves appear, and repeat every seven to ten days.

Watch out for the disease that is deadly to all blackberries.

 I've heard that a newly introduced rust disease may kill the weedy Himalayan **blackberries** in the

Northwest. I'm delighted to hear the disease might wipe out the weedy blackberries trying to take over my back forty, but what about the special thornless blackberries that I spent an arm and a leg for so that I could enjoy the delicious fruit? Are thornless blackberries susceptible as well?

A It's true that a rust disease bred to kill the weedy Himalayan blackberry overseas somehow found its way into Oregon and Southwest Washington. The disease kills all varieties of blackberry and has already decimated populations of weedy Himalayan blackberry, as well as commercial and homegrown varieties. Scientists are busy searching for fungicides to protect desirable varieties in commercial and home gardens, and hopefully there will be a list of effective sprays in the near future. The symptoms begin with yellow pustules on the undersides of leaves, followed by leaf drop and plant death. If your garden is being taken over by weedy Himalayan blackberries, you'll be delighted to learn that the disease is deadly to the rampant spreading vines and will probably wipe them out. If you're a pie lover like me, you're undoubtedly depressed to know that these wild vines, along with the special hybrid blackberries, may soon be a thing of the past. So pick all you can next summer. As long as you wash them, the berries of infected plants are reported to be edible. If scientists can't come up with a cure, it might be the last blackberry pie you'll eat for a long time.

Net blueberries and stay friends with the robins.

Q I love birds and I love **blueberries**. Unfortunately, the birds also love my blueberries. How do I be nice to the birds but keep them from eating the berries?

A My robin friends Robby and Rebecca follow me around hoping that I'll expose a fat worm or blow a moth's cover while I'm working in the garden. Much as I like them, I draw the line at allowing them to eat my blueberries. There's flat-out nothing better than blueberry pie à la mode (except maybe a brussels sprout casserole). Bird netting is inexpensive, and covering blueberries is easy. Do it before the berries begin to ripen. Robins often eat blueberries just before they're ripe, so if you don't get your netting on in time, it could ruin a beautiful friendship.

Plant bare-root blueberry bushes in February, and eat blueberry pancakes for the rest of your life.

Q When is the best time to plant **blueberries**, and do they need to be planted near a different variety for cross-pollination? What conditions do they prefer?

A The best time to plant blueberries is in January or February, when you can find them bare-root at the nurseries or in mail-order catalogs. Although they will produce with only one variety, blueberries do best with cross-pollination, so plant two varieties in one hole for bigger fruit. Peat moss is the magic ingredient when it comes to growing healthy blueberries. Add lots to the soil when planting. Make sure they get lots of sun, adequate water, and a shot of organic rhododendron food every spring; then expect to get a lot of practice in making blueberry pancakes. Blueberry bushes often remain productive for more than a hundred years!

Brighten up your perennial garden with Swiss chard.

Q I'm thinking about planting **'Bright Lights' Swiss chard** in my perennial garden to add color. It might be nice to cook with as well. Is 'Bright Lights' only an ornamental, or is it edible as well?

A The 'Bright Lights' strain of Swiss chard is colorful and delicious, yet tough and easy to grow. Just give it a sunny spot, and 'Bright Lights' will add interest and beauty to your perennial garden as well as to your veggie patch. Who says you can't have your cake and eat it too?

Start fall and winter vegetables in July for a spring harvest.

Q I want to try growing **broccoli** in winter to be harvested in spring. Should I sow directly into the garden, and when do I need to sow the seeds?

A Sow the seeds of broccoli, cabbage, and cauliflower indoors in early July to be transplanted into the garden in mid-August. Don't delay too long; these plants need to grow sufficient roots, and obtain sufficient size, before the cold, rainy days of winter are upon us. Use winter-hardy varieties, available in many nurseries, and you'll be eating delicious veggies from February through April.

Beware bronze fennel.

Q I recently planted **bronze fennel** to add a soft textural look in my mixed border, but a friend told me that it can become a horribly aggressive weed. If that's true, is there any way that I can grow it without allowing it to become a menace?

A Bronze fennel (*Foeniculum vulgare* 'Purpurascens' or 'Smokey') is an attractive perennial herb that can reach 6 feet tall, with bronzy purple-filigreed foliage and interesting flat-topped umbel flowers. The leaves and seeds have a licorice flavor and are often used in vegetable dips, cream sauces, and grilled fish recipes.

Fennel was even used to calm hiccups in medieval medicine. The pollen-rich flowers attract beneficial insects such as lacewings and lady beetles. If you grow bronze fennel, remove the flowers before they go to seed. The seedlings have been known to come up as thick as a lawn, and bronze fennel has a taproot that's similar to its relative the carrot, but a lot harder to pull. If you let it go to seed, buy a cookbook that specializes in recipes using fennel. You'll need it.

Brussels sprouts discovered to be brain food.

Q Are **brussels sprouts** really that good for you? Are you serious when you say you love them that much, or is that a bunch of bahooey?

A Brussels sprouts were already well regarded for turning a well-known TV and radio gardener, who just happens to be a *Seattle Post-Intelligencer* columnist and the author of this book, into an incredible physical specimen. But now scientists have discovered that brussels sprouts may also be the reason he is so intelligent. New research has found that brussels sprouts contain bull-tweetle, a substance known to cause massive proliferation of brain cells, especially on the right side of the brain. I was worried that release of this information could cause a run on brussels sprouts and result in a severe shortage, but followers of my writing, TV, and radio shows inform me that there's little danger of my running out of B.S. anytime soon.

Scientific studies recently found that brussels sprouts are among the healthiest of foods. If you don't want to eat them, try giving them out as Halloween treats. You'll be amazed at the interesting places you'll find them the next day.

Start your brussels sprout seeds during the last week of March.

Q Obviously I'm an intelligent person, because I share your love for **brussels sprouts**. When should I start my seeds indoors, and when should I transplant them outside?

A Yep, if I do say so myself (humbly, of course), loving brussels sprouts is a definite sign of genius. Start the seeds indoors during the last week of March, and transplant the plants into the garden in mid-April. Oh, la, la! Be careful not to drool all over this book in anticipation.

Brussels sprouts haters, chill out.

Q I'm crazy about **brussels sprouts**, but my husband hates them and calls them nasty names. We just moved into a new house, and wouldn't you know it, there are a quite a number of brussels sprouts plants in the veggie garden. I confess I've never grown them. When and how do you harvest these delicious vegetables?

A Brussels sprouts: You either love or hate them. OK, you non-believers: Give them another try. If possible, wait to harvest until temperatures turn cold. The sprouts can easily withstand light frosts, and cold snaps trigger changes that make them taste sweet as sugar. Harvest the ripe ones at the bottom, snapping them off and removing any leaves in your way as you work your way up the stalk. The sprouts higher up on the stalk will continue to mature. If your sprouts aren't sizing up well, pinch out the growing point at the top of the stem. As long as the lower sprouts are close to a half inch in diameter, most of the sprouts will increase to full size within about two weeks. Brussels sprouts are tough, cold-hardy plants, but they can't take temperatures below 20 degrees. If a big freeze is expected, extend the harvest for a few weeks by pulling the plants up and hanging them upside down in a cool place. Thrill your brussels sprouts–hating partner by dropping a few of the little delights into whatever they're cooking when they leave the room. I do this to my wife, and it's so fun to see the look on her face when one of the little depth charges emerges during dinner!

Be bad on Thanksgiving.

Q I'm thinking about serving a **brussels sprouts** casserole this year at Thanksgiving, but I'm afraid some of my guests might find it disgusting! I'm thinking it will help if I can tell my guests that brussels sprouts were part of the first Thanksgiving dinner. Do you know if they were? And do you have a favorite recipe that my guests might like?

A I'm sorry to disappoint you, but they probably didn't serve brussels sprouts at the first Thanksgiving dinner in 1621. Brussels sprouts would have been too sinfully delicious for those innocent Puritans. They might have risked the temptation, however, had they known about all the vitamins and disease-fighting qualities in those decadent minicabbages. So this Thanksgiving, live on the wild side and serve my brussels sprouts casserole with caramelized onions and pecans!

Brussels Sprouts with Caramelized Onions and Pecans

> 1 large Walla Walla or sweet onion
> 1 pound brussels sprouts
> ¼ cup butter or margarine
> 1 cup pecan pieces
> ¼ teaspoon salt
> ¼ teaspoon pepper

• Cut onion in half, and thinly slice. Cut brussels sprouts in half, and cut each half crosswise into thin slices. Place vegetables in separate plastic bags, seal, and chill for eight hours.

• Melt butter in a large, heavy skillet over medium-high heat, add pecans, and sauté for 5 minutes or until toasted. Remove pecans from skillet.

• Add onions and cook, stirring often until caramel-colored, about 10 minutes. Add brussels sprouts and cook until tender. Takes about 4 minutes. Add pecans, heat, and sprinkle with salt and pepper. Serves 8.

Store carrots the way Grandma did.

Q Bugs Bunny would go crazy with desire if he saw the bumper crop of **carrots** I grew this season. Now it's getting cold, and I'm not sure what to do. Will they keep if I leave them out in the garden?

A You can usually leave carrots in the ground anywhere temperatures rarely dip below 20 degrees, as long as they're under a blanket of straw or compost. If a really cold freeze comes or your drainage is less than perfect, however, you could lose the whole batch. Also, leaving them in the garden can increase attack by carrot rust fly maggots, which mine into the carrots. My mother-in-law taught me how her family harvested and stored carrots on the Canadian prairie when she was a little girl: When harvesting, don't use a spading fork, as that could bruise the roots. Water well and then hand-pull, using a trowel if necessary to loosen the soil. Twist off the tops, and layer the undamaged carrots in sand. Make sure they are not touching each other. Left in a cool dry place, carrots will keep for up to five months if you use this technique.

Sow carrot seeds in summer for harvest in fall and winter.

Q It's only midsummer and it seems as if I just planted my spring garden, but am I right that it's already time to plant **carrots** for harvest in fall? Any tricks when it comes to sowing carrots in summer?

A I know, mid-July does seem too early to be thinking about fall and winter, but that's the perfect time to plant carrots for fall harvest. Carrots resent transplanting, so seed them directly into the garden as space becomes available. Plant about a quarter inch deep, and cover the seeds with a thin layer of peat moss. Carrot seeds must stay moist to germinate. Carrots tend to look like a grandpa's nose when they get too much nitrogen, so go easy with the fertilizer, and use a high-phosphorus product.

Test seeds before you sow.

Q This spring I planted a big patch of **carrot seeds** left over from the year before, and very few came up. I don't want to waste time planting leftover seeds if they're not going to grow. Is there a way to tell if the seeds are still good?

A Test the germination rate before you sow by wrapping a number of seeds in a moist paper towel, placing them in a plastic bag, and setting the bag in a warm spot inside your house, out of direct sunlight. Check the paper towel every day for the next several days to see how many seeds have sprouted. If germination is low, it's time to buy new seeds.

Cherries don't have to be monsters.

Q **Cherries** are my favorite fruit, but they cost a mint at the grocery store. I want to plant my own tree, but I don't want it to take over the whole yard. Are there any varieties that don't get so big? Also, is it true that I have to plant two different varieties in order to get cherries?

A Sweet cherries do cost a mint at the grocery store, but in the past if you grew your own, you needed a lot of room and an appreciation for shade. Most sweet cherry trees topped out at around 40 feet tall, and you had to plant a second, different variety to provide cross-pollination. Now, self-pollinating sweet cherries are available on dwarfing Gisela rootstock and can easily be maintained at 10 feet tall. Here are a few of my favorites: 'Lapins' is a heavy producer of delicious, black, crack-resistant cherries; 'Glacier', a recent WSU introduction, has huge, incredibly flavorful dark red fruit; and 'Sweetheart', a new one from British Columbia, is covered with big, bright red, irresistible cherries. Now you can have your cherry pie and enjoy sunshine too. (That is, if you can beat the birds to the fruit!) These and other self-fertilizing dwarf sweet cherries are available bare-root at local nurseries, or order online from Raintree Nursery at www.raintreenursery.com.

Read this before you prune your cherry tree.

Q My **cherry tree** is supposed to be a semidwarf, but it's so tall that the birds are getting more cherries than I am. When is the best time to prune it, and how far can I lower the tree by cutting it back so that I can get the cherries before those darned birds do?

A You can prune your sweet cherry tree anytime it's dormant during winter, but do it only on a dry day to reduce disease problems. And I'm sorry to tell you that your trees will be better off if you share the bounty with the birds. Cherry trees need only light thinning of crowded and crossing branches, and the removal of dead, diseased, and damaged branches. Don't lower the height drastically, or you'll get serious decay and will be battling sprouts for the rest of your life. Semidwarf cherry trees should be pruned using the central leader method. The goal is to make your cherry look like a Christmas tree, with equally spaced layers of branches growing out at 45-degree angles. The lowest branches are left the widest, with each successive layer of branches pruned shorter than the one below. The central leader can be headed back each year, about a foot above the last branch, to maintain a height that can be reached using a ladder.

Priests can help you with your chicken problems.

Q My wife insists on raising **chickens** in our urban garden. I wouldn't mind, but they keep escaping and causing havoc in my vegetable garden. Is there anything I can spray on the plants that will keep the poultry from eating them?

A It's legal to raise as many as three chickens in most urban localities, and a growing number of city gardeners are giving it a try. If you aren't careful, however, chickens can do serious damage to your garden. I don't know of any sprays you can apply to keep chickens from eating your plants. However, there are ways to prevent the chickens from escaping and causing problems, one of which I learned from my old buddy Jose, whom I worked with at Seattle University for many years. After retiring, Jose was one of the first urban gardeners to raise chickens in Seattle. The problem was that Jose had two roosters, and before long he had a whole lot of chickens. One day when I came to visit, I was surprised to find neither a rooster nor a chicken in sight. When I asked Jose where they were, he answered: "Chickens got in vegetable garden last night, priests eat chicken tonight!" If you're thinking about raising chickens, or are already raising them and are having problems (and don't live near a Jesuit university), learn all about how to raise chickens successfully by attending a City Chickens 101 class. They're offered periodically by organizations such as Seattle Tilth, an outstanding organization dedicated to helping folks learn to garden organically. Contact Oregon Tilth (www.tilth.org) or one of the several regional chapters in Washington (www.tilthproducers.org/wta.htm) for information. After a few years of raising chickens, you'll think that little Gertrude is so cute, you'll enter her in the ever-popular city chicken beauty contest.

Sow cilantro in fall.

Q I love **cilantro** but my partner hates it, and I'm beginning to wonder if she's putting a curse on it. Every spring I plant the seeds, and every spring it flowers and goes to seed. I'm following the directions on the seed package exactly. Is cilantro impossible to grow from seed in the Pacific Northwest?

A Cilantro, also known as coriander, is one of those "love it or hate it" herbs. Maybe it will help to tell your partner that the Chinese once thought it conferred immortality. Its sweet-spicy flavor is great in curries, but I like it best in salsas and Latin dishes. Fortunately, I don't think your problem is being caused by a curse from your partner. Cilantro bolts (goes to flower) in warm weather. To prevent that, sow it directly in the garden in early September, and thin to 4 inches between plants. It rarely bolts in fall. Go easy on the fertilizer; too much nitrogen spoils the flavor. Break the curse: Plant cilantro in fall, and even if you don't live forever, the life you live will be more interesting and tasty.

The only difference is in the way you use this spice.

Q What's the difference between **cilantro and coriander**? What's the best time to plant these spices, and are they hardy enough to live through the winter in the Pacific Northwest climate?

A Cilantro (*Coriandrum sativum*) is the same plant as coriander. The only difference is that the leaves (cilantro) are used fresh in salads or cooked in many dishes, while the crushed seeds (coriander) are used to flavor sausage, beans, stews, and baked goods. If you prefer to use the leaves, then the best time to plant *Coriandrum sativum* is in early to mid-September. When it's sowed in spring, the warming weather triggers it to bolt and go to seed, but that rarely happens in fall. Cilantro has a taproot and is difficult to transplant, so it's better to sow the seed directly into the garden. It's a semihardy annual, so how long it will last in the winter garden depends on the weather. If conditions remain mild, you could be harvesting it fresh to flavor your favorite Mexican or Asian dishes all winter long.

Eat your lemon meringue pie and smell the flowers, too.

Q I've heard it's possible to grow a hardy **citrus tree** that produces edible fruit here in the Northwest. Will it survive year round outside, or do I have to bring it inside to keep it alive in winter?

A The improved Meyer lemon tree is the most popular citrus tree grown in the Northwest and makes a great container plant. The compact tree produces fruit that is a cross between a mandarin orange and a lemon: It looks and tastes like lemon, but the flavor is sweeter. Be warned that a Meyer lemon meringue pie is so delicious that a single bite can make one's hair stand straight up. Don't serve it if you suspect that your dinner guest might be wearing a wig! Although they're hardy, Meyer lemon trees can withstand only limited exposure in the low 30-degree range and must be brought in for the winter. The tree will survive in a brightly lit unheated garage or a cool greenhouse, but most folks bring it into the house to ripen the fruit and to enjoy the powerfully fragrant blooms that appear in all seasons, including winter. If you bring it in, place the tree in a cool room in direct sunlight, stand it on a pebble saucer, and mist constantly. A Meyer lemon tree requires at least 50 percent humidity, or it will be plagued with spider mites and drop its leaves. If you can give it the conditions it needs, your house will smell like a citrus grove, and you'll be able to bake some hair-raising pies.

Companion planting can discourage pests.

Q Does **companion planting** in the vegetable garden really work to repel insects? I've heard some gardening experts swear by it, while others say it's of little or no value. Who's right?

A No one can say for sure if companion planting really works in all situations. That's because there's little scientific evidence to prove the effects of companion planting; most recommendations are based on folklore. A few studies have shown that plants with strong odors—such as basil, rue, marigold, scented-leaf geranium, and garlic—repel or confuse insects that rely on smells to find their target plants. Many gardeners swear by these pairings: Basil, French marigolds, or catnip heavily planted around brussels sprouts and other members of the cabbage family reduce aphid populations. Thyme planted around potatoes, eggplant, or cabbage repels flea beetles. Onions or garlic planted in the same rows with carrots discourage carrot maggot. Tomatoes, parsley, or basil growing alongside asparagus repel the dreaded asparagus beetle. By the way, there are some bad companions, as well. Beans won't grow well near garlic or onions, and keep tansy away from cabbage or you'll attract cabbageworms.

Patience is a virtue.

Q When I was a kid, we bought **corn on the cob** from stands right at the farm. It's so much sweeter when it's fresh. I don't live near any farmers now, and I find the stuff you buy at the grocery store to be pretty flavorless. I tried growing my own last spring, but the seeds never came up. What's the trick to growing my own corn on the cob?

A There's an old saying, "The patient person gets the first corn." OK, I made it up, but there should be such a saying. If you plant corn before the soil temperature is at least 60 degrees, it simply rots or is so maimed that it never amounts to anything. If you start your own corn indoors, or buy starts at the local nursery, find that meat thermometer you hardly ever use, test soil temperatures with it, and wait to transplant into the garden until the soil is warm enough. Plant in blocks of at least four rows to take advantage of wind pollination, and mix in about 6 pounds of a nitrogen-rich fish fertilizer per 100 square feet before planting. Use the same fertilizer as a foliar spray on a weekly basis until tassels form, cutting back on applications only if the foliage becomes dark green. Mulch heavily to control weeds, and water deeply and regularly. For the sweetest corn you've ever tasted, harvest minutes before you cook it, or for a real treat, eat it raw!

Clear up the confusion.

Q Can you clear up the confusion about which plants **cross-pollinate**? I save seed from my garden, but I've been told that I shouldn't do that if I plant melons, pumpkins, or squash in the same bed. Evidently they can cross-pollinate, and plants from those seeds will produce strange, inedible fruit. Do I have to worry that my cucumber will cross with my watermelon?

A Despite the popular misconception, it's scientifically impossible for a cucumber to cross with watermelons, cantaloupes, pumpkins, or squash. Watermelons and cantaloupes won't cross with squash either. So feel free to save the seed from watermelons, cantaloupes, squash, and cucumbers without worry, even if they are growing side by side in your garden. On the other hand, if you grow various kinds of squash in the same area, the seed you save from them may produce bizarre, most likely inedible fruit next summer. For instance, if you grow summer squash in the vicinity of other varieties of summer squash, or near pumpkins, they may cross with one another. And winter squash won't cross with summer squash or pumpkins, but they can cross with each other. There's no way of knowing whether a cross occurred by looking at the seed, unfortunately. You'll only know when zucchapumpkins show up on your zucchini plant next summer. If you think it's hard to give away oversized zucchinis, wait until you try to get someone to take these Frankensteins off your hands!

Cut down everbearing raspberry canes.

Q I understand that there are two ways to prune **everbearing raspberries**, and that one way will produce two crops, while the other only one. Can you explain the difference? Which method do you recommend?

A The canes of everbearing raspberries, which grow during summer, produce a steady crop on the top half of the cane from August until frost, and then produce a smaller crop on the bottom half in the following spring. Although it's possible to remove the top half in fall and wait to cut the rest of the cane to the ground until after you've harvested the spring crop, it's easier to cut all of the canes to the ground after the harvest is over in fall. You'll sacrifice the spring berries, but you'll get a great fall harvest on sturdier canes that won't require trellising.

Eat a Mediterranean treat.

 While visiting Italy this summer, I ate my first fresh fig right off of the tree. Wow, was that tasty! Can I grow these Tuscan treats here in the Northwest?

You don't have to go to Italy to eat yummy figs. It's just as easy to grow them here in the Northwest, provided that you live on the west side of the Cascades. The most reliable variety is 'Desert King'. Give your fig a warm, sunny location; they do best against a sunny southern wall. Depending on how sunny the summer is, the figs will begin to droop in late July, or by mid-August at the latest. Once they droop, they're ripe as soon as they become soft. Pick them right away, especially if you hear crows and yellow jackets shouting "Oh, la, la!", or they'll be the only ones to enjoy your Tuscan treats. Withdrawing water after harvest will reduce winter damage. Eat a fig fresh off the tree in the morning, and you'll think you've woken up in Tuscany.

Try not to squeak when you eat one.

The first time I ate a fig right off the tree, I literally squeaked with joy! I now have my own fig tree and it produces well, but it's getting a little bigger than I expected. When and how should I prune it to make it smaller?

It's been scientifically proven that figs are so tasty it's impossible to eat one without squeaking. Don't overprune, however, or you'll significantly reduce the number of figs you'll receive.

That's because most figs are produced on the previous season's growth, so try not to remove more than half of what grew last season. You can easily maintain your fig tree with light annual pruning while the tree is dormant during winter. Begin by removing dead branches and twigs. Height can be maintained, but concentrate on thinning by removing suckers and wayward or crossing branches. If you must prune back to bare wood with no branch, leave an inch stub on the branch you cut. New twigs will sprout in summer. If your tree is too big for the location, consider replacing it with the very productive dwarf 'Petite Negri'.

Give Frost peach a healthy start.

Q I planted a **Frost peach tree** because it's supposed to be resistant to peach leaf curl. The following spring the leaves curled up, became fuzzy, and fell off. New leaves grew to take the place of the ones that fell, but many of them became swollen and contorted as well. Why did my "resistant" Frost peach get peach leaf curl? Will it grow out of this problem?

A Every year hundreds of Northwest gardeners plant Frost peach trees because they're known to be resistant to peach leaf curl. Unfortunately, when growth begins, these peach lovers are surprised and disappointed to see their newly planted tree developing symptoms of the disease. The Frost peach becomes resistant as it ages, but it needs to be covered or receive fungicide applications for the first three years after planting. If you don't protect it, the tree will most likely survive and develop resistance as it matures, but preventing the disease early will result in a healthier, more vigorous tree in the future. Unfortunately, if you help your Frost peach grow into a healthy, productive tree, you'll need to buy a Jack Russell terrier to prevent those greedy little squirrels from stealing all of the peaches before you get any.

Don't be a swine.

 Q Is it true that **garlic** is a great health food? I'm going to try to plant my own. When and how do you plant and care for it, and what's the difference between soft-neck and hard-neck garlic?

A Garlic has long been believed to have magical powers against evil and disease. It saved Odysseus from being turned into a pig, and as long ago as 2000 BC, garlic was used as a remedy for some twenty-two health problems, including headaches, worms, tumors, pimples, and heart ailments. October is the best time to plant garlic. Plant cloves 2 inches deep in well-cultivated, rich organic soil. Don't fertilize until growth starts in spring. Then feed with a high-nitrogen fish fertilizer every two weeks. Keep the soil slightly moist. With the summer solstice, the days begin to get shorter. The bulb will have formed and won't get any bigger, so discontinue fertilizing and begin to reduce watering, allowing the soil to dry out slightly between waterings to prevent mold problems. Once there are only three leaves left on the plant, usually in July, it will be time to harvest. Soft-neck garlic is the kind you braid, and it stores for up to a year. Hard-neck has stronger flavor, but can't be braided and usually keeps for only five or six months. Avoid possible fungus disease problems by ordering garlic cloves from a gardening catalog, or buy them at a nursery. Plant lots of garlic; you never know when someone may try to turn you into a pig!

Share your health food with your dog.

Q Is it difficult to grow **garlic**? I want to feed it to my dog to keep fleas away.

A I have a friend who was convinced that feeding his dog garlic would keep the fleas away. Unfortunately, it did little to deter the fleas, but old Beauregard lived a good long life, no doubt due in part to the health benefits of eating all of that garlic. Who knows, if my friend had served Beauregard a few brussels sprouts with that garlic, the old hound just might have lived to be 100!

Grow your own edible ginger.

 Is it possible to grow edible **ginger**? I'd like to try it just for fun.

It's easy to grow a piece of edible ginger root (*Zingiber officinale*) bought right from the grocery store. Edible ginger is native to Asia and Australia and goes dormant when days get shorter and temperatures drop in fall. Buy the rhizome you are going to plant in spring so that it's fresh. Plant the ginger root horizontally, about 4 inches deep in a five-gallon pot. Provide warmth in early spring by locating the pot next to a southern wall in full sun on nice days, but bring it back into a garage or sunroom on cold nights. Water lightly and infrequently until the plant begins to grow, but once growth starts, water enough to keep the soil moist and fertilize regularly with a soluble houseplant fertilizer. The canes will grow to about 15 inches tall but rarely flower in our region. By late fall, your five-gallon pot will be filled with ginger plants and ready for harvest. Pull the plant out of the pot and slice off sections of the underground roots. Leave a few of the rhizomes planted in the pot over winter and allow them to remain dry and dormant in an unheated garage. Those sections should begin to grow again when warmer weather returns next spring.

Don't eat your grapefruit: Wear it.

Is it possible to grow a **grapefruit** plant from the seed of a grapefruit I purchased at the grocery store? If I can get the seed to grow, will my plant actually grow edible grapefruit?

A It's easy and fun to grow your own grapefruit tree from a seed. Place the seed just below the surface in a pot of soil and keep the surface moist. Before too long, the seed will germinate, and soon you will be growing an attractive grapefruit plant. In time, the plant will flower, and although it's a long shot, it might even form fruit. The plant will not be hardy, however, so you'll need to bring it inside and keep it next to a bright window during winter to keep it alive and to give any fruit that formed a fighting chance to ripen. In the unlikely event that you ever grow a grapefruit, depending on your gender, you may prefer to wear it rather than eat it. Don't ask me how they got the idea, but researchers in Chicago discovered that when women smell like grapefruit, they appear 5 years younger to men. Interestingly, when men wore the scent, smelling like a grapefruit did little to make women think that the men were younger. Other scents tested, such as grape and cucumber, lacked the effect. Early reports state that a significant number of women are considering wearing "eau de grapefruit." Men: Aren't you glad it wasn't brussels sprouts that caused this effect?

Grow grapes for fall color.

Q Last fall I saw what looked like a **grapevine** growing to the top of a huge tree. The leaves had turned a fantastic shade of scarlet. Are there grapevines with leaves that turn beautiful colors in fall?

A There are more reasons to plant grapevines than to enjoy the fruit or to make wine. Some grapevines do indeed develop stunning fall colors that rival anything in the autumn garden. *Vitis vinifera* 'Purpurea' (purple ornamental grape) grows to about 20 feet, with 6-inch leaves that emerge downy green, mature to deep purple, and then turn dark wine-purple in autumn. For dazzling summer-long color (with a fine finish), grow it up a tree with golden foliage, such as *Acer pseudoplatanus* 'Brilliantissimum'. Even showier is *Vitis coignetiae* (crimson glory vine). This vigorous native of Korea can reach 50 feet or more and is covered with 12-inch green leaves that turn radiant scarlet in fall. This vine is better suited for pairing with a large tree. For a vintage autumn display, train it to scamper up a mature *Betula utilis* var. *jacquemontii* (Himalayan birch). You'll find the contrast of bright scarlet grape leaves against the airy golden foliage and brilliant white bark as intoxicating as drinking a bottle of fine wine, and you won't suffer a hangover.

Eat, drink, and be merry.

Q My **grapevines** are taking over the whole back garden, but the fruit never seems to ripen. Should I just eat stuffed grape leaves and give up on my dream of making wine?

A The fruit needs to be in bright filtered sunshine to ripen, so if your grapes are growing under an umbrella of foliage, it will be helpful to remove some of the excess leaves. Cut the vine at the second leaf after the last cluster of fruit. Use the leaves that you cut off to make a batch of dolmas. Then get ready to take off your shoes and make some wine!

Manure never smelled so good.

Q I've heard of covering vegetable gardens with **green manure cover crops.** What's the advantage of sowing a cover crop, and which of the many types of cover crop should I grow to increase soil fertility? Also, do I have to wait to sow the cover crop until I've harvested all of my vegetables in fall?

A Sowing a fall cover crop (green manure) on your vegetable plot has several advantages, and it doesn't even smell bad. Green manure prevents the pounding winter rains from compacting the soil and leaching out nutrients. When spring comes, the cover crops soak up extra moisture, making your soil workable much earlier. Cover crops in the pea family, such as crimson clover, Austrian peas, and vetch, increase fertility by fixing nitrogen in the soil. The process relies on special bacteria that capture nitrogen and make it available to the plant. Large populations of nitrogen-fixing fungi must be present in the soil to raise fertility effectively, however. Sometimes there just aren't enough of these beneficial organisms present to do much good. Luckily, you can buy mycorrhizal fungi at good nurseries and from seed catalogs. There are different types, so make sure you order the right bacteria for the cover crop you're using. Moisten the seeds slightly with milk or water before sprinkling them with the mycorrhizal fungi to encourage it to stick to the seed. To maximize fungi survival, sow seed as soon as possible after inoculation, and minimize contact with direct sunlight. It's important to plant your cover crop between early September and mid-October. Don't worry if you still have crops in your garden; the seeds can be worked in around your tomatoes and other plants before you harvest. In spring, till in the cover crop when it's in full bloom but before it goes to seed. Then stand back! Your vegetables will grow like the dickens in healthy, fertile soil.

Special treats for Halloween tricksters.

 Any suggestions for healthy Halloween treats from the garden? I don't think candy is good for 'em.

Surprise trick-or-treaters by offering them brussels sprouts as a treat this Halloween! It's quite amusing to see the amazed (disgusted?) looks on their little faces. I strongly recommend a backup bowl of candy bars so you won't find brussels sprouts in undesirable locations the following morning.

Add sizzling color to your vegetable garden.

 I love hot peppers, the hotter the better. Can we grow the really hot ones in the Northwest?

Many quality nurseries carry hot pepper starts that produce sizzling hot, colorful fruit. Mid-June is the perfect time to plant because hot peppers won't grow in cold soils and may never snap out of the funk they experience if night temperatures drop below 50 degrees. Hot peppers grow equally well in the garden or in a container. Choose a hot, sunny location, as heat is the name of the game. Create extra warmth early in the season by covering your hot peppers with floating row crop cover, but don't forget to remove it when temperatures rise in summer: Even peppers can burn up in too much heat. Give peppers plenty of room, planting no closer than 20 inches apart. Trigger lots of early growth by applying about a half cup of high-nitrogen fish fertilizer below and around each pepper during the planting process. When the plants begin to flower, work in a half cup of an organic high-phosphorus vegetable food around each plant to encourage fruit set. If you like it hot, plant 'Habañero'. It's the hottest kind of pepper, so be ready to shout "Oh, la, la!" when you take a bite.

Grow juicy fruit.

I can't seem to grow juicy fruit on my pear, apple, and other fruit trees. The trees are growing in full sun, flower well, and appear to be well pollinated. Do I need to water them?

Fruit trees need at least an inch of water per week in hot, dry weather to produce sweet, juicy fruit. Mulch around the trees, and use a soaker hose to give them a deep watering every week in the heat of summer. I suspect you'll be rewarded with large, succulent fruit. If all of that watering seems like a lot of work, think of all the sweet juice that will be running down your chin when you bite into a magnificent pear.

Hand-pollinate kiwis for bigger fruit.

Q Every year one of my fuzzy **kiwis** produces an abundant crop, but the fruit is small, hardly bigger than large grapes. How do I get bigger fruit? Will it help to thin the fruit in spring? Also, I have a second kiwi patch in another area that has been there longer than the first one, yet it has never produced fruit at all. The kiwi is growing in full sun, and I give it the same care. Why isn't it producing any fruit?

A You don't need to thin kiwis to get big fruit. The problem is that your flowers are not getting pollinated well enough. Fuzzy kiwis (*Actinidia deliciosa*) usually bloom in June, and female kiwi flowers must receive adequate amounts of male pollen to set large fruit. Unfortunately, there aren't always enough pollinating insects flying around when the plants bloom. To get big fruit, pick off some male flowers and rub the pollen-laden stamens against the central part of the female flower. Each male flower can be used to pollinate about five female blooms. Your kiwis will get so big that New Zealanders will mistake them for grapefruit (well, almost). Regarding the lack of fruit on your second vine, if you're getting flowers and no fruit, you probably lack a flowering male vine for pollination. The male vines sometimes die or get mislabeled at the nursery where you bought them. Raintree Nursery has good pictures of the male and female flowers in their catalog; order a catalog at www.raintreenursery.com.

Have your ornamental vine and eat fruit too.

Q I'm looking for an attractive vine that will add color and cover a shady fence. Someone mentioned a hardy **kiwi** that is supposed to have attractive leaves and edible fruit. Do you know anything about it?

A *Actinidia kolomikta* (kiwi vine) earned the common name "Arctic beauty" in its native Russia because the ornamental leaves are splashed with striking combinations of green, pink, white, and red variegation. The vines are hardy to –30 degrees, and as long as both sexes are in proximity for pollination purposes, the female will produce delicious kiwi-flavored fruit about the size of an oblong grape that you can eat right off the plant without peeling. However, it's the male that is the good looker, so make sure to plant it where you can appreciate its colorful leaves. Arctic beauty will burn in full sun, but will thrive in partial shade. Less vigorous than other kiwi vines, *A. kolomikta* grows rapidly to 15 feet or more. Give it a sturdy support that it can twine into, but don't plant it in a crowded area. Once they're entangled, it's practically impossible to extricate the branches of other delicate plants from its powerful grip. Don't be in a hurry to rip out the male plant if it seems like a dud and won't color up. It takes a few years before the spectacular variegation shows up, but once it does, your male *A. kolomikta* kiwi will be the showpiece of your garden.

When to harvest kiwis depends on the kind you have.

Q I have a **kiwi** vine, and for the first time it's covered with fruit. I've heard that kiwis don't ripen on the vine. If so, how do I know when to harvest them?

A Some types of the hardy varieties of kiwis, such as *Actinidia arguta issai*, *A. kolomikta*, and *A. arguta*, can be picked and eaten right off the vine, as soon as they're soft. But the fuzzy kiwi (*Actinidia deliciosa*) is picked when it's still hard. Don't rush; fuzzy kiwis are much sweeter if they're hit by two or three light frosts. Pick by Thanksgiving even if no frost has occurred, and be ready to harvest earlier if temperatures are expected to dip into the lower 20s. A hard freeze will ruin your kiwis. Store them in individual plastic sandwich bags (not zip-lock) that are folded over (but not tied) to allow for air circulation. Placed in boxes with newspaper between layers, kiwis can be stored for six months or more in an unheated garage. Even after storage, it can take weeks for a kiwi to ripen on the kitchen counter. Put a few in a paper bag with a couple of apples, and they will ripen in a couple of weeks.

Rid your fruit tree of Medusa.

Q My fruit tree looks like **Medusa**. It has a beautiful umbrella shape, but every spring an incredible number of sprouts grow straight up out of the top. The sprouts ruin the look of the tree, and it's a lot of hard work removing them. Two questions: Do I really need to remove the sprouts every year, and is there anything I can do to stop them from forming?

A The Medusa effect is the result of a growth-promoting hormone that always moves to the high point in the branch. In an umbrella-shaped tree, in which the branches hang down, the hormone migrates to the center to instigate sprout growth because it's the highest point. Removing these sprouts is a real pain in the kazutski, but you've got to do it. Not only are the sprouts unproductive, but if they're left in the tree, they will soon shade out lower growth, causing thinning, dieback, and reduced fruit production. Break the Medusa syndrome by pruning to upward-facing branches at the point where the limbs begin to bend downward. Eventually the growth hormone will migrate away from the middle of the tree out to the ends of the branches where growth is desired. It's a long process, but it's worth it. The reward will be less work, and more fruit for fruit crisps smothered in whipped cream.

Grow your own mushrooms indoors.

 What do you think of those indoor mushroom-growing kits? I really miss vegetable gardening in winter, and thought I might give one of those a try. Have you ever tried growing mushrooms indoors?

Growing mushrooms in your kitchen is just the solution for the frustrated gardener who's itching to grow a food crop in winter. Kits that produce large crops of nutritious and delicious mushrooms are for sale at most good nurseries. The one hang-up is that the nutrient block is anything but lovely. If you can endure looking at something that makes the Creature from the Black Lagoon look pretty, however, you'll enjoy a crop of delectable mushrooms approximately once a month for the next six months. Each flush can produce up to a pound of mushrooms, but be warned: The harvest can consist of many small mushrooms or just a few big ones. (My last crop consisted of only one mushroom, but it was the size of the *Queen Mary*!) My wife wouldn't try a taste of these homegrown 'shrooms until I survived a day after eating one. Now I have to race her at harvest time to get enough mushrooms for my brussels sprout casserole.

Size matters when it comes to onion sets.

What causes some of the onion sets I plant to go to seed instead of forming a bulb?

A Onions are biennial. They normally form bulbs the first year, then flower and go to seed the second year. Unfortunately, many frustrated gardeners watch in dismay as their onions planted from sets bolt by flowering and going to seed the first year. Avoid this by only planting onion sets that are about a half inch in diameter. Sets containing larger bulbs tend to bolt, while sets with bulbs smaller than a half inch often result in very small onions.

Start a new housing development.

Q On your advice I began raising **orchard mason bees**. I'm happy with the results, but I'm worried about the bees. I've noticed that some are so covered with mites that they can't even fly when they emerge from their homes. I'm aware that I should replace the mite-infested blocks, but even though I put out new boxes, the bees seem to go right back to the old infested blocks before all the bees have even emerged. Is there a trick to replacing the old blocks?

A Mites are a problem. They build up in the boxes, and just as you described, sometimes emerging bees are so covered that they can't even fly. Hence it is important to remove the old blocks and replace them with new ones to prevent a buildup of mites. The problem is that the bees prefer the old blocks to the new ones, and they move right back in before you get a chance to remove them. There is a solution, though. As soon as the bees begin emerging in force, place a cardboard box over the blocks. The box must be located solidly against the wall so that the bees cannot enter through any gaps. Then cut a dime-sized hole in the front of the box. The bees can follow the light to find their way out, but they won't be able to find their way back in. As long as there are plenty of new nesting blocks available, the bees will move right into their new homes. Soak the old blocks in a 10 percent bleach solution, and rinse out the holes with a powerful spray from the hose. Store the old boxes for use next spring. By then the effect of the bleach will be long gone, and you can use them again.

Don't let peach leaf curl ruin your tree.

Q I bought a **peach tree** (I don't recall the variety), but the very first year, instead of forming fruit, the leaves got all puffy and twisted, turned a dusty white, and then fell off. Even the branches seemed to get puffy. Can I save my peach tree, or should I start over with a new one?

A Your tree was infected by peach leaf curl. It's one ugly disease, but if you apply sprays in a timely manner this winter, you should be able to save your tree and enjoy peach pies in the future. In spring the leaves of infected trees become thick and contorted, then turn yellow and red, and finally end up covered with a coating of dusty white spores. Soon the leaves fall from the tree, leaving only unappetizing reddish fruit on puffy branches. If you don't get it under control, severe infections will generally kill a tree within two or three years. Peach leaf curl is a fungus that infects buds in the dead of winter. A plethora of effective fungicides are available at garden centers, but they must be applied at exactly the right time to prevent the disease. Apply the first spray during the first week of January, and follow up with two more sprays, three weeks apart. Write yourself a note and put it where you can't miss it, since it's practically impossible to remember to apply sprays in the dead of winter, when few of us have gardening on the brain.

"Eaves-drop" on an old English idea.

Q I know you're supposed to spray for **peach leaf curl disease** in the middle of winter, but I always forget and I about die of guilt in spring when the poor tree suffers distorted, swollen leaves. Worse yet, I don't get any peaches. Is there any other way to protect my peach tree so it will produce fruit and I won't feel so guilty?

A Gardeners in England experience the same wet springs and winters that we do, but they never spray for peach leaf curl. That's because long ago they learned to prevent it by simply planting and espaliering peach trees in sunny locations under the eaves of their houses; then they drop plastic down from the eaves to keep the trees dry. Infection can only occur if the branches and buds are wet when spores are present. As long as the tree remains dry, disease can't occur. Even if your tree isn't growing under the eaves, you can use the English method to prevent peach leaf curl and a host of other diseases that attack stone fruits. Build a simple framework and cover it with clear plastic to allow light in. You can either make the cover wide enough to prevent rain from hitting the tree, or drape plastic down to cover the sides. Don't forget to open the plastic sheeting during the bloom period to allow free access to pollinating insects and during the heat of summer to prevent burning the foliage. Most people only cover dwarf or young trees, but constructing a roof over your big peach tree might be just the penance for all of that misery you've put your old tree through.

Plant some fast-growing veggies for fall harvest.

Q I love to eat fresh veggies out of the garden in all seasons. Are there some good-tasting, nutritious vegetables that I can **plant in late summer** to enjoy eating in fall?

A Despite my love of brussels sprouts, eating so much spinach could be the real reason that I'm the best-looking and most muscular gardener at KING5 TV (not counting Meeghan). Spinach is a great late-summer crop. Plant it in August, and you'll be eating baby spinach in salads within two to three weeks. You'll be harvesting full-grown spinach for cooking and steaming within about 40 days. August is also a great time to plant lettuce, arugula, and some of the delicious mustards and Oriental greens. Swiss chard adds beauty to the vegetable garden and is very nutritious. Try a variety called 'Perpetual', available from Territorial Seed (www.territorialseed.com). It's resistant to bolting, often becomes a perennial, and has been known to survive for several years in gardens west of the Cascades. If you're a cilantro fan, try sowing the seed in August. The cool weather will arrive before the plants bolt, and you'll be enjoying this wonderful little herb well into the fall.

Check your pears to see if they're ready for the picking.

Q I'm ready to give up on my **pear tree**. The fruit takes forever to ripen on the tree, and once it softens up, I bite in and it's rotten in the middle. Is this tree a dud?

A When I was a kid, I was always disappointed when I raided my neighbor's pear trees. The pears were hard as a rock, or if they were soft, they were rotten in the middle. Unlike apples, European pears cannot be allowed to ripen on the tree, or they rot from the inside out. They must be picked before they're ripe and allowed to ripen off the tree. When a pear begins to size up and change color, cup your hand under it and lift. If the pear stem breaks, the pear is ready to pick. Pears that ripen in early September, such as Orcas and Ubileen, need only be put on the counter for a few days to ripen and be ready to eat. Those that ripen in late September or October, such as Bosc and Comice, must be stored in a refrigerator for at least a month, and then put on the counter to fully ripen. I love pears and can never wait a whole month. Try bringing them out at various time intervals. They may be just fine after only a couple of weeks in cold storage.

Mmm mmm good: finger food in your garbage can.

Q I've heard you rave about how much fun it is to grow **potatoes** in a garbage can. How does one go about this? Can you grow any kind of potato in a garbage can?

A Every year I grow potatoes in a garbage can. Of course, I always use a clean container, not one that ever had garbage in it. Kids love this. In early April, plant seed potatoes 5 inches apart in potting soil 6 inches deep in the bottom of the can. (Make sure the can has plenty of drainage holes.) Work Osmocote or another slow-release fertilizer into the soil when you plant the spuds, or fertilize every two weeks with a soluble houseplant fertilizer such as Miracle-Gro. Every time the vines grow about 4 inches, cover all but 1 inch with soil, straw, or compost. Water enough to keep the soil evenly moist all season long, and keep covering the vines until they come out of the top of the can. Once the potatoes bloom, you can reach in to find and harvest new potatoes to eat right away (they don't keep long), or you can wait until the vines die back at the end of the season and harvest the whole batch of keepers in one shot. This year, I'm trying something different. I'm growing fingerling potatoes. These easy-to-grow spuds are famous for use in potato salad, but there's nothing better than a few of these long, skinny spuds mashed up with plenty of butter and served with . . . asparagus. (Fooled you, didn't I?)

Late summer is the time to prune your fruit trees.

Q When is the best time to **prune fruit trees**? I always do it in the winter, when the trees are dormant. Now I've heard that August is best. Can you give me a few hints on how to go about pruning fruit trees?

A August is now considered the best time to prune fruit trees. Removing the water sprouts in August helps reduce shoot growth the following year. That's because pruning in August removes many of the little food factories (leaves) that transfer energy when the leaves die back in fall, which would otherwise encourage rampant sprout growth in the spring. Late-summer pruning has also been shown to reduce disease problems, especially on trees with stone fruit. As long as you don't remove more than a third of the foliage, the energy loss will not harm the tree. August is the best time to limit height, remove sprouts, and cut out branches crossing into the center of the tree. Thinning in this way will allow sun to penetrate into the canopy to reach and ripen fruit. Cut back some of the small water sprouts to about 2 inches to promote fruit spurs. Remove larger water sprouts and any that crowd existing fruit spurs by cutting them back to the main branch. Take your time, and you won't knock fruit off in the process. There are a few important rules to remember: Always cut to an upward-facing branch to preserve a vase shape rather than that of an umbrella; don't try to make up for twenty-five years of neglect in one pruning; and don't let your male partner loose with the pruners until he attends a pruning seminar! Yes, pruning is a lot of work, but think about all of the scrumptious pie à la mode you'll be eating in September.

Harvest a champion.

Q I need your help to win the bragging rights in a **pumpkin-growing contest** with a bunch of my garden-loving friends. It's the first time I've ever grown a pumpkin, and I must have done something right because it's getting pretty good-sized. I'm already bragging because I'm pretty sure I'm going to win. I want to let it grow as big as possible, but the nights are getting colder, and I'm worried that a freeze might harm it. When is the best time to harvest to win the trophy, not to mention bragging rights?

A I wouldn't brag too much before the trophy is in hand. I once challenged the gardeners at Seattle University to a high-stakes pumpkin-growing contest. The prize for growing the biggest pumpkin was a peanut-butter chocolate chip cookie from each contestant. By the end of summer I realized I had a real honker, and I was so sure of victory that I bragged for weeks leading up to the day of the contest. I'll never forget the morning of the contest, when I sauntered over to harvest my prize specimen and found a can of pumpkin pie filling in its place! Harvest your pumpkin as soon as the skin gets hard and the vines begin to wither. It takes only a few nights of freezing weather to rot a pumpkin when it's growing on the vine. Cut the stem to 3 or 4 inches long and leave the pumpkin in the sun for 10 days, covered with a blanket to prevent cold damage at night. If it's raining or freezing cold, the best method is to bring the pumpkin into the furnace room to cure for at least four days at temperatures between 80 and 90 degrees. Then it can be moved to a cool garage or basement, where it can be stored for up to six months at around 50 degrees. If I were you, I'd borrow your neighbor's Doberman for the next couple of nights, just in case.

There is life after raspberries.

Q I planted **raspberries** last year and enjoyed my first harvest this summer. The only problem is that now I'm really bummed that they're all gone. What do I need to do to my raspberries this summer to make sure I'll have a bumper crop to cheer me up next summer?

A We're kind of down at our house every year when the June-bearing raspberry season comes to an end. By "we," I mean my wife, Mary; me; and the robins. The robins are so bummed that they won't even sing! Work is the best cure for depression. Cut off the old canes right to the ground. Thin the new canes to about 4 inches apart, keeping only the sturdiest ones to produce next year's crop. Feed with a good organic vegetable fertilizer early next spring.

Think about planting a patch of everbearing raspberries this winter. Then you and your robins will have plenty of raspberries to keep you cheerfully eating (and tweeting) into the fall season.

Pick raspberries every day, and get to know your bird friends.

Q I'm thinking about growing **raspberries**. What's your favorite variety, and is there an easy way to beat birds to the harvest? I like to eat them fresh.

A Mmmm, raspberries! Dish out a hefty portion of ice cream; then cover it with tons of homegrown raspberries, and feast. My only problem with raspberries is that I tend to eat them at the same rate that I pick them; hence, I have none left for the ice cream. My favorite variety is Tulameen: sweet berries the size of my thumb! Tulameen raspberries begin to ripen in early June and often last until at least mid-July, but you may not get many if you wait to harvest, as the birds may gobble them up first. Any time it's a lousy year for cherries, the robins are going to be regular visitors at the raspberry patch. You could cover everything with bird netting, but I prefer to get out there and harvest every day. That way you'll get your share, plus you'll have happy, chubby robins to keep you company.

Keep fruiting plants growing strong.

Q My **raspberries** seem to be pooping out. There aren't as many new canes as there used to be, and the ones that grow aren't getting as tall as they used to. My rhubarb also seems less vigorous than it used to be. Do I need to fertilize them?

 Raspberries and blackberries need nutrition in order to keep growing new productive canes. Apply a good organic flower food before growth begins in spring. Generally about a half cup per 10-foot row is sufficient. Rhubarb is a much bigger eater. Feed with a cup of high-nitrogen fish fertilizer in March to promote strong growth and to discourage flowering. Better yet, put bunny power to work in your rhubarb patch. If you have access to bunny manure, stick a chunk of the pellets into the ground about every 4 inches around the drip line and watch your plant take off. Don't forget to ask the bunny owner for permission to take some pellets. I know from experience that it's embarrassing if your neighbor catches you pilfering bunny *guappa* at midnight.

Lock undesirables out of your vegetable garden.

Q How can I keep those horrible **root maggots** from ruining my radishes, turnips, and carrots? They've also been tunneling into the roots of my cabbage and cauliflower, preventing them from forming heads. I don't use poisons. Should I give up trying to grow these crops?

A Cabbage maggot and carrot rust fly can ruin a crop faster than you can say *yuck*. (And you're likely to say something worse than that if you bite into a radish, turnip, or carrot that's full of maggots!) Use floating row covers, which are made of ultra-light spun polypropylene fabric and can be placed directly over seeded rows or on top of transplants. Bury the edges of the fabric, so the adult flies can't get in to lay their eggs on or near the base of the plants, but leave slack in the fabric to allow room for it to expand as the crops grow. Be sure to rotate the location where you grow your cabbage-family vegetables and carrots when using crop covers. The flies pupate under the plants, so if you don't rotate, you're liable to have undesirable garden tenants that will definitely lead to expletives when you chomp into your carrots.

Rotate veggie crops.

Q My grandpa always told me to **rotate my vegetable crops**. Why is it important to change the location of where you grow your vegetables, and how often should you do it?

A There are good reasons why you should change the location of your vegetable crop at least every three years. Many insects and pests are specific to only one plant family. If you continue to plant vegetables from the same plant family in the same place year after year, harmful insects and soil-borne pathogens that zone in on that particular family will build up to harmful populations. If you plant vegetables from a different family, the pests lose their food source, and pest populations usually diminish rapidly. At the same time, it usually takes a few years before the pests specific to the new crop find them and begin to build up troublesome populations. The other reason to rotate crops is to manage soil nutrition. Members of the pea and bean family tend to fix nitrogen by transferring it from the air to the soil, making it available for other plants to use. If you plant big feeders such as corn or squash where you previously grew peas and beans, you'll significantly reduce the amount of nitrogen fertilizer you'll have to add to grow healthy productive plants.

According to European folklore, if you have a beautiful rosemary growing in your yard, a woman is the head of the household. My wife heard me say that in a garden talk, and the next day there was a huge one growing right by the front door.

Develop a taste for rosemary chicken.

Q How the heck do you prune **rosemary**? My wife planted a whole bunch of it, and the plants are getting so big that they're taking over the whole garden.

A According to European folklore, if you have a beautiful rosemary plant growing in your garden, it means a woman is the head of the household. My wife heard me say that in a garden talk; the next day, I stumbled over a huge rosemary bush that had suddenly appeared right next to our front door! Happily, you don't have to let that rosemary become dominant in your garden. You can cut about 4 inches off each branch tip once a week, as long as you don't remove more than 20 percent each time. You'll have to come up with your own explanation for your sudden infatuation with rosemary-seasoned barbecued chicken, though.

Sow veggies in July for your Thanksgiving feast.

Q I've harvested my early-season crops, and I'd like to plant a **second crop** that will be ready to harvest and serve at my Thanksgiving dinner. What can I sow directly into the garden around July that will be ready to harvest in late November?

A Mid-July is the time to sow fast-growing crops for fall and winter harvest. Chinese cabbage, collards, and kohlrabi can be sowed directly into the garden in midsummer for harvest by late summer and fall. These are fast-growing plants that can withstand cold and often will thrive well into winter. Mid- to late July is also a great time to plant spinach and lettuce. These can be sowed directly into the garden, but they won't germinate if soil temperatures are too warm. Shade cloth (a woven fabric available at most good nurseries) can be laid over beds to cool the soil until the seeds germinate, after which it should be removed. Lettuce can be planted in the shade of taller plants, such as tomatoes and potatoes. Remember to keep the soil moist, especially during the warm summer weather.

Get out your orchard mason bees.

 Every year I seem to have smaller fruit on my apple and pear trees, and much of it falls off before it ripens. Why is this happening?

Your fruit is not getting pollinated. Orchard mason bees to the rescue! They are small blue bees that are native to most of the Western states and that just happen to be some of the best pollinators on earth. Get them going in your garden, and you'll get bigger and better fruit. During winter, you can buy starter blocks with bees in them at most good nurseries or at the Northwest Flower and Garden Show. Then make additional bee condos by drilling ⁵⁄₁₆-inch holes in blocks of untreated wood. A deep hole provides more housing for the bees, but remember that the back of the house needs to be solid (either don't drill all the way through or screw a wooden board onto the back). Space the holes as evenly as you can, but don't worry if they aren't perfect. My blocks generally end up looking like tenements, but the bees don't seem to mind. They prefer a clean house to fancy digs. The blocks should be placed outside on a south wall beginning in early March. Place them where they'll receive as much sun as possible. I call these gentle pollinators my little teddy bees. They are not aggressive and almost never sting. A friend sat on one and said he found it to be a very uplifting experience, however!

Grow a healthy treat.

 My kids are crazy about strawberries, but I've heard the ones you buy at the store are heavily sprayed with

pesticides. I'd like to try to grow my own so I don't have to worry, but I've never done it. Any advice on how to grow them would be greatly appreciated (especially by the kids).

 It's no surprise that strawberries are the most popular berries in the world. They're not only delicious but also high in phenols and antioxidants that help protect your heart, prevent cancer, and even make you more intelligent. It's true that unless they are grown organically, the strawberries for sale at the grocery store may have been heavily sprayed with pesticides—so you're better off growing your own. June bearers produce the biggest, best-tasting berries. They are available bare-root and ready to plant at quality nurseries in February and March. Keep the roots cool and moist until you are ready to plant them in a sunny location with well-drained soil. Cut the roots back to 5 inches and plant the swollen crown just above the soil surface. Plant individual strawberries about 20 inches apart in rows spaced at least 36 inches apart. Allow runners to form until the rows are about 14 inches wide. Strawberries aren't heavy feeders. Before planting, work in a cup of organic, high-phosphorus veggie food per 10 square feet and apply the same amount of veggie food on the planting area again immediately after harvest. Provide adequate water, but avoid overhead watering during the bloom period, as that can lead to fruit rot. Now that you know how healthy organic strawberries are, you can let your kids eat that second helping of strawberry pie à la mode guilt free!

A little effort will pay tasty dividends.

I've always grown **strawberries** that produce fruit in June; now I'm considering the day-neutral type, and I'm hoping they'll taste as good as the June berries. Do you grow them the same way as the June-bearing kind?

Day-neutral strawberries produce delicious fruit from June until frost. The most popular variety, 'Tristar', tastes so good that it outsells all of the other varieties of strawberries combined.

Day-neutral strawberries have a limited productive life and should be replaced every two years. A few important tasks will reward you with bigger, more abundant berries. The first step is to remove the first set of blossoms. Sacrificing the earliest fruit will enable the plant to store the energy it needs to produce an abundant crop of big berries all season long. On first-year plants, remove the runners as well. If you want to make new plants, pull a few of the second-year plants out of production and allow them to form starts at the ends of the runners. Runners rob the plants of valuable energy, resulting in much smaller fruit. If the foliage turns light green in late July and August, fertilize lightly with a nitrogen-rich fish fertilizer. You might be disappointed at first, because day-neutral strawberries produce light crops of small fruit in June. Don't let that worry you. By July your day-neutral strawberries will produce big, incredibly delicious berries that will keep coming all summer long.

Be bad in spring and enjoy big juicy fruit in the fall.

Q I know I'm supposed to **thin my apples and other tree fruit**, but pulling off all of that baby fruit makes me feel like a bad person. Is it really that important to thin the fruit?

A No one enjoys thinning fruit. I think it's because we feel like criminals yanking off and doing in all of those poor baby fruits. You'll get over your guilt at harvest time. The yield will be the same, but it'll come in the form of fewer and substantially bigger, better-quality fruit. Thinning also helps break the every-other-year pattern of production by reducing the energy drain that occurs when trees bear overly heavy crops. Thinning is only effective if you do it before the fruit exceeds the size of a nickel. Thin apples and European and Asian pears by removing all but the largest fruit in each cluster. Peaches, nectarines, and apricots produce individually rather than in clusters. Thin the fruit to 4 to 6 inches apart.

Japanese plums set tons of fruit, which could result in broken branches from the excess weight load. Thin to 4 to 6 inches apart to prevent damage and encourage bigger plums. Most other types of plums usually don't require thinning, but if the tree sets a bumper crop, the plums will be extraordinarily small. Improve fruit size by thinning to 4 inches apart. You'll definitely overcome any lingering feelings of guilt next fall, when it takes three people to carry one apple into the house!

Avoid cracked tomatoes.

Q I grew all of these great-looking **tomatoes**, but then I noticed that the skin on most of them was cracked. What causes this?

A Nothing's more frustrating than going out to harvest a bunch of delicious tomatoes only to find that they're full of cracks. And cracked tomatoes are not only unappetizing but also quick to spoil. Uneven watering causes the problem. When water is applied after the soil has been dry, the thirsty plants tend to take up too much water too quickly, and the excess is stored in the fruit. The fruit cracks because as the skin turns red, it also loses flexibility and can't expand to accommodate the excess fluid. To solve the problem, irrigate regularly and apply mulch to keep the soil evenly moist. 'Early Girl' and 'Roma' are two crack-resistant tomato varieties.

Prevent frustrating blossom-end blight.

Q Help! I'm unbelievably frustrated. A disease is turning the bottom ends of most of my **tomatoes** brown and hard. Am I going to have to buy my tomatoes at the grocery store this year?

A Considering the cost and insipid taste of store-bought tomatoes, it's frustrating to put so much work into growing tomatoes, only to find that the bottom half (blossom end) of the fruit has turned brown and leathery. Fortunately, as long as you cut off the leathery bottom, you can eat the rest of the tomato. The condition, referred to as blossom-end blight, is not a disease. It's a physiological problem caused by a lack of calcium uptake during fruit development. It helps to work ten pounds per 100 square feet of agricultural lime into your garden every fall; but even if there is adequate calcium available, plants can only absorb it if there's adequate moisture in the soil. It only takes the slightest dry soil conditions for blossom-end blight to occur, so mulch around your tomatoes and water regularly to maintain evenly moist soil. Also avoid using high-nitrogen fertilizers, which can exacerbate the problem. By the way, pick off the affected tomatoes right away: This will encourage new, hopefully unaffected tomatoes to grow in their place.

Prevent late blight before it's too late.

Q Last year my entire **tomato** crop was destroyed by what I assume was a disease. One day I casually noticed black streaking in the leaves, and by the next day the plants were dead. What can I do to prevent this disease from ruining my tomato crop next year?

A The disease called late blight is the fungus that caused the great potato famine in Ireland in the 1840s and is the reason my grandma Maude O'Hara was born in this country. The disease usually attacks potatoes and tomatoes, but it can attack peppers and eggplant as well. Symptoms begin with black streaking in the leaves and stems, but by the time you notice that, your tomato is on the way out and will collapse into a slimy mess within hours. Once infested, the fruit is inedible. The key to controlling late blight is to prevent the leaves from staying wet for long periods. Begin by spacing your tomatoes far enough apart to allow for good air circulation. When you water, use a soaker hose. Stake your tomatoes and allow no more than four main stems per plant. Prune off all leaves within 5 inches of the soil and remove sprouts growing from branching points to prevent crowded foliage. Sprays are available at garden centers, but they must be used on a regular basis before the disease is present to be effective. For a 100-percent-effective, nonchemical method to control the disease, build a structure that you can cover with clear plastic to keep dew and rain off the stems and leaves.

Watch out for catfacing on tomatoes.

Q I think my **tomatoes** have been taken over by a creature from outer space. Several of them are contorted and look like Martians. If I eat them, will an alien life form take over my body?

A Your tomatoes aren't being taken over by an alien life form—they're suffering from a physiological problem known as catfacing. Sometimes it shows up as unappetizing, dark indentations on the blossom end of the tomato, but more often it causes interesting contorted shapes. One of my favorite catfaced tomatoes ended up a dead ringer for Elvis Presley. The condition is usually caused by poor pollination resulting from low temperatures during flowering. Excess heat, herbicide injury, and erratic soil moisture may also be to blame. Too much high-nitrogen fertilization can also cause this disorder. The good news is that you can eat the tomatoes as long as you cut off the contorted and leathery parts; although if you eat them, I can't guarantee that that an alien life form won't take over your body.

Don't pick the first tomato.

Q I'm frustrated to tweetle, as you're fond of saying. My neighbor has been eating **tomatoes** for a week and bragging about it, but only one of mine is even close to being ripe. Is there anything I can do to hurry the ripening process? I can't stand the thought of hearing more of her bragging!

A That first tomato may be calling your name, and picking it might temporarily stop the bragging, but don't do it! Left to ripen until it almost rots, that first tomato will give off a gas that will cause the rest of the tomatoes to ripen much more quickly. So wait a wee bit longer. Your neighbor will stop bragging when she sees the rest of your tomatoes ripen sooner than hers.

Fried green tomatoes are yummy.

Q It's late in the season, and my **tomato plants** are loaded with green tomatoes. Is it true that if I hang the vines upside down in the garage, the green tomatoes will turn red and ripen?

A I once told my radio audience that the idea of tomatoes ripening by being hung upside down in the garage was a myth. Boy, did I get massacred for that one! I must have received a thousand emails telling me I was full of bull-tweetle. Evidently it does work for most people. At the risk of once again bringing the wrath of the upside-down tomato-hanging crowd upon me, I must say that I've found that even if you hang them upside down, unless the green ones have begun to soften inside, they will never turn red and ripen. In any case, by mid-October it's time to hang the vines upside down in the garage and harvest any fruit that have sized up and have at least a touch of red coloring. Once in the house, you don't need to place tomatoes in a sunny spot to ripen them. All that's needed is warmth. Even if you hang them up and they don't turn red, don't throw the hard green ones away. Fry them up with brussels sprouts. The kids will love 'em!

Give tomatoes a big head start.

Q Is there something I can cover my **tomato plants** with that will enable me to plant them earlier in the season? I want to get a head start this year so that I'll be eating homegrown tomatoes earlier than ever.

A Wallo'Water, available at nurseries and garden centers, is a self-standing plant protector that you fill with water. The water absorbs heat during the day and remains warm enough to protect tender tomatoes from being harmed during cold nights. Generally, tomatoes should not be planted out until Mother's Day, but with the Wallo'Water, they can be successfully planted outdoors by mid-April. Set the Wallo'Water up a few days before planting to allow it to build up adequate heat. Remove it a week or two after Mother's Day, when temperatures have warmed up sufficiently that the added protection is no longer needed. You'll be eating homegrown tomatoes while the rest of us are drooling over the thought of 'em.

Don't prune to allow light into tomatoes.

Q It's getting late in the season, but most of my **tomatoes** aren't ripening up. They're getting big, but they aren't turning red at all. Should I prune the vines to allow more sunshine to reach them?

A Next year, choose tomato varieties that require less time to ripen. There just isn't enough heat to grow the big late-ripening ones in the Pacific Northwest. If we experience a cool summer, even early varieties don't always ripen well. Unfortunately, pruning your tomatoes to allow more sun to reach the fruit in an attempt to get them to ripen won't work; it will only ruin the fruit. Direct sunlight gives tomatoes a sunburn, which shows up as an unappetizing white blotch that soon turns hard and black. Fortunately, the heat of the average house is sufficient to ripen tomatoes. That's why you can bring green tomatoes into the house and ripen them on a dark counter.

Tomatoes are the most popular homegrown vegetables in the United States, but did you know that until the mid-1800s they were thought to be poisonous? A women's magazine finally put the matter to rest when they reported that you could eat tomatoes—you just had to boil them for 2 hours first.

It's OK to eat (and plant) tomatoes.

Q I've dabbled with ornamental gardening in my home, but I've never grown vegetables. I want to start with **tomatoes** because they're expensive, and the ones I buy at the store aren't nearly as tasty as those given to me by friends who grow their own. Are tomatoes difficult to grow? I plan to buy starts at the nursery. When and how should I plant them?

A The tomato is the most popular homegrown vegetable in the United States, but did you know that until the mid-1800s, tomatoes were thought to be poisonous? A women's magazine finally settled the question when they reported that you could indeed eat tomatoes; you just had to boil them for two hours first. (That must be how pasta sauce was invented.) Now that we know they're safe, early May, around Mother's Day, is the time to plant them outdoors. When you're choosing which tomatoes to grow, pick varieties that ripen within no more than 85 days. If you buy starts at the nursery, the stocky ones are better than the tall, leggy ones. Mix about a half cup of a good organic vegetable food in the hole before planting. Plant the tomato on its side and bend it so that only the top 4 inches of the vine are sticking out of the ground. The entire stem will root and make for a much stronger tomato plant. Be sure to plant it in a sunny spot, and try using plastic red mulch (available at nurseries and in catalogs) to reflect infrared rays and increase harvest. Then, be a risk taker: Eat them raw!

Grow tomatoes in a container.

Q I've always grown my own **tomatoes**, but since I moved into a condominium I now have to do all of my gardening in containers on my balcony. Fortunately, it's pretty sunny out there. Is it possible to grow tomatoes in a pot?

A You can grow great tomatoes in a pot. Choose one that is at least two-thirds the size of a whiskey barrel and locate it in the hottest, sunniest spot available. Make sure you choose tomato varieties that ripen early. Most folks grow determinate tomatoes like 'Legend' or 'Patio' because you don't need to stake them. Determinate tomatoes all ripen at once, however, and then the plant dies. If you can figure out a way to stake tomato plants, try a few of the delicious indeterminate varieties such as 'Stupice', 'Early Girl', and 'Sun Gold'. Indeterminate varieties continue to grow and produce fruit all season long. When you plant, work in a half cup of all-purpose organic vegetable food; supplement as needed with a high-phosphorus soluble houseplant food such as Miracle-Gro if leaves yellow or appear small as the season progresses. Keep the soil evenly moist, and you'll be picking salad tomatoes right out of your pots all summer long.

Start tomato seeds early for tasty delights later.

Q How do you grow **tomatoes from seed**? I tried it last year, but the starts grew tall and fell over. What did I do wrong?

A Start your tomato seeds indoors in mid-March, so that you can get the plants out into the garden before Mother's Day. Sow the seeds in flats of seed-starter soil covered with plastic domes to keep the seed from drying out. Remove the domes as soon as a majority of the seeds have germinated. As soon as the first set of true leaves has emerged, pot them up into 4-inch pots. Avoid the mistakes that home gardeners often make when propagating tomato seeds in the house: Don't plant the seeds any deeper than a quarter inch. Maintain cool air temperatures in the 60s, but provide bottom heat; the optimum soil temperature for germination is between 70 and 90 degrees. Keep the transplants in cool conditions. Most important, keep the starts in bright light or under grow lights. Warm air and low light are a prescription for leggy, weak-stemmed tomatoes. Get the tomatoes ready to put into the garden by putting the starts outdoors for seven to ten days in mild weather to harden them off. Be careful not to drool all over the starts in anticipation of biting into a juicy tomato come July.

Give cool-season veggies what they need to survive.

Q I'm relatively new at vegetable gardening, but I enjoy the challenge of trying to grow my own. What are the earliest **vegetables** I can plant in spring, and what conditions do they need to flourish?

A Peas, Oriental greens, mustard, parsley, and spinach can all be directly sowed into the garden anytime the soil is workable. Each vegetable has a key requirement that must be satisfied to produce productive crops. Peas require constant moisture (work in lots of compost for moisture retention) and a balanced fertilizer with higher amounts of phosphorus than nitrogen. Oriental greens also need constant moisture, but require fertilizers higher in nitrogen than phosphorus, to encourage leaf growth rather than flowering. Parsley is easy to sprout in cool, damp soils. It also needs fertilizer higher in nitrogen, but requires acid soil. Mulch parsley with coffee grounds to lower soil pH. Spinach needs uniformly moist soil that's rich in nitrogen, to prevent bolting. Spinach often fails in our acid Northwest soil because it requires a pH between 6.5 and 7.5. Every autumn, work in dolomite lime to sweeten the soil by the time you plant in spring. Plant as soon as the soil is about as moist as a squeezed sponge, and you'll be eating fresh vegetables and greens right out of the garden in no time.

Grow your own to get the best varieties.

Q You often recommend growing your own **vegetables from seed**. What's the advantage of doing this rather than growing them from starts available at my local nursery?

A There are several. It's less expensive, for one, and you can try all sorts of new and interesting varieties that rarely show up at nurseries. For instance, here are a few of the hard-to-resist plants in Territorial Seed's catalog: 'Pink Accordion' tomato is a new introduction with ruffled fruits that look as if you could use them to play Lawrence Welk champagne music, yet are purported to be so sweet that one bite makes grandmothers jump up and break into a wild polka. 'Bulgarian Carrot' is a new hot pepper that would be worth growing just for the fluorescent orange fruit. The crunchy flesh is perfect for roasting, and its flavor begins intensely fruity but finishes in flames. Tired of fighting powdery mildew on your summer squash? 'Success PM' is said to be highly resistant, yet it pumps out delicious, buttery-tasting yellow squash all summer long. There are many more new and exciting vegetables to choose from. Order a catalog at www.territorial-seed.com. Then your only problem will be where to plant all the veggie starts that you've raised.

Apply dormant oils in winter to prevent insect problems in spring.

Q Every spring my fruit trees drip with **wet, sticky stuff**. What is causing this, and can I do anything to prevent it during the winter?

A The sticky liquid (honeydew) is a sign that you've got a sucking insect, such as scale or aphids, in your trees. Inspect them for potential insect problems during the winter months. Look for woody-looking bumps on branches and twigs (a sign of scale) and tiny, black, shiny aphid eggs, usually on the ends of branches. If your trees have one or both of these problems, an easy way to solve them is to apply a delayed dormant oil spray in mid-February. Supreme or Superior brand oil is available at most garden outlets. The oil will suffocate the scale crawlers and prevent the aphid eggs from hatching to become a major problem in spring.

Give winter gardening a try.

Q I understand that some types of vegetables are hardy enough to survive the winter to be harvested in spring. Which veggies are the best ones for **winter gardening**? Do you plant them in fall?

A Quite a number of vegetables are hardy enough to survive the winter to produce a late winter/spring crop, and most of the good seed catalogs carry them. Most winter-hardy veggies need to be sowed in early July. The goal is to allow the plants to develop deep roots to survive the winter cold. Sow hard-to-transplant root vegetables such as carrots, rutabagas, and turnips directly into the garden. Work in about 1 cup of balanced organic vegetable fertilizer per 10 feet before planting. Unfortunately, it isn't easy to keep garden soil moist enough for good germination in the heat of summer. To aid germination, water regularly and cover the soil with shade cloth, a finely woven fabric designed to cool the soil and slow evaporation. Remove the shade cloth as soon as the majority of the seeds have germinated. Start the seeds of easily transplanted vegetables such as broccoli, cabbage, cauliflower, and kale indoors under lights. Fertilize lightly with a good organic vegetable fertilizer when the starts are planted out into the garden. Wait to fertilize again until spring, and then only if the plants look peaked. Most vegetables that are listed as cold-hardy will survive the winter with little or no winter protection. If you hear that an Arctic Express is bringing subfreezing temperatures, however, build a quick frame around the plants with stakes; then drape a sheet or mattress cover over the stakes. Remove the cold protection as soon as milder temperatures return. One last note: Remember to eat your winter crops when they're ready to harvest in spring. It's amazing how easy it is to forget they're out there, and to let what would have been delicious vegetables sit and rot.

CHAPTER THREE

Other Trees, Shrubs, and Grasses

Grow a desert plant.

Q I recently returned from Arizona and fell in love with those big **agaves**. Can we grow those gorgeous plants here, or are they too tender?

A Anyone who has seen these colossal succulents growing in the mountains and deserts of the Southwest, Mexico, and Central and South America can't resist growing agaves here in the Pacific Northwest. These colorful, wickedly spined succulents make a formidable statement as an addition to a rock garden, or even in the mixed border. Agaves are easy to grow and, surprisingly, many of the most colorful ones are hardy here and can be planted out into the garden in extremely well drained soil. *Agave americana* 'Marginata' is an architectural masterpiece. It can develop as many as twenty 5- to 8-foot-long lance-shaped gray-green leaves with creamy yellow margins. If you prefer something that will stay a little smaller, the variety 'Protoamericana' is upright and compact, featuring ghostly blue foliage. For something unusual, try growing *A. parviflora*. This one grows in a symmetrical whirl of narrow, white-marked, dark-green leaves edged with hundreds of white, threadlike spines. If you find it hard to grow an agave, you can always distill it: Agaves are used to make tequila in Mexico.

Take the hedge by the chain!

Q Our old **arborvitae hedge** took a hit this winter. It's all splayed out from being crushed by heavy snow, and about half of the plants are bent to the ground. I guess some weren't in very good shape to start with. Most of them are brown and look half-dead. I hate to give up on my plants. How can I get this hedge looking good again?

A The only thing uglier than a rusty old car in the driveway is a half-dead hedge in the front of the garden. I understand the reluctance to remove old plants, but half-dead hedges can rarely be renovated, and they detract horribly from the appearance of the garden. Show no mercy! Get out the chain and pickup truck, and put your hedge plants (and your neighbors who have to look at them) out of their misery. Nurseries have great deals on hedge plants, and either spring or fall is a great time to plant a new hedge. You'll be amazed by how much better your garden will look.

Monitor for mites on arborvitae.

Q Every summer the foliage on our **arborvitae hedge** turns brown, and the hedge looks as if it's dying. Then winter comes and it turns green and looks great again. What's causing this?

A Your *Thuja occidentalis* (commonly called arborvitae or pyramidalis) may be suffering from an infestation of spider mites. Find out by inserting an open manila file folder inside the plant, placing most of it under last year's needles. Then beat the living beetle hopper out of the branches above the folder. Pull the folder out, tip it to clear out needles and debris, and look for little dust particles that crawl. These are spider mites that thrive in dry conditions and suck moisture out of the plant. Often, your hose is all that's needed to prevent the problem. Starting in spring, blast a powerful spray into the interior of the shrub at least a couple of times per week. If the problem continues, suffocate the mites by spraying with a highly refined, environmentally friendly horticultural oil such as Superior or Supreme, available at garden centers. Your hedge should begin to green up within a few weeks.

Keep your barberry a manageable size.

Q My **barberry** is getting huge. I need to prune it, but I don't want to turn it into an ugly mess. Can barberries be pruned, and when and how should I do it?

A Barberries such as *Berberis julianae* (wintergreen barberry) are meant to be big, and no one in their right mind would even try to take on that prickly monster. Many of the other barberries, however, such as the attractive red Japanese variety (*B. thunbergii* 'Rosy Glow') and *B. verruculosa* (warty barberry), are quite manageable if pruned soon after the flowers fade in spring. The key with all barberries is to resist cutting the top growth. Instead, cut about a third of the individual canes to the ground. These guys are the porcupines of the plant world, so wear the thickest gloves available, protective glasses, and thick-soled shoes.

Bare-root is better.

Q I've noticed that more plants are becoming available **bare-root**. Is this a good way to plant? Do you plant bare-root plants differently from plants in containers?

A It's true: More and more bare-root deciduous trees and shrubs are becoming available in nurseries in late winter and early spring. There are several advantages to planting bare-root. Bare-root plants generally cost less because pots and soil are not required. They are lighter and easier to handle for the same reason. Bare-root plants usually have fewer long-term problems because the roots are less likely to be kinked or rotted. Best of all, the roots of bare-root plants generally develop much faster than do those of potted plants. That's because the roots don't have to make the transition from the soil in the root ball into the existing garden soil. Be sure to dig a wide planting hole, and spread out the roots to give the plant a good start. Incorporate compost by working it into a large area rather than only into the planting hole. Then stand back! Your bare-root plant will grow so fast that it's liable to knock you over.

Black is in fashion.

Q I'm intrigued by a plant I saw in one of the display gardens at the Northwest Flower and Garden Show. It was about 6 inches tall and looked like grass, but the leaves were black. Is this **black grass** something we can grow in our gardens here?

A Black plants are "in." The spectacular dark-foliaged plant you saw at the show is *Ophiopogon planiscapus* 'Nigrescens', commonly known as black mondo grass. It is easy to grow, and most quality nurseries carry it. Although it looks like grass, it's actually a member of the lily family. The evergreen, black foliage looks incredible in combination with apricot-flowered pansies or the white marbled leaves of *Helleborus argutifolius* 'Janet Starnes'. Black mondo grass is usually recommended for shade, but it turns green if it doesn't get sufficient sunshine. It thrives and looks its darkest in full sun, where it will spread to form a large clump as long as it gets sufficient moisture. Keep it looking good by removing any brown foliage damaged by winter cold. Black mondo grass is easy to divide in spring. Remove offshoots or slice off sections from clumps with a digging spade.

Cut your buddleia down to size.

 My **butterfly bush** is getting way too big. How and when can I prune it?

Butterfly bushes (*Buddleia*) are popular because they attract both hummingbirds and butterflies, and they are invincible shrubs that can thrive in the driest of conditions. However, as many a gardener has learned, all buddleias, including the supposedly dwarf varieties, quickly become trees unless they are pruned hard every year. To keep them a manageable size, cut these ambitious shrubs practically to the ground in early April. They will grow back and bloom in summer. How far to cut them back and how tall they will grow in one season depend on the variety and the growing conditions. Be careful when cutting back huge old ones. Cut only to where there is live growth. I once cut an old one practically to the ground, and that was the last I ever saw of it.

You can't hurt a camellia.

My **camellia** is getting so big that I can't see my house anymore. When is the best time to prune it, and can I cut it back practically to the ground?

Prune your camellia soon after it finishes blooming. Camellias look their best when the branching is thinned out. A wise old gardener taught me to prune camellias so that a bird could fly through them, but by the time he was done, it always looked as if an eagle could fly through. Don't worry: You can't overdo it. Cut them anywhere to lower the height. They always grow right back.

Try growing your own tea.

Q Is it true that tea comes from a **camellia bush**? Which camellia is used for tea? Can I grow it in my garden here, and if so, how do I make tea out of it?

A Not many folks are aware that the black or green tea they drink comes from a camellia that has been cultivated for centuries in China. *Camellia sinensis* is a lovely little evergreen bush that grows about 4 feet tall and has small, fragrant, nodding flowers in autumn. This camellia prefers sun and will do great planted in well-drained soil or in a container. The leaves must be fermented to make black tea, but to make green tea, pick only the new growing tips, and spread and dry them in the shade for six hours. Then heat on low in an open pot for a couple of hours, frequently stirring. Pour boiling water over a few leaves, and you're drinking the same delicious tea that Confucius enjoyed centuries ago.

Don't get carried away pruning ceanothus.

Q I love my *ceanothus* plant. It has blue flowers and the evergreen leaves look great in my dry border, but it's getting too big. How far can I cut it back without hurting it?

A *Ceanothus* is often called California lilac. The blue spring flowers are attractive to butterflies and bees. It's the ideal shrub for a sunny, well-drained location. The problem is that they almost always get bigger than desired. Don't overdo the pruning. Cutting back hard will drastically shorten the life of *ceanothus*, and shearing them gives them an artificial, "lollipop" look. Branches can be pruned back, but never cut wood that is wider in diameter than a pencil, and always cut to another branch, never leaving a stub. It's much better to control height by starting when the plant is young.

What to do if your *ceanothus* is huge? Enjoy it: They generally live for only five to ten years. Begin pruning its replacement when it's still small.

There are ornamental cherries with bark showier than flowers.

Q While visiting an arboretum, I saw a **cherry tree** with shiny red, peeling bark. What kind of cherry has this kind of showy bark? Are they easy to grow?

A Most gardeners plant flowering cherries for the spectacular spring flowers, but there are two standouts planted primarily for their colorful bark. *Prunus maackii* (Manchurian cherry) is a rarely seen, small tree famous for its magnificent, shiny, golden-red papery bark. It usually reaches about 25 feet tall. The leaves turn a lovely shade of purple in early fall. The profuse fragrant white flowers appear in May and are followed by black, bitter cherries greatly loved by birds. Not all *Prunus maackii* specimens develop the attractive peeling bark, so make sure to pick one that is already shedding at the nursery. *Prunus serrula* (Tibetan cherry) is also a small tree rarely exceeding 30 feet tall, with thin, willowlike leaves that turn golden yellow in fall. The small white flowers are barely noticeable, and there's rarely fruit, but the glossy mahogany-red bark is superb. These cherries are as easy to grow as any other type of ornamental cherry. All they require is a sunny location in deep, well-drained soil. Even though the bark looks super shiny right after it peels away, resist the urge to peel the bark by hand. If you pull off the bark before it's ready, it will significantly delay the time it takes for natural exfoliation to occur in the future.

If you prune the tweetle out of your tree to reduce its height, it will exact revenge by producing 5,439,721 sprouts right where you made the cuts—every year, for the rest of your life.

Clumping bamboos are fantastic.

Q I love the look of bamboo, but I'm not willing to risk planting a running bamboo. Recently I've noticed that nonrunning **clumping bamboos** are showing up at nurseries. What can you tell me about them? Are they hardy in the Northwest? How big do they get? Are there any good ones that you recommend?

A It's not surprising that clumping bamboos are becoming one of the hot new choices for Northwest gardens. These non-running bamboos sport magnificent culms and feature finely cut leaves that add a tropical flair to the garden. Since they are evergreen and come in a variety of sizes and shapes, they work equally well planted as a specimen or as a privacy hedge. One of the most attractive clumping bamboos is *Chusquea culeou*. This Chilean native is hardy to zero degrees, reaches anywhere from 12 to 20 feet high, and features colorful bluish culms adorned with white leaf sheaths. Another spectacular clumping bamboo is *Fargesia muri-elae* (umbrella bamboo). As is true of all *Fargesia* species, this bamboo prefers light shade. Hardy to –30 degrees, it can reach 12 feet tall, but culms bend down from the top, creating a striking umbrella form. Another equally hardy, spectacular clumper is *F. nitida*, with showy purple-striped culms, contrasted with powdery white nodes. The queen of the fargesias is the new and extremely rare *F. scabrida*. This "Oh, la, la!"–inspiring bamboo features bright orange sheaths among steely blue and purple culms. The leaves are long and narrow, giving the plant a uniquely tropical aspect. Unfortunately, only a fool or a madman would fork out the $200 it costs for a small start of this bamboo. I can't wait until UPS delivers mine next week!

Plant the Ross Perot of plants.

Q While at the nursery, I happened upon a large-leaved plant called *Colocasia* or elephant ears. There wasn't much information about them. What do the flowers look like, and are they good container plants?

A *Colocasia esculenta* (elephant ears) will add a lush, tropical flair to your garden or containers. The rarely seen flowers resemble those of a greenish calla lily, but it's the mammoth, heavily veined, heart-shaped 2- to 3-foot leaves that make this a magnificent plant. The species is a showpiece with shimmering gray-green leaves, but it's hard to beat the variety 'Black Magic', featuring colossal dark purple leaves all summer long. *Colocasia* can be planted as a bulb in spring, but even with adequate fertilization, it will take until midsummer before the plant will grow to full size. Fortunately, most nurseries carry potted elephant ears that you can plant out into the garden any time after Mother's Day. Whether you place them in the open ground or in containers, they require filtered shade and fertile, moist soil. The bulbs come from the tropics and are not hardy, but there are a couple of things you can do with them in winter: Either store the bulbs dry in peat moss, or, better yet, dig up the plant and water it just enough to keep it growing by a sunny window in an unheated garage. After the danger of frost passes, replant it in the garden, and in no time you'll have huge leaves to add a tropical touch to your container or shaded garden nook.

Check blue spruce for aphids in winter.

Q My **Colorado blue spruce** tree was so majestic when I planted it, but now it's ugly. The only needles are at the end of bare branches. What ruined my spruce, and is there hope for a recovery?

A Colorado blue spruce (*Picea pungens glauca*) is a great tree, if you live in Colorado. In areas with milder climates, unbelievable numbers of small green aphids attack in the middle of winter. (I've seen as many as twelve aphids per needle!) By the time you see the foliage dropping in March, the aphids have left and the damage is done. After a bad year, the only needles left are those on the ends of the branches. There are better choices: *Picea orientalis* (Caucasian spruce) is never bothered by insects, sports glossy forest-green foliage, and grows slowly to about 40 feet tall and 20 feet wide. The slightly pendulous branches extend all the way to ground level, adding elegance to an attractive silhouette. Another handsome spruce that fits perfectly in the smaller garden and is resistant to pests is *P. omorika* 'Pendula' (weeping Serbian spruce). This tree evokes a mountain scene, even though it only grows to about 25 feet tall and 5 feet wide. It is amazingly colorful; the tops of the leaves are bright green, but the suspended branches sweep up at the tip, revealing the blue and white undersides of the needles that create a shimmering blue cast throughout the tree. The combination of color and form is hauntingly beautiful. Send the Colorado blue spruce back to Colorado and plant a much easier tree that will remain beautiful for years to come.

Do the Dinosaur.

Q Any suggestions for an interesting **conifer tree** that I can plant in front of a bare wall in baking hot sun? I want to hide the wall, but I don't want a tree that will get so big that I have to fear it falling on the house someday.

A One of my favorite landscapes at Seattle University was nicknamed "The Dance of the Dinosaurs" by the students. The star players were five 20-foot-plus Hollywood junipers (*Juniperus chinensis* 'Torulosa'). I don't like many types of junipers, but these magnificent, dark green trees with upright, angular, twisted branches create an amazing effect. Blowing in the wind, they resembled a gang of *Tyrannosaurus rex* swing-dancing in the heart of campus. Hollywood junipers rarely exceed 40 feet tall, so it's worth planting two or three, especially if you like birds. Your feathered friends won't show much interest in the prolific berries until winter, but then they'll descend like locusts, stripping every berry from the tree. So plant a Hollywood juniper, and both you and your bird friends can dance the Jurassic twirl.

Earn an apple from Father McGoldrick.

Q I'm feeling guilty as can be for allowing the branches of my street trees to grow into the sidewalk. I haven't cut them back because I don't want to harm the trees, but if I wait much longer, they're liable to put someone's eye out. Will it harm the trees if I **cut the branches back** while they're in leaf during summer?

A Every night I take a promenade with Mary and our pups Fred and Ruby. As we weave and duck around branches of trees and shrubs growing over sidewalks, I'm reminded of my early days as a gardener at Seattle University. If I didn't control the growth of trees and shrubs next to walkways, I'd get a lecture from old Father McGoldrick, but if I kept them cut safely back, I'd receive an apple as a reward. Even though the much-loved Father McGoldrick has long since passed away, I'm sure he continues to keep an eye out for foliage growing over sidewalks. It doesn't harm trees and shrubs to cut them back at any time of year, as long as you cut to a branch or a main stem. Just remember that the bigger the branch you cut, the more decay will enter the tree, so try to avoid cutting off entire branches that are more than a couple of inches in diameter. Instead, cut large branches back to smaller side branches to avoid making major cuts. Constant pruning along walks will do no harm to the trees and shrubs, your plants will look better, and you won't have to worry about angry neighbors. So you'd best get out there and cut those trees and bushes back; I guarantee you'll prefer an apple to one of Father McGoldrick's scoldings.

The nose knows. Plant a *Daphne odora*.

Q While out on a walk, I was smitten by the **fragrance of a shrub.** The plant was about 4 feet tall, with thick, glossy, 3-inch-long green leaves edged with white. The flowers occurred in pink clusters at the ends of the branches. Please tell me what this plant is; I have to have that fragrance in my garden!

A In late winter, *Daphne odora*, the diva of fragrant plants, casts a spell on anyone who walks by while it is in bloom. Oh, la, la! The flowers on this Chinese native smell even better than roasted brussels sprouts. Be warned, though: This plant is somewhat of a prima donna. It will thrive or die; there's no in-between. Plant *D. odora* in well-drained soil, where it will receive morning sun until about noon but will be shaded after midday. Add plenty of organic compost, and work a cup of agricultural lime into the planting hole. Mulch lightly with compost or wood chips, and feed right after it blooms with an organic, nonacid fertilizer. Once it's established, water as infrequently as the plant will allow. Then, if you always talk nicely to it, your *Daphne odora* might thrive and cast its fragrant spell for years to come.

Don't prune the queen of fragrant plants.

Q Last spring I purchased what I consider to be the queen of fragrant plants: ***Daphne odora***. I planted it in a sunny location, and it grew beautifully the entire summer. Then winter came and my royal plant came to look more like the court jester: Practically all of the leaves fell off. Should I prune it back to encourage it to leaf out again?

A *Daphne odora* often takes a hit in extra-cold winters. The plants usually suffer burned leaves, but sometimes they defoliate. The damage is always worse if the daphne is growing in full sun. Don't dig it up and move it; daphnes are notoriously difficult to transplant. The good news is that the leaves will grow back. Resist the temptation to cut back hard to make your daphne branch out. That will reduce the number of intensely fragrant flowers, and could lead to dieback. Wait to prune until after flowering, and then cut only to active buds close to the ends of the branches.

Desert plants love pots.

Q At my local nursery I've noticed an array of **desert plants** that are labeled as hardy. What are the best ones for growing outdoors year round? Will they really survive our wet, cold winters?

A Gardeners all over the Northwest are discovering the unique effect that desert plants can add to the garden. Agave, with its colorful, fleshy leaves, has been popular for some time, but now other desert plants in the agave family are coming into fashion. One of the most interesting is *Dasylirion*. Native to the Southwest and Mexican deserts, these evergreen perennials feature long, narrow leaves that form a grassy head at the end of a round woody base that eventually can form a 3-foot trunk, giving older plants an exotic palm tree look. *Dasylirion wheeleri* (desert spoon) is a must-have with stiff, bluish-gray 3-feet-long leaves. Another star in the agave family is *Beschorneria yuccoides*. The 3-foot clumps of blue-gray leaves are ornamental in their own right, but the real fireworks come in spring when 6-foot coral-red stalks rise up to bust into green bell-shaped blooms, surrounded by spectacular red bracts that drive gardeners and hummingbirds mad with desire. Considering the freezing winter nights in the deserts where they come from, it isn't surprising that these succulent plants are often quite hardy. Unfortunately, on the west side of the Cascade Mountains, if they're planted in the garden, they often succumb to the soggy, wet soil conditions that occur in a typical winter. Potted up in a light, gritty soil, however, they rarely suffer damage when left out in the weather all winter long.

Don't suffer a mite-infested Alberta spruce.

Q I thought **dwarf Alberta spruce** would make the perfect centerpiece in the containers by my front door. I changed my mind when the needles turned an ugly brown in the middle of summer, making it look dead. Is there anything I can do to green it up again?

A Dwarf Alberta spruce (*Picea glauca albertiana* 'Conica') is a bushy, compact, cone-shaped shrub that makes a popular container plant. Unfortunately, it also attracts spider mites. Although they don't kill the plant, these little menaces build up incredible populations, resulting in ugly brown foliage that makes the plant look dead. Powerful sprays of water from a hose-end nozzle are usually all it takes to defeat spider mites, but spraying won't win the battle in Alberta spruce. The only way to prevent this pest is to apply horticultural oil sprays before the mites gain a foothold. But you may end up spraying all summer long. Unfortunately, once the needles turn brown, you may have to live with your dead-looking plant for at least a month before it sheds its brown leaves and new ones take their place. Better yet, rip your Alberta spruce out by the ears and replace it with a dwarf variety of Hinoki cypress (*Chamaecyparis obtusa*), white cedar (*Chamaecyparis thyoides*), or Monterey cypress (*Cupressus macrocarpa*). There are several forms of these conifers to choose from that make great container plants, and you won't have to spend the rest of your life spraying to keep them looking good.

Plant a little lilac with big fragrance.

Q I planted a beautiful lilac at my condo, but despite my best efforts to keep it small, it quickly outgrew the space available. Is there any such thing as a **dwarf lilac**?

A Lilac trees are among the most popular of all fragrant plants, but they have a frustrating habit of growing taller than expected, with blooms only at the top where you can barely smell them. Fortunately there are dwarf Korean lilacs (*Syringa meyeri*) that thrive in a pot or out in the garden. These small, sturdy shrubs are drought tolerant and rarely reach 6 feet tall. The trees may be smaller, but the flowers are every bit as fragrant. *Syringa meyeri* 'Palibin' is the smallest of all lilacs, maxing out at about 4 feet. It's one of the first to bloom with pinkish lavender blossoms in spring and often repeats in fall. The variety 'Superba' gets only a smidgen taller, and its sweetly scented, deep-pink flowers are among the longest lasting of lilacs. The newly introduced *Syringa* × 'Bailbelle' (Tinkerbelle lilac) rarely exceeds 6 feet and is an olfactory delight. The deep-pink single flowers emit a rich, spicy fragrance guaranteed to please. Give your lilac full sun and well-drained soil, and apply lime every few years to prevent the soil from becoming too acidic.

Grow choice plants under eaves.

Q Everything I plant under the **eaves** of my house dies. Is there anything that will grow there, or should I be content with plastic plants?

A One of the most difficult areas to keep plants alive in is under the eaves of the house. Even weeds struggle. Under eaves, near the wall of the house is actually a great place to plant semihardy plants such as the hummingbird-attracting *Abutilon* or tender varieties of *Canna*. The walls absorb heat during the day and unleash it on cold winter nights to keep relatively tender plants from freezing. The problem is that the eaves block the moisture and, despite all of the winter rain, the plants die of thirst. Worse yet, by early winter, the hoses are generally stored away and the outdoor faucets covered for the season—so you're stuck watering by hand. Buy a big watering can and stick a note on the wall that reminds you to water under the eaves every two weeks. Come spring, you'll delight in showing off those rare, semihardy plants that died for everyone else.

Flavor your garden with chocolate.

Q Can you tell me about the new **elderberry** that has lacy leaves and dark foliage? I've heard it looks fantastic and will grow almost anywhere. How tall does it get? Does it maintain its dark leaf color all season?

A The recently introduced 'Black Lace' elderberry *Sambucus nigra* 'Eva' is creating quite a sensation. Hardy to –30 degrees, 'Black Lace' has finely cut chocolate-burgundy leaves, giving the plant a look similar to a Japanese maple. Plant it in full sun and the leaves purportedly maintain the rich, dark coloring all summer. Large heads of slightly scented pink flowers complement the dark foliage in early summer, followed by black berries that are lusted after by birds in fall. 'Black Lace', like all elderberries, will thrive in almost any type of soil, including clay. The mature height is around 8 feet, but you can easily prune it to keep it smaller. To keep it bushy, prune back growth from last season to a few inches, or if a smaller, bushier shrub is desired, cut it back to the ground every spring. It will quickly grow back to about 4 feet tall, with fresh, colorful foliage.

Delay the winter blues by planting *Camellia sasanqua.*

Q The gray winter skies are bumming me out. I'm looking for an **evergreen plant** that will flower all winter long in a whiskey barrel–sized container next to my front door. The container is in full sun. Is there any plant that will fit the bill and chase away my winter blues?

A Suffering the winter blahs? Let the fall blooms of *Camellia sasanqua* cheer you up. These dark-leaved evergreens flower reliably all winter as long as they're planted in a sunny location. There are numerous varieties to choose from. Two of my favorites, 'Apple Blossom' (single white flowers, flushed with pink) and 'Yuletide' (cheery bright red flowers on a dense upright plant), have lightly fragrant flowers. 'White Dove' is a new variety with big, double white flowers sporting yellow stamens topped with orange anthers. Sasanqua camellias make wonderful container plants, and they're easy to espalier against a wall or fence. Next year, thin buds in early summer, and you'll get such big, showy flowers that winter will become your favorite season.

Get friendly with your ferns.

 I have a wide variety of **ferns** growing in my garden. Is it true that one should remove all of the fronds of any type of outdoor fern in spring? When should this be done? Also, can ferns be divided?

A In about mid-March, the old fronds on all types of ferns should be cut back to keep the plants looking fresh and attractive. This will not weaken the fern or harm it in any way, as long as you are careful not to cut off the new fiddleheads that are just beginning to grow. March is also a good time to divide ferns. They rarely *need* to be divided, but it's a good way to get new ones if you'd like more ferns. As long as it is healthy, any good-sized hardy fern can easily be divided in spring. Simply lift the clump and slice the plant in half with a digging spade. Keep the new sections well watered and voilà, you now have two for the price of one.

Invite a touch of spring into your home in winter.

Q I've heard it's possible to **force the branches** of flowering trees and shrubs by bringing them into the house in winter. Do you need to do anything special to get them to flower? What type of plant is easiest to force?

A Impress the living tweetle out of your family and dinner guests by bringing cut branches of spring-blooming shrubs into the home to create colorful bouquets in the middle of winter. It's easy to force spring-flowering shrubs into bloom, but it can take several weeks unless conditions are right. The trick is to wait until the buds swell, generally at the tail end of winter; some years, however, warm winter temperatures cause the buds on many late winter–blooming shrubs to plump up early, making it possible to force them as early as in January. Once the buds have swelled, branches of forsythia, flowering quince, and pussy willow are likely to burst into flower within three weeks or less. Cut the bottom of the branch with a sharp pruner, remove any buds or twigs that would be underwater, and place the branches in a vase filled with warm water. Every few days, cut about one-quarter inch off the bottom of the branch and change the water. Once the flowers open, place the vase in a cool location out of direct sun to extend the bloom period. Mix and match branches of different shrubs to create such spectacular combinations.

'Forest Pansy' redbud trees need water.

Q I planted a **'Forest Pansy' redbud tree** at my home a couple of years ago. At first it was incredibly beautiful, with red leaves and unusual red flowers that seemed to come right out of the branches, but in its third year the leaves came out but never grew. The following spring it never leafed out at all. What killed my lovely tree?

A The 'Forest Pansy' redbud (*Cercis canadensis* 'Forest Pansy') is a gorgeous small tree with beautiful red heart-shaped leaves and attractive flowers in spring. I liked it so much that I featured it in a "Favorite Small Trees" talk I gave at the Northwest Flower and Garden Show, and told everyone that they simply must have one. To my great chagrin, almost all of these trees died within a few years of being planted! Thanks to the renowned plant pathologist Olaf Ribeiro, I learned that redbud trees need adequate moisture. Those that suffer drought stress are highly susceptible to potentially fatal soil-borne fungus diseases. So keep the soil moist, but be careful not to drown your tree. Then you may be able to grow a healthy, long-lived 'Forest Pansy' redbud, and I won't be so embarrassed for having recommended them.

Go to battle with your forsythia.

 Sometimes I wish I had never planted my **forsythia**. I love the cheery yellow flowers, but it's become so huge that it's crowding out half of the plants in my garden. I prune it constantly, but it just grows back faster than I can cut it. Don't bugs ever attack this plant and slow it down? How can I get this monstrosity under control?

A The only pests I know of that harm forsythia are unskilled pruners. The problem is that most folks give the plant a buzz cut, trimming it into a big ball in an attempt to control the rampant growth. Inevitably, the forsythia gets revenge by putting out 1,730,027 sprouts right where the cuts were made. Then the plant both looks horrible and becomes a bigger thug, taking over more space than ever. Instead of pruning it into a ball, symmetrically cut one-third of the branches to the ground. By May, plenty of new suckers will have grown out of the ground to try to replace the ones you removed. Cut out most of the suckers, allowing only a few well-spaced ones to fill in as replacements. Do not cut back top growth. Your forsythia will develop a pleasing fountain shape, and you'll be rewarded with beautiful blooms next spring. If the beast is totally out of control, cut the entire shrub to 6 inches and let it start over again! Believe me, even if you want it to, that won't kill it!

Gunneras thrive in mixed borders.

Q While on a garden tour in England, I was introduced to an enormous perennial called **gunnera**. The head gardener told me that in England they call it the dinosaur plant, and I can see why: The huge leaves give it a prehistoric look. He also told me that it is hardy enough to grow in the Northwest. Is it possible to grow these monsters in good perennial garden soil? I'd like to plant one near my palm tree to add a tropical look.

A Few if any plants look more prehistoric than *Gunnera manicata*. With huge, sharply toothed leaves that can reach more than 8 feet across, *Gunnera manicata* looks like it's straight out of *Jurassic Park*. Even the corncob flower spike, studded with tiny reddish and green blooms and fruit, looks like something a dinosaur would dine on. This plant requires moist soil, but it'll thrive in a mixed border as long as you mulch heavily and provide a daily watering to ensure that the soil never dries out. To help it achieve honker status, feed at least three times per year with an organic fertilizer high in nitrogen. Gunnera will survive temperatures as low as zero degrees if you protect the crown. When the leaves begin to die back in October, cut the stems where they emerge from the plant; then turn the huge leaves over and use them to cover and insulate the crown from the cold. Remove the leaves when growth begins again in early spring. While you're out performing these tasks, keep an eye out for any *Tyrannosaurus rex* that might be in the area.

Make new plants the thrifty way.

Q When I was a kid, my father would go out in the middle of winter to take **hardwood cuttings** to make new plants. I should have watched closer, because I never learned how he did it. What is the procedure, and what plants does it work best on?

A One of the easiest ways to propagate new plants is to take hardwood cuttings from dormant plants. This method works best on roses and other deciduous flowering shrubs. Cut 8- to 10-inch-long cuttings the thickness of a pencil from the branch ends. Be sure that each contains at least three nodes, and make the cut about a half inch below a node. Cutting diagonally, prune away the top 2 inches of the cutting. The top of the branch you are removing will not survive, and the slanted cut will tell you which end is the top. Dip the bottom end in rooting hormone and insert each cutting into a pot filled with a 50-50 mix of peat moss and perlite, leaving only the top bud exposed. Then bury the containers up to the rim in an area of the garden protected from direct sun and wind. Make sure the rooting medium remains moist at all times. Your newly rooted shrubs should be ready to plant out in the garden by next fall.

Hardy bananas can take the cold.

Q I've got the fever, and **hardy banana** is the cure. I love the tropical look of these huge plants, but it's hard to believe that something that looks so tropical can really be hardy here. Am I going to have to go to all sorts of extremes to protect it from the winter weather?

A The spectacular hardy banana (*Musa basjoo*) is undoubtedly the main reason that "jungle fever" is raging in the Pacific Northwest. The huge leaves and palmlike habit of *Musa basjoo* exude a tropical flavor, yet this Japanese native needs little protection from the cold in our climate. The roots are hardy to zero degrees, and the trunklike stem (actually a pseudostem made up of leafy tissue) is hardy to around 17 degrees. The big leaves are the least cold-tolerant part of the plant; they're maimed after only a few hours of freezing weather. Once frozen, they'll be anything but beautiful, but leave them on for extra protection. In spring, trim off the leaves, and if the stem looks mushy, trim it back inch by inch until you see new growth—look for a pale green circle in the mushy stem. Your banana will quickly spring forth from the live tissue. Even if the stem is killed right to the ground, your banana will grow back to at least 10 feet tall the following season. If we experience a mild winter, you may need to buy yourself a safari hat and a machete: By the end of next summer, your hardy banana will tower to almost 20 feet tall and might even produce a bunch of 4-inch, bright yellow bananas.

Cut back hardy fuchsias in spring.

Q I'm getting into **hardy fuchsias**. I planted some last year, but I'm not sure how to prune them. Some are getting rather tall. Can I cut them back, or will that harm them?

 Few plants can beat hardy fuchsias for colorful, long-season blooms—especially if they're planted in full sun in rich, fertile soil. Best of all, hummingbirds find the flowers irresistible. One of my favorites, *Fuchsia* 'Genii', is a hybrid of the tough *Fuchsia magellanica* from the mountains of South America. It is hardy to zero degrees and drought-tolerant once established. This gem contrasts golden leaves with flaming red stems and small but showy dark red and purple flowers. Give it full sun to bring out its golden color. Fuchsias bloom only on new growth, so unless you want a monster shrub with blooms predominantly on the ends of the branches, it's best to prune them back to promote a lower-growing shrub with plenty of blooms throughout. Most of the small-flowered fuchsias are hybrids from a tough species that grows in Chile and Argentina. These rock-hardy fuchsias can be cut to the ground when growth starts in early spring. However, some of the larger-flowering varieties, such as 'Mrs. Popple' and 'Jingle Bells', are slightly less hardy. Wait to prune until you see new growth appear, and don't cut below live growth on the stem.

Heathers need a haircut.

Q My **heather** is developing bare, woody stems that look horrible. How can I stop that? Will it help to cut the bare stems to get them to branch out?

A Although heathers bloom in summer and heaths bloom in winter, both need to be sheared in spring to encourage new growth and help prevent them from developing bare stems. Heathers should be sheared in February or March. Shear to within a half-inch of bare stems. Trimming will retard flowering by two or three weeks, but will encourage vigorous new foliage. Wait to shear heaths until late April or early May. Trim back as far as possible without cutting into bare wood to encourage new growth and keep the center from dying out. If your plant has developed dead-looking stalks, it won't work to cut them back to encourage branching. Instead, plant a new heather or heath next to the one with bare wood, allowing it to grow over and cover the dead-looking stems.

Plant a ray of sunshine in the winter garden.

Q What's the difference between **heather and heath**? I'm particularly looking for a variety that will add interest to my winter garden.

A Heathers (*Calluna*) bloom in summer; heaths (*Erica*) bloom in winter. Heaths in flower make colorful additions to the winter garden and containers, but don't avoid heathers just because they aren't in bloom. Several heather varieties sport fiery winter plumage that warms up the winter landscape. Some of my favorites are 'Robert Chapman' and 'Wickwar Flame' (gold turning orange-red), 'Beoley Gold' (golden yellow), 'Firefly' (brick red), and 'Sunset' (golden yellow in spring, orange in fall, and red in winter). As do heaths, heathers need an open, sunny site with well-drained soil. Like their close relative the blueberry, they prefer an acid soil, so work in plenty of peat moss when planting. Plant enough heathers with flaming foliage, and you'll be going out to the garden to warm up this winter.

Go to therapy with your heavenly bamboo.

Q I'm interested in a plant called **heavenly bamboo**. Does it spread like other bamboos? What can you tell me about this exotic-looking plant?

A *Nandina* (heavenly bamboo) is an incredibly attractive evergreen plant that turns beautiful shades of red and purple, especially in winter. Nandina is not actually related to bamboo and does not spread. It's in the barberry family and prefers well-drained soil, a sunny location, and average watering. It is able to withstand very cold temperatures. Nandina comes from Japan, where it's believed to have magical qualities: Whenever you have a problem, you just tell it to the nandina, and your problem disappears. I must admit that I have frequent sessions with my nandina, such as the time I put a two-ton rock through the side of the house and followed it with the bulldozer! Check out some of the great new varieties such as 'Bay Breeze', 'Gulf Stream', and 'Plum Passion'.

Take another look at English hollies.

Q I really want to plant a **holly tree**, but my wife says they're too common and that buying one would be a waste of money. Are there any varieties with colorful leaves or different colored berries that are special enough to change her mind?

A The standard English holly (*Ilex aquifolium*) is rarely purchased these days. Who in their right mind would pay for a tree that birds plant practically everywhere for free? Well, get out your wallet: There are spectacular varieties of holly available, and the birds aren't going to plant these rarities for you. One of my favorites, *Ilex aquifolium* 'Argentea', sports glossy green leaves outlined in white. English holly thrives in dry shade, and this one glows creamy white in a dark corner. Another candidate to light up dry shade is 'Bacciflava'. It's a dead ringer for the standard, except the berries are sunshine yellow. The birds aren't as fond of yellow berries, hence the luminous fruits usually remain on the tree all winter long. The showiest variety of them all has to be 'Ferox Aurea'. Its wickedly prickly leaves are edged with brilliant gold. Plant 'Ferox Aurea' in full sun to bring out the brightest colors. This well-armed holly is the perfect candidate for an impenetrable clipped hedge, but don't back up if you weed near it! 'Ferox Aurea' is a male clone and will not produce fruit. Most English hollies are dioecious: Trees are either male or female, and you must have a male nearby for pollination or the females will not produce the showy berries. Fortunately, thanks to the birds, there are usually plenty of male suitors in the neighborhood, and lack of pollination is rarely a problem.

Plant *Melianthus* deeper than it comes out of the pot.

Q On a recent nursery tour, I about swooned when I saw an incredible tropical-looking plant called a **honey bush**. I wanted to buy one, but they cost an arm and a leg, and I don't want to fork out all of those bucks unless there's a fair chance it will survive in my garden. What does honey bush need? Can the average gardener keep one alive and attractive?

A Few, if any, plants in my garden garner more attention than *Melianthus major* (honey bush). This 4- to 6-foot-tall South African perennial boasts deeply divided and serrated blue-green leaves that exemplify Tropicana. Recent introductions featuring rich colors are guaranteed to drive perennial gardeners into fits of uncontrollable plant lust. The stems of 'Antonow's Blue', named after the late, great plantsman Steve Antonow, can reach 6 feet, carrying leaves drenched in luxurious, incandescent blue. The lower growing 'Purple Haze' will only reach 2 or 3 feet tall, but it forms a kaleidoscope of rich blues and lavenders overlaid with reds and golds as leaves mature. *Melianthus* requires a sunny, well-drained location. After a cold winter, if the foliage has frozen or looks ratty, cut the stems to the ground in mid-March to enable fresh foliage to grow anew. Plant these semitender perennials 6 inches deeper than they came out of the pot to increase hardiness and long-term survival. Even if your honey bush lasts only one season, it will be worth buying one of these new colorful forms—but with a little bit of luck, it will add a touch of tropical paradise for years to come.

Protect plants from snow and ice damage.

Q Last year a horrible **ice storm** left my trees and shrubs broken and bent over. It looked like a war zone when the whole thing was over, and although we pruned some, many of the trees broke in half and had to be removed. I know we haven't seen the last of Mama Nature's fury. Is there anything we can do to prevent, or at least minimize, damage when the next ice storm occurs, and can broken branches be mended in any way?

A You never know when winter storms laden with heavy snow and ice will damage trees and shrubs. The first defense is to have a good broom ready to gently knock heavy snow off the branches of your favorite trees. Unfortunately, that doesn't always work. Just in case, have a variety of lag bolts, wide washers, and nuts available. If a small tree splits down the middle, call some strong friends to help lift and push the sides of the tree back together. While your friends hold the split parts together, drill three or four holes (not lined up in a straight line) through both sides of the split trunk or branch. Use the hardware to bolt the tree together. As long as you get it done within a day of the break, not only will your tree survive, but in a number of years the trunk will grow right over the bolts and you won't be able to tell where the break was.

Don't get stuck with a dud.

Q Last spring I bought a **Japanese maple** expecting that it would put on a beautiful color display in fall. Instead, the leaves turned brown in fall—no color at all. The other trees in the neighborhood put on magnificent shows. What's going on?

A When it comes to trees with great fall color, "Some what's got it, some what's ain't!" I bought two vine maples one spring a while ago. I planted them across from one another in almost the exact same conditions. Every fall, one of the trees puts on an incredible show, displaying every color in the rainbow. The other is a dud: The leaves inevitably turn an ugly brown and fall from the tree. The only way to be sure you will get a great show is to buy your tree in fall. Choose the one with the best fall color of its type in the nursery. Then your new tree will likely be one "what's got it," one that will put on a gorgeous display every autumn.

Lose ten pounds on the hedge-pruning diet.

Q I'm thinking about planting a **laurel hedge** along about 125 feet of my property line as a privacy screen. Am I making a lot of work for myself?

A If you want to stay fit as a fiddle, plant a laurel hedge. You're guaranteed to lose weight because for the rest of your life you'll be climbing the ladder with shears in hand at least once per month to keep it under control. If you don't do this, you'll be forced to do a major pruning at least once a year to keep it from taking over the whole garden. Laurel hedges are like people: They get wider as they get older, and there's nothing you can do to stop them. I recommend a fence instead. Fences make wonderful backdrops for mixed borders and work great as privacy screens. They never grow and require very little maintenance. Of course, you'll be exercising less and will have to cut down on those hearty brussels sprout casseroles.

Neaten up your hedge, but don't overdo it.

Q Is fall a good time to neaten up a **laurel hedge**? Ours looks horrible, and I'd like to trim it before it gets too cold outside. How far can I cut it back without harming it?

A Fall is a good time to prune your hedge. Once a cold snap has caused evergreen plants to go dormant, you can prune without fear of triggering tender new growth. Remember to trim hedges so that the bottom is slightly wider than the top, or the lower section will become bare for lack of sun. Although laurel and photinia hedges can be cut back practically to the ground in spring, don't get carried away and cut to bare wood in fall. Your hedge won't grow back until spring, and you (and your neighbors) will have to look at your handiwork all winter long.

A hedge made up of plants such as English laurel is a Sisyphus hedge (remember the guy who constantly rolled the rock to the top of the hill?), and keeping it under control is never ending work. The best way to prune it is with a chain and a pick-up truck.

Shear lavender to keep it from becoming woody.

Q I planted a whole row of **lavender** a few years ago. The plants looked wonderful at first, but now they've all developed unsightly, bare woody stems. They're planted in full sun in well-drained soil. Can I cut them back hard to force new growth at the base?

Lavenders tend to become woody and bare at the base in only a couple of years unless they're sheared back every year. Trim them back by as much as two-thirds every spring, but avoid cutting into bare wood. As a last-ditch effort, you can try to get your lavender to sprout at the base by cutting back a few of the oldest branches to a couple of inches tall. Then cut back a few more old branches if new growth appears where you made the original cuts. If this doesn't work, listen to Edith Piaf records while you peruse garden catalogs for a suitable replacement.

Don't be fooled by brown spots on lilac leaves.

There are big ugly brown spots on the leaves of my lilac that look like they're caused by some horrible fungus disease. How can I kill the fungus before it does serious harm?

Those ugly brown blotches certainly look like a fungus disease; cut into one, however, and you'll find that the larvae of a small brown moth have hollowed out the leaves. Unfortunately, it's too late to solve the problem this year, and you'll have to live with the unsightly leaves until they drop in the fall. Next spring apply Bioneem (available at local nurseries or at Ace and True Value hardware stores) to repel the moths. Spray when the leaves are about half out and again when they're full size. This safe, environmentally friendly product repels leaf miners and will prevent the moths from laying their eggs, and you won't have to live with ugly brown blotches on the leaves.

Patience has its limits.

Six years ago I planted a lilac and a mock orange that were in full bloom when I brought them home from

the nursery. They haven't flowered since. They're in good soil and full sun, so why won't they bloom? I'm loosing patience. How much longer should I wait before I rip them out?

A *Syringa* (lilac) and *Philadelphus* (mock orange) are famous for taking years to bloom in the garden, even if they were in bloom when you planted them. They bloom at the nursery because of the stress caused from being trapped in small nursery pots. Once you plant them in better conditions, however, they are in no hurry to raise a family; instead, they put their energy into growing a healthy, strong root system. Usually it takes five to seven years to begin flowering, but even fifteen years before blossoming is not unheard of. Make sure the plants are in full sun and don't cut them back. Shade and hard pruning can prevent bloom. If, after seven years, your plant fails to bloom, here's what you can do: In June, dig the plant out as you would if you were going to move it, but instead replant it right back in the same spot. This should stress the plant enough to convince it to start a family by blooming and forming seed the following year. If that doesn't work, walk in front of it with a chainsaw and smile menacingly!

Replace the old with the new.

Q The **Mexican feather grass** that I planted last summer barely made it through the winter, and it looks horrible now that it's spring. If I cut it to the ground, will it grow back and look attractive again?

A Mexican feather grass (*Nassella tenuissima*) is a natural for the mixed border. This native of the Southwest and Mexico produces a dense green fountain of thinly textured foliage, followed by silver, feathery inflorescences from June until September. A clumping grass, *N. tenuissima* rarely exceeds 2 feet tall by 3 feet wide. Some gardeners don't like it because after a hard winter the plant often resembles a boxer that spent too much time in the ring. Don't bother cutting it back: The plants lose their attractive shape and become floppy the second year anyway. Instead, dig it out and replace it with one of the many seedlings that come up in spring. The seedlings will delight you with upright delicate foliage that moves constantly in the lightest breeze. To create stunning contrast, plant Mexican feather grass near bold foliage or next to a rock.

Prune your *Choisya* hard if need be.

 Q What types of **Mexican mock orange shrub** make a good hedge? How far down can you prune it, and when is the best time to do it?

A *Choisya* (Mexican mock orange) is a popular evergreen broadleaved shrub. It's drought tolerant, loves full sun, and displays aromatic foliage and pleasantly scented star-shaped flowers. The Mexican species *Choisya ternata* grows rapidly to 8 feet tall. Its fragrant flowers open in spring, followed by a second flush in late summer. 'Sundance' is a golden-leaved variety, but it requires protection from afternoon sun. 'Aztec Pearl' is a newly introduced hybrid that shares the tough constitution and growth characteristics of the species, but features lush green, narrow leaves that resemble bamboo and bigger flowers that smell pleasantly of almonds. Any of the varieties make good privacy hedges. Generally, little pruning is needed, but a light shearing once per year after the first flush of flowers helps retain a dense, full habit. *Choisya* will grow back, even if frozen to the roots, however, so if hard pruning is necessary, cut it back two-thirds after it finishes blooming in May to give the shrub time to grow back and harden up before next winter.

Prune your mock orange correctly and it will return the favor.

Q I need to prune our wonderfully fragrant **mock orange**, but I'm not sure how to do it. I'm worried that I'll do it wrong and it will stop blooming. When and how should I prune it?

A There aren't many shrubs with flowers as wonderfully fragrant as those of *Philadelphus* (mock orange). The attractive 1- to 2-inch cream-colored blossoms range from single to fully double and sweeten the air in late spring or early summer. Unfortunately, the fountain-shaped shrubs are vigorous growers, and left unpruned, a mock orange can outgrow its space in no time. If it's pruned incorrectly, the heady fragrance soon becomes a distant memory. Prune just after the bloom finishes, but don't make the common mistake of lowering the shrub by cutting all of the branches down part way. The flowers are formed on laterals that grew the previous season, so lowering the shrub not only prevents bloom the following season but also causes a riot of sprouts that ruin the look of the shrub. Instead, thin the shrub: Remove at least a third of the oldest branches by cutting them out at ground level. Leave the remaining stems intact: Cutting them back will result in unattractive sprouting where you made the cuts.

Be daring: Plant orange roses this year.

Q I used to be afraid of planting **orange roses** because they clashed with my pink garden. Now I've become braver and am growing mostly hot-colored plants. I want to liven up my garden with some orange roses, but all I can find at the nurseries are yellow, pink, and red ones. I've seen them in gardens, so I know they're out there. What are some good ones, and where can I find them?

A Yes, it does take courage to change to hot colors. The good news is that plenty of great orange roses are available in mail-order catalogs and at quality nurseries. Call ahead, or visit the nurseries in December and early February, when the bare-root roses become available. The climbing rose 'Westerland' has huge, apricot-orange flowers which are so fragrant that bees faint when they land on one. Cool the fire by pairing it with the velvety purple flowers of *Clematis* 'Gypsy Queen', and you'll faint when you see the combination in bloom. The fragrant climbing rose 'Royal Sunset' is unusual in that it blooms on both new and old stems, creating an abundance of peach-shaded flowers all summer long. English roses are naturals in the mixed border. My favorite orange English rose, 'Pat Austin', features unusual nodding flowers that resemble little gossamer petticoats. It should be encouraged to grow tall to show off the large blooms. One sniff of the fragrant flowers, and you'll order twelve!

Eat up if you plan to divide ornamental grasses.

Q With the coming of winter, most of my **ornamental grasses** have died back and look like straw. When should I cut the old foliage down? Also, do ornamental grasses need dividing? What is the easiest way to do it?

A Deciduous ornamental grasses (the ones that look like straw in winter) should be cut back to the ground every spring just as the new grass blades begin to grow. Never cut back or divide ornamental grasses in fall; it makes them prone to rot. Besides, many ornamental grasses save the best show for last, in early winter, when they turn captivating shades of red and orange. When the leaves turn to straw, the constant motion and sound of their rustling adds interest to the winter garden. Don't be in a hurry to remove the spent flowers. They look beautiful covered with frost, and the seeds are a highly nutritious food source for our winter birds. Don't forget to cut deciduous grasses back in spring, however. Nothing looks worse than dead strawlike leaves mixed in with emerging live foliage. Evergreen grasses (the ones that don't turn straw colored) should never be cut back. Groom them anytime they look bad by combing your gloved hand through the foliage to pull out dead leaves. Any grasses that are beginning to go bald in the middle, or any that are getting too big for their space, need to be divided. It's easiest to lift the entire clump and slice it into chunks by sawing the roots with a bow saw or, if you're big enough, by jumping on the root ball with a sharp digging spade. Replant the vigorous outside growth and discard the worn-out middle. If you decide to use the jumping technique, eat lots of brussels sprouts (and ice cream) before you take on this project. You'll need to gain all of the weight you can to help you slice through the nearly impenetrable root ball.

Be nice to the roots when you plant a palm tree.

Q It seems like every **palm** I bring home does well until I transplant it, then it inevitably dies. I score the roots just as I do my other plants, and I'm careful to put it in a pot that is only 1 inch bigger than the last one. The rest of my plants thrive with this treatment. Is there a trick to transplanting palms?

A The general rule when planting a root-bound plant is to slice off the roots twirling around the bottom of the root ball and to score the roots on the side by cutting into them; this allows them to break free and grow into the surrounding soil. But palm trees are different. If you cut a root, it won't grow back. If you cut too many roots, you may inhibit the plant's ability to absorb water, causing the plant to die before it can grow replacement roots. If you buy a tropical palm for the house, or a hardy one for the garden, submerge the root ball in warm water and gently work the roots free. If it's too huge for a bath, you're better off planting it in its root-bound state than scoring the roots. Also, it is critical to plant palms at the same depth as they came out of the pot. The only exception is *Trachycarpus fortunei* (Chinese windmill palm): This palm can be planted up to a third deeper, as it will grow new roots on the buried part of the trunk. Don't try this with any other kind of palm, or it'll soon be heading to the giant dumpster in the sky.

Prune the Pfitzer juniper before it eats your house.

Q They should sell **Pfitzer junipers** with a warning tag attached. I've never seen a plant grow so big, so fast. The little shrub I planted grew into a 12-foot monster overnight! How do I prune it to keep it from taking over the neighborhood?

A The *Sunset Western Garden Book* warns that Pfitzer junipers can become trees in time. As far as I'm concerned, it should say that they can become trees overnight! The tags say the trees will reach 5 to 6 feet tall and 8 to 10 feet wide, but at Seattle University we had Pfitzers 16 feet tall and wide that showed no sign of slowing down. Junipers can be pruned most anytime, and there are only a few rules to follow: Try to resist the drive in all human beings to turn junipers into balls and doughnuts. Prune each branch at a different length to reduce the buzz-cut look. Cut only to live growth, and try not to remove more than a third of the foliage in one shot. Consider using the truck-and-chain method of "pruning" if the monster is more than a third bigger than you ultimately desire.

Phormium is a great seaside plant.

Q I've heard that **phormium**, or New Zealand flax, is able to survive salt spray. I live along Puget Sound, and I'm looking for a spiky plant that can withstand the coastal winds. I've noticed that they often look pretty beat up, however. If phormium is a good choice for a seaside garden, how do you keep them looking tidy?

A Phormium is a natural for seaside gardens, thriving in wind and salt spray. The swordlike leaves, which can reach 6 feet tall, make a bold statement in the fall and winter garden. By late summer, though, phormium often has a number of unsightly leaves that give the plant a ratty look. Your pruners are mightier than the sword. Arm yourself with sunglasses for eye protection; then cut any unattractive leaves as close as possible to the ground. New ones will take their place next year, and your phormium will cut a dashing figure along the windblown coast.

Trim your phormium.

Q Is **phormium** hardy in the Northwest? I paid a bundle for one last summer, but after the cold winter, it looks horrible. Most of the swordlike leaves are brown or covered with ugly brown spots. Did the winter kill my expensive plant?

A Phormiums are borderline hardy in the Northwest. If you live in an especially cold area, they can be killed by the winter. On the other hand, they almost never die if your garden is located by the sea or in a warm urban area. But a cold winter can hammer them into unattractiveness, as you've experienced. Remove the ugly leaves by cutting them to the ground in April. That will thin your plant, but new leaves will grow back during the summer to fill in. If all of the leaves are ugly and brown, you have to make a decision. You can either cut them all down or dig up and replace your phormium. If you cut all of the leaves down, they most likely will come back, but it will take a long time and you'll be stuck with a pretty ugly plant in the meantime. You could dig it up and put it somewhere out of the way, and then move it back when it recovers; but if you live in an especially cold climate, the same thing is likely to happen again the next time a cold winter comes along. Maybe it would be better to spend that money on a hardier plant with a similar growth habit. A spectacular variegated yucca or an attractive ornamental grass would add a spiky look without looking like gradoo (Wischeescin talk for ugly as can be) after a tough winter.

Let your phormium bloom.

Q Does **phormium** ever bloom? I've had one growing in my garden for years, but have yet to see it blossom. What do the flowers look like?

A The colorful, evergreen, spiky leaves of *Phormium* (New Zealand flax) make it a perfect focal point in the mixed border or container planting. Although flowering rarely occurs in our Northwest climate, occasionally when conditions are right, branched clusters of inch-long, chartreuse tubular flowers bloom on a stem that rises high above the foliage. In fact, while I was at Seattle University, one of my gardeners ran in excitedly shouting that the phormiums were blooming. I surprised her by asking her to cut them off, telling her that the flowers are short lived and quickly turn ugly and brown, and that I'd seen way too many of the hideous spent flowers while leading garden tours in Australia and New Zealand. She quickly returned and told me something that made me change my mind about cutting off the blooms. There were about twelve hummingbirds fighting over every flower! If your phormium blooms, grab the camera rather than the pruners and get ready for a great show. You probably will want to cut the flower stalk off once the hummers have enjoyed their feast.

It's OK to prune your *Pieris*.

Q I've looked in pruning books and searched on the Web, but I can't find a word about how or when to prune **Pieris**. Can it be pruned?

A Pieris are elegant, easy-to-grow relatives of the rhododendron. Most varieties reach at least 10 feet tall and 10 feet wide. Superb dwarf varieties are available, but even the smallest varieties always seem to get bigger than listed on the tag, yet it's almost impossible to find information on how to prune them. If your pieris is getting too tall, the best time to prune is right after the flowers fade. Symmetrically cut back about a third of the tallest branches to branch whorls lower down inside the plant. Just don't cut individual branches back more than two-thirds. This method will leave holes, but the foliage will fill in quickly. It will take about three years, but thinning the plant in this way will allow you to control its height without ruining its natural appearance.

De-geezer your pine trees.

Q Most of the innermost needles on our **pine tree** have turned yellow and look dead. Is this something to worry about?

A My wife told me that the hair sticking out of my ears is a sign that I'm becoming a geezer. In my opinion, pines have a geezerly look when they are filled with those yellow and brown needles. After dry summers, evergreens are anything but evergreen, and old needles turn brown and die in vast numbers. As long as it's the inner needles that are dying, and not the ones at the end of the branch, it's a natural process and not a problem. It doesn't look good, however. Climb in there and clean out those ugly dead needles. The last thing you want is a pine tree that looks like a geezer all winter long.

Cistus is well adapted to drought.

Q I'm looking for a plant to help **prevent erosion** on a hot, sunny bank that gets blasted with sea spray. It would be nice if it flowered, but it will have to be drought tolerant, because it is about impossible to water that area. Any suggestions?

A If you are looking for a spectacular evergreen flowering shrub to plant on a hot, dry hillside, or to add color, texture, and fragrance to your drought garden, *Cistus* (rockrose) is your plant. Once established, these tough Mediterranean natives rarely require supplemental irrigation. Most varieties are hardy to 15 degrees, and because they are tolerant of salt spray, rockroses make great seaside plants. The showy flowers resemble single roses, and although each flower lasts only one day, new ones emerge every day over a long blooming period. In addition to the attractive flowers, the leaves of some varieties contain a sticky resin called labdanum that is used to make incense and perfume, giving the leaves a delightful spicy fragrance.

Make new plants.

Q I understand that winter is a good time to **propagate roses** and other flowering shrubs. How is it done?

A The dormant season is the time to take hardwood cuttings. This method of propagation is relatively easy and works great on roses and many other deciduous plants, such as dogwoods, figs, and grapes. In December or early January, using a sharp knife or pruning shears, take 1-foot-long, pencil-width cuttings containing two or three nodes from the ends of branches. Make all cuts about ½ inch below a node. Prune away the top 2 inches, using a slanted cut. (The end of the branch won't survive, and using a slanted cut will help you remember which end is the top of the cutting.) Dip the bottom end in a rooting hormone and plant the cuttings in a trench. You can also plant in a container filled with a 50-50 mix of peat moss and perlite, and bury the container in the soil. Firm the soil around the cutting, leaving only the top bud exposed. During the following spring and summer, make sure that the rooting medium stays moist, and protect the cuttings from direct wind and sun with shade cloth or a lattice. Your new plants should be ready to plant in the garden in fall.

Protect valuable trees and shrubs from construction damage.

Q We've just signed the contract to add a second floor on our home. I'm worried that the equipment and general construction might damage the beautiful old-growth trees and valuable shrubs growing near the house. What should we do to **protect our plants during construction?**

A It's wise to ask this question before the work begins, because once the damage is done, it's usually too late to save a tree or shrub. Before construction begins, meet with the contractor and determine which trees and shrubs can be saved. Then write and agree upon a plan to protect them. Nothing kills roots faster than being run over by heavy equipment. Wherever possible, fence off valuable trees and shrubs that are planted inside the drip line. Keep this space off limits to everything, including heavy equipment, foot traffic, and stored supplies, including soil and debris. Roots outside the drip line also need protection. Cover all areas where equipment will cross with a foot-deep layer of wood chips. Avoid changing soil elevations near existing trees, and keep trenching as far away from tree roots as possible. Any trenching within the drip line should be hand dug, with every effort made to excavate under roots. Cut any injured roots cleanly before replacing the soil. If a tree is too big to relocate and too close to the construction site to be protected effectively, consider removing it as part of the construction process. It'll save you money to do it as part of the project, and it's better to put a tree out of its misery than to watch it slowly die.

Prune like a grand master.

Q I love the ethereal cloud-layered look of the pines I've seen in famous Japanese gardens, but as hard as I try, I can't seem to re-create the effect when I **prune my own pines**. Do I have to receive years of training from a grand master, or are there tricks I can use to help achieve that look?

A I was lucky enough to receive lessons on pine pruning from a famous grand master. He told me that one should never bend a tree to one's own will. Instead, one must prune to bring out the natural character of the tree. (Then he commenced to tie bamboo canes and hang rocks all over the tree to bend the branches every which way!) If you want your pine tree to look as if it were pruned by a Japanese master, it's best to use the ancient art of tip pruning. The ideal time to prune pines is when the candles at the ends of the branches have elongated, but before the new needles begin to appear. Cutting the new candles by half will promote a shorter, bushier tree perfect for creating a cloud-layer effect. Removing some of the candles will cause the remaining candles to grow longer, and will result in a thinner, taller tree. Doing a little of both, combined with the removal of some crowded branches, will create a tree worthy of the imperial garden in Kyoto.

To deadhead or not to deadhead . . .

Q For years I've heard that it's necessary to deadhead **rhododendrons** to get a good flower display the following year. Recently I heard an expert say you don't need to do it. I don't want to climb the ladder to deadhead the spent flowers if I don't need to. Who's right?

A Both opinions are correct. It's not necessary to deadhead rhododendrons to get flowers the following year, so if it's dangerous (or even just a pain in the kazutski) to climb up a rickety ladder, you don't have to bother. You will get more branching, however, and therefore many more blooms, if you remove the spent flower clusters soon after flowering is finished. Also, rhodies definitely look better if the spent flowers are removed, so if it's not a 15-foot monster, it's probably worth the effort. You'll find that the old flower trusses snap right off, but take care not to injure the new buds at the base of the spent flowers in the process.

Feed your rhodies.

Q Is it necessary to fertilize **rhododendrons**? Mine aren't looking very green, and the blooms are sparse. I'm wondering if it's because I haven't been feeding them.

A Rhododendrons that bloom well and are healthy rarely require fertilizer. However, if your rhododendron has yellowing leaves, or if its new leaves are smaller than normal, it might need a feeding. Use only organic fertilizer; rhododendrons have airy surface roots that can easily be burned if synthetic fertilizers are used incorrectly or too liberally. Scratch the fertilizer into the ground around the outside of the drip zone, being careful to avoid digging into surface roots under the foliage. Feed in March, and again when the blooms begin to fade. You should notice an improvement in leaf size and color soon after bloom. If your rhododendron doesn't respond to fertilizer, it may be growing in too much sun or suffering from root rot. Take a sample to your local Master Gardener clinic for diagnostic assistance.

Prune your rhododendron right after the blooms fade.

Q I have a several spectacular **rhododendrons,** but they need pruning. A few are getting thin and leggy, and others are growing too tall and blocking windows. When is the best time to cut them back?

A The best time to prune your rhododendrons is soon after they finish blooming. I prefer thinning them by removing about a third of the small branches, but if your rhodies are getting leggy, they can be cut back hard. Rhodies contain barely noticeable buds that will break to become new branches almost anywhere you cut. Rather than whacking your rhododendron back to preserve a view through a window, consider removing the lower branches and allowing it to grow tall. Many rhodies have spectacular exfoliating bark. You'll be able to look out through attractive trunks while enjoying a canopy filled with flowers blooming above.

Transplant the monster.

Q Something tells me you've been asked this question before. When is the best time to transplant **rhododendrons**, and how do you do it? I've lived in the same home for about twenty years, and some of the rhododendrons I planted when I moved in are getting way too big for the spot where I put them. These are gorgeous plants and I don't want to lose them, so I want to do it right.

A Ever since I arrived in Seattle in 1972, the question I'm most frequently asked has been "When can I move my rhododendron?" You can move rhodies any time when it isn't hot and dry out, and any time they aren't putting out new growth, but if the plant is a big old one, you're in for a struggle. Dig in around the drip line until you run into the tightly packed roots that resemble a bird's nest underground. Dig a trench around the roots until you can dig underneath. Keep digging, and rock the plant from side to side until the shallow root ball breaks free. Dig a gradual slope on one side of the hole. Once you're sure the root ball is free, place a big piece of plywood on the slope. Put a blanket around and under the root ball, station really strong folks on each end of the blanket, and pull the root ball up the plywood to get it out of the hole. Then you can turn the rhody on its side and roll it to its new home. Treat yourself to some extra brussels sprouts for dinner. You earned them!

Ignore the books—prune your *Cistus*.

Q My **rockrose** is growing over my walkway, but my gardening book says you're not supposed to prune it. If I don't cut it back soon, I won't be able to get into the house. Will I kill it if I cut it back?

A Most books tell you that *Cistus* (rockrose) shouldn't be pruned. I don't know what rockrose they are talking about. Over the years, every variety I've planted has turned into a monster that grew over the walk or suffocated its neighbor plants. Cistus can be pruned, but it doesn't take well to hard pruning, so begin when it's young. As soon as flowering begins to slow down in mid-summer, remove about a third of the older stems by cutting them to the ground or to a stem near the ground. This allows air and light to penetrate the plant and promote new growth within the shrub. Then control branches that are growing too tall or too wide by cutting back to live growth farther back in the shrub. If you prefer a hedge, you can shear one-third off the top and sides, but avoid cutting to dormant wood. If your rockrose has become a gigantic woody geezer, you probably are better off replacing it with a new one that you can keep under control from the start.

Rosa rugosas need pruning.

Q I practically gave up trying to grow roses until I discovered **Rosa rugosa**. Now I can finally grow roses without diseases ruining them! The person who sold the plant to me at the nursery told me I'd never have to prune it. Is that true? I thought all roses needed pruning. What if it gets too tall?

A Most folks don't realize that the rugged *Rosa rugosa* needs annual pruning to keep it attractive and productive. Rugosas are tough shrub roses that originated in China. They're becoming increasingly popular because they rarely suffer disease and are as drought tolerant as a rock once established. Best of all, the flowers are extremely fragrant, and they form huge rose hips that are delicious and nutritious if eaten raw or used to make herbal tea. Left unpruned, the center of the plant becomes crowded with dead or old, less productive canes. Every year, in early March, remove one-third of the oldest canes. This will promote the growth of plenty of new, highly productive canes to take their place. It's not a good idea to cut the canes back to reduce the size of a *Rosa rugosa*. It's better to move a big one to where it has elbow room and replace it with a variety that tends to stay smaller, such as 'Fru Dagmar Hastrup', with single silver-pink blossoms on a shrub that reaches only 3½ feet tall. Other nice varieties include 'Scabiosa', with single pink blooms, which reaches 4 feet tall; and 'Hanza', with reddish purple blooms on a 6-foot shrub. The only problem with rugosas is that the petals fall off when the flowers are cut, thus rendering their blooms useless for arrangements.

Don't overdo rose pruning.

Q Why can't I grow **roses**? I buy disease-resistant roses and plant them in a well-drained, sunny location. I spray, fertilize, and water religiously, and I prune them down hard every spring. Yet before I know it, they begin to go downhill. If I'm lucky, my roses live for about five years. What am I doing wrong?

A Back in the 1800s, roses were planted along the Oregon Trail to commemorate folks who died while trying to make the difficult crossing. Why is it that most of those uncared-for roses still thrive in the middle of nowhere, with no care at all, while the roses in many of our home gardens go downhill despite the heaps of attention we give them? Perhaps we're pruning our roses to death. Roses store energy in their canes, which is needed for strong growth and renewal. Pruning them to 6 inches year after year deprives the plants of critical energy supplies and turns them into Pee-wee Hermans. Turn them back into Arnie Schwarzeneggers by cutting the canes back no farther than two-thirds. Perform drastic pruning to 6 inches or less only every few years, as necessary to force branching if the rose becomes leggy and bare on the bottom.

Take it easy on roses.

Q Is it a good idea to prune **roses** in fall? If not, when should I prune them? Also, do I need to cover the bottom third of each of my roses with compost to protect them from freezing winter weather?

A The only reason to prune roses in fall is to cut canes back far enough to keep the wind from blowing the plant over. Wait to do the hard pruning until growth starts in spring. If you live on the east side of the Cascade Mountains, it's generally necessary to protect roses from the cold by covering the bottom third of the plants with compost. If you live on the west side, however, you don't have to worry about that; it's usually necessary only if temperatures dip into the teens. Save a few extra bags of compost just in case, though, and be ready to cover the bottom third if a rare Arctic Express is forecast.

Hybrid tea and floribunda roses know they're on earth to reproduce.

Q My hybrid tea and floribunda **roses** bloom magnificently in early summer, but barely bloom again all summer long. Instead, they produce only rose hips. I prune my roses in March, they're in full sun, and I fertilize regularly with a quality organic rose food. Why do they bloom only in spring instead of all summer long, as they're supposed to?

A The reason your roses are not producing flowers is because they're putting all of their energy into producing seed instead. By allowing the spent flowers to remain, you're encouraging them to form rose hips filled with seed. The rose knows it raised a family, kicks back, gets a good suntan, and stops blooming. Cut back spent blossoms to a branchlet with five leaves facing outward. If only a few blossoms in the bunch are spent, remove those by cutting them off individually, but wait to cut to the branchlet until the rest are over the hill. Deadheading your roses every evening will frustrate the tweetle out of them. They'll keep trying to raise a family by blooming away all summer long, and as an added benefit, deadheading will make your garden look its best because visitors will never see a spent rose on your plants.

In fall, let your rose be a proud papa.

Q It's getting cold out, but my **rose** is still pumping out flowers like there's no tomorrow. What can I do to persuade it to stop growing and get it to harden off for winter?

A By mid-October, stop deadheading your rose and allow it to form seed-bearing hips. Your rose will know that it has raised a family, so it can kick back and begin to harden off for the long, cold winter.

Cut out old canes on climbing roses for better flowers.

Q **I think I've mastered pruning my perpetually blooming hybrid tea and floribunda roses, but I haven't figured out how to prune my perpetually blooming climbing roses. What's the trick?**

A The best time to prune any perpetually blooming roses is in early March, and climbers are no exception. Old canes become unproductive over time. Prune one or two of the oldest canes all the way back to the graft union, the spot where they come out of the stem at the base. This will entice new canes to grow. Wear thick clothes and leather gloves. Getting these old canes out is like wrestling a prickly anaconda. When new canes grow up to take the place of the ones you removed, while they are still flexible, bend them around the structure or along a fence to promote flowering. Prune the smaller laterals, which grew out of the bigger canes and bloomed all last summer, back to two buds. These will send up shoots that will flower all summer long. You and your rose will be friends again when you see all the blooms.

Use Grandma Maude's trick to prevent black spot on roses.

Q **No matter what I do, my roses are covered with black spot. I spray constantly and avoid overhead watering, but it doesn't seem to help. I know I probably should replace many of the worst-hit plants with more resistant varieties, but I inherited many of these roses from my mother, and beyond the sentimental value, many have beautiful flowers and wonderful fragrance. Is there anything I can do that will help me keep this raging black spot under control?**

A When I was a kid, I gardened with my fiery grandma, Maude O'Hara. She was famous for her quick Irish temper and wielded a nasty broom if you made her mad. If she were still around, I'd be running for my life for sharing her secret trick with you. After Maude did the spring pruning, and as soon as new growth reached about a foot tall, my job was to remove all of the new leaves within 11 inches from the ground. Maude knew that the black spot spores that fell to the ground during winter become active in spring and are splashed onto the lowest leaves by the rain. Without leaves, the black spot can't get a foothold. It isn't a panacea—susceptible roses eventually require sprays as the summer wears on—but the onset of the disease is significantly delayed. The method was so successful that Maude's neighbors always said her roses were the best-looking in the neighborhood. (Especially if her broom was nearby!)

Don't let the big three get the jump on your roses.

Q I love the smell of **roses**, but I don't like the looks of them when they're covered with powdery substances, black spots, and orange pustules. Is there any environmentally friendly spray that will control all of these maladies?

A It sounds as though your plants are being besieged by the big three fungus diseases that can weaken roses, causing reduced flowering and a shorter life span. Worst of all, they make roses look like gradoo (Wisconsin word for "not good"). Powdery mildew resembles a coating of powdered sugar on the leaves and stems, and it weakens the plant by interfering with photosynthesis. Black spot shows itself by spotting the leaves and causing them to turn yellow and fall off early. Severe infestations can shorten the life of a rose by reducing energy reserves and causing dieback. And rust causes orange pustules on the underside of the leaves; the infected leaves turn ugly and brown and soon drop, further weakening the shrub. It's best to replace highly susceptible roses with ones that are disease resistant. If you have a favorite that always seems to get hit, however, environmentally friendly neem oil (found in products such as Rose Defense) can help prevent these diseases. Neem oil is a vegetable oil squeezed out of the seeds of the neem tree from India. It's safe for humans, pets, and birds as long as you follow the directions on the label, but it will kill any insect on your rose, so remember to move ladybugs to another plant before spraying. At the first sign of problems, remove any infected leaves and spray thoroughly, making sure to cover both sides of the leaves. Avoid overhead watering, and chances are that once the dry weather comes, you won't have to spray again until fall.

Plant a tough rose.

Q I keep buying **roses** that are supposed to be disease-resistant, but before I know it they're covered with black spot, mildew, and rust. Are there any that are truly resistant, or should I just give up on roses for good?

A Oh, la, la! Don't give up. Two kinds of roses are almost never affected by diseases, and they're spectacular to boot: *Rosa rugosa* and a new line called the Easy Elegance collection, which includes only hardy, repeat-blooming roses grown on their own roots. They come in a wide variety of colors, and most have fragrant blooms. During the development phase, newly hybridized roses are sprayed with a mixture of powdery mildew, black spot, and other disease spores, and any roses that show problems are eliminated from the collection. 'Love and Peace', a yellow and pink blend, was the All-American Rose Selection award winner in 2002. Look for Easy Elegance roses at quality nurseries, and throw away the spray can!

Bare-root roses fare better.

 Is there any advantage to planting roses bare-root rather than from a container? Do you plant them the same way?

 Many folks plant bare-root roses because they're cheap (the plants, not the people). There are other advantages, however. Bare-root roses generally grow better than those that come in containers. That's because the roots don't have to make the difficult transition from the soil in the root ball to the soil in your garden. Plunge the roots in warm water for a couple of hours before planting to rehydrate the plant. Work in lots of compost, and plant the rose with the graft union about a half inch above soil level. Remember to plant your rose where it gets plenty of morning sun, so its leaves will dry before fungus diseases such as black spot and rust get a chance to gain a foothold.

> The only roses worth growing are the ones with flowers that are so fragrant it's been scientifically proven that no one can smell them without their socks rolling up and down.

Steal an idea from English gardens.

 Why am I getting so few blooms on my rosebushes? I prune as recommended in spring, I fertilize with alfalfa meal, the roses are in good sunshine, and I water regularly. What can I do to my roses bloom more?

 Do what the English do in many of the famous gardens to greatly increase rose blooms: Bend the canes down and peg the ends to the ground. Your rose will look like a dome tent, but the

hormone that makes growth happen only at the highest point on the branch will be evenly distributed throughout each cane. Instead of blooms only on the end, there will be an explosion of flowering branches all along the length of the cane. You will get so many blooms that you'll hardly be able to see the leaves. Impress your visitors by telling them you learned the technique at Sissinghurst, the famous castle garden in England.

Get your roses off to a galloping start with a shot of horse food.

 Now I've heard everything. Is it true that you feed horse food to your roses?

Alfalfa meal is good for horses, and great for roses and other blooming plants such as peonies, dahlias, delphiniums, clematis, and a host of other perennials. It doesn't contain high amounts of the major nutrients, but it's packed with micronutrients, growth regulators, and amino acids that tell your rose, "Bloom, you fool, bloom!" Two cups will feed the average-sized tea rose. Be sure to work it into the ground. Fertilize your rose once every six weeks beginning in March, but substitute a good organic rose food for one feeding to ensure that all nutritional needs are covered. Wear a bandana; as with any dusty grain, you don't want to breathe too much of it. Also, keep it in a metal can. If you don't, you'll hate those "mieces" to pieces. I found out how many mice live in Western Washington because they all feasted in my garage the same night. The mouse poop was 2 feet deep! The good news is that alfalfa meal won't attract rodents once it's worked into the soil. Give it a try and enjoy watching your roses make blooming fools out of themselves.

Treat your roses to a cuppa.

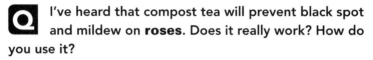

Q I've heard that compost tea will prevent black spot and mildew on **roses**. Does it really work? How do you use it?

A Many home gardeners brew their own compost tea or purchase it at nurseries and apply it as both a foliar spray and a soil drench to help combat black spot, rust, and mildew on roses. Although there's little scientific proof that it works, many home and professional rose growers rave about the results. The tea is not a fertilizer; rather, it's a source of microorganisms that duke it out with, or crowd out, any disease-causing organisms on the leaves and in the soil. The idea is to use it in combination with a good feeding program, to help fight disease and keep the plants healthy and strong. To be successful, it may be necessary to apply foliar sprays of full-strength tea weekly during wet, rainy months. Then, during the drier months, if you're careful not to wet the leaves by overhead watering, only monthly treatments are required to keep roses healthy and disease-free. Be prepared to apply tea more often when dew-laden conditions return in fall.

Divide sedge in fall or spring.

Q What is the difference between **sedges and ornamental grasses**? What are some good varieties of sedge?

A They look like ornamental grasses, but sedges (*Carex*) are unrelated. Unlike ornamental grasses that tend to rot if they are divided in fall, sedge divides easily in spring or fall. In fact, fall is one of the best times to plant and transplant sedges. Two sedges that thrive in dry shade are the attractive white-and-green variegated *Carex morrowii*, and the finely textured *C. albula* 'Frosty Curls'. A terrific variety for sun is *C. buchananii* (leather-leaf sedge). This New Zealand native features unusual reddish bronze grasslike leaves. The unique color will prompt visitors to ask if it's dead, but the color and fine leaves are especially effective coupled with bold blue or silver foliage. My current sun-loving favorite, *C. muskingumensis* 'Little Midge' (dwarf palm sedge) reaches only a foot tall. With its textured bright green leaves, this plant looks like a little palm tree, making it the perfect companion planted next to a Chinese windmill palm.

Here's a great small tree for winter interest.

Q Are there any **small trees that bloom in winter?** I want to make my winter landscape more interesting. I'm looking for something that will remain less than 20 feet tall that can take semishade.

A Witch hazels (*Hamamelis*) are wonderful small trees with blooms that resemble colorful spiders covering the bare branches in the middle of winter. Plus, most have lovely fall color. A number of great hybrids rarely exceed 15 feet tall, including 'Diane' (red flowers), 'Jelena' (coppery orange), and 'Arnold's Promise' (bright yellow), to name just a few. Witch hazels are tough and easy to grow. They thrive in sun or shade and are not picky about soil. The flowers attract the Anna's hummingbird, which often remains in areas with moderate temperatures during winter. Many varieties have fragrant flowers and can be combined with greenery to make wonderful, sweet-smelling midwinter bouquets. Do the sniff test first, though. I once made a bouquet from an unidentified variety, and the whole house ended up smelling like a wet dog!

Where there's a smoke tree, there's fiery foliage.

Q I want to grow one of the colorful **smoke trees** in my mixed border, but I want to keep it small. Is it true that I can cut it back hard to keep it in proportion with the other plants in the border?

A For a spectacular color spot in your mixed border, or a centerpiece in your container garden, cut smoke trees back to within a couple of feet of the ground, anytime from when they drop their leaves until mid-March. You won't get the flowers that resemble puffs of smoke; instead, you'll get a low-growing (less than 5-foot-tall) explosion of color that can be used for wonderful combinations from spring until fall.

Plant a smoke tree for the best fall color.

Q I'm looking for a tree with great fall color. I've heard that **smoke trees** stay small and color up nicely in autumn. What varieties are available to liven up my garden?

A It's hard to find a tree with better fall color than *Cotinus* (smoke tree). The big daddy of the species is an American native (*Cotinus obovatus*) that can grow to more than 35 feet tall. It's also one of the most colorful trees in fall, when the leaves turn glorious shades of red, purple, and orange. Better suited for the small garden is *Cotinus coggygria* from Eurasia. Depending on the variety, these trees come with colorful foliage ranging from golden yellow to dark burgundy. They reach only about 15 feet tall, but if you don't mind sacrificing the smoky flowers, these small trees can be cut practically to the ground to create low-growing explosions of color in the mixed border. The best show comes in fall, when the leaves turn rich violet, orange, and coral. Two sensational *Cotinus* *coggygria* cultivars are 'Royal Purple', with dark burgundy leaves in summer that turn dark purple and orange outlined in bright red in fall, and 'Golden Spirit', a newly introduced hybrid that sports bright yellow leaves in summer, turning rich red-tinged gold in fall. A favorite of mine is a recent cross between the Eurasian and American species. *Cotinus* 'Grace' will reach more than 20 feet tall, but can be cut back hard to restrict height. In spring, the new leaves emerge reddish purple, turn pewter blue in summer, and finally change to magnificent shades of red and orange in autumn. Best of all, 'Grace' tends to hold on to its fall plumage late into the season, and you can depend on its attractive leaves to add color and interest well after Thanksgiving.

Give your St. John's wort a new lease on life.

Q There's something wrong with my **St. John's wort** groundcover. The leaves develop orange spots and then turn brown. What can I spray to save it?

A Practically every type of St. John's wort (*Hypericum*), including the groundcover and the many varieties of attractive shrubs, is susceptible to rust fungus. The leaves develop yellow, red, or brown spots; then the undersides become covered with orange spores. Eventually the leaves turn an ugly brown. No chemical control has been found to be effective against this airborne disease. The bad news is that your hypericum will probably develop rust every year by early summer. The good news is that all you need to do is cut the plant down to about an inch from the ground. The foliage will grow back disease-free. Remove the infected foliage from the garden and avoid overhead watering. Your hypericum should remain free of rust for the rest of the summer.

You can eat the fruit, but don't let it get you into trouble.

Q I'm thinking about planting a **strawberry tree** to create a privacy screen that will block the view of my neighbor's ugly garage. How big does it get, and what conditions does it require? One other important consideration is the fruit. Is it poisonous? I don't want to plant anything that might harm my kids.

A The fruit won't harm your kids, but it could get you into trouble. Years ago while working at Seattle University, I made live weekly appearances on a TV noon news show. The parking enforcement person in the area was a big fan and was somewhat lenient about where I parked. She brought me some fruit from her strawberry tree (*Arbutus unedo*) to identify and was amazed when I told her that years ago while on a hiking trip in Yugoslavia where the strawberry tree is native, I dined on delicious jams and tarts made from its fruit. The next morning she surprised me by giving me a jar of homemade jam made from fruit off her tree, so I decided to bring the jam and a few branches of strawberry tree to show on TV that day. On the show I described the strawberry tree as an attractive, drought-tolerant evergreen plant in the rhododendron family. It produces pretty, creamy bell-shaped flowers in fall, and features red bark, dark green leaves, and spectacular red fruits that hang on the tree throughout winter. As long as it is planted in well-drained soil it thrives in sun or shade. The species truly is a tree and can reach 35 feet tall, but the variety 'Compacta' stays under 10 feet tall and is easy to prune in spring to keep it small, or it can be sheared to form a hedge. The news show appearance went great until the host and I tried the jam. It tasted terrible, and we got carried away making jokes about the parking enforcement person's cooking skills. Guess what other surprise the parking enforcement person left waiting for me on the windshield of my car.

Dress your garden in green and red and yellow and . . .

Q My garden explodes into color in spring with rhododendrons, azaleas, and all sorts of spring-blooming plants, but when the show is over everything reverts to boring green. Are there **summer-blooming shrubs** that would add color all season?

A A garden that blooms beautifully in spring but then reverts to only green foliage for the rest of the season is a wee bit bland. Give your garden a fashionable flair by adding some shrubs that not only bloom but also feature colorful foliage that last all summer long. Many of the most colorful shrubs are also drought tolerant and easy to grow. Few shrubs are tougher than weigela, but don't overlook varieties such as 'Gold Rush' with dark red flowers and yellow margined foliage, and 'Midnight Wine' with burgundy-purple leaves and deep pink flowers. Even tougher is *Sambucus* 'Black Lace' (elderberry)—with almost black, finely cut foliage—or 'Sutherland Gold', with leaves that emerge copper red and then turn and stay golden yellow until fall. *Forsythia* 'Golden Peep' is clothed in yellow leaves on an indestructible dwarf shrub, and the recently introduced *Caryopteris* 'Sunshine Blue' holds its bright yellow foliage throughout the season, providing the perfect backdrop for rich amethyst-blue flower clusters that appear in late summer. So give your garden a makeover by adding shrubs that will remain colorful all summer long.

Cut back twig dogwoods.

Q I'm the world's biggest bird lover, so I'm always looking for plants that will attract the little avian wonders into my garden. Recently I heard that **red twig dogwoods** are attractive to birds and that the colored stems are attractive all winter long. What type of conditions do twig dogwoods need?

A Twig dogwoods are drought-tolerant shrubs that thrive in most soil conditions and are tolerant of clay soil. Most of us grow this plant for its colorful branches, which stand out in the winter garden. As an added attraction, many varieties display colorful variegated leaves during summer. In addition, the nutritious berries are known to feed twenty-three different species of birds; furthermore, cats can't climb in the thick branches to attack nesting birds.

Twig dogwoods like a haircut.

Q My **red twig dogwood** is getting huge, and there's little color in its once fiery stems. How do I prune it to limit height and encourage it to develop red twigs again?

A Left unpruned, twig dogwoods can reach 18 feet tall and make great bird habitat. Only the new growth displays the incredible colorful twigs, however, so if you want a spectacular winter display (and a much shorter plant), you need to prune hard in spring. Coppice the shrub by cutting the branches back to about 4 inches from the ground, about the time that growth begins. You won't get as many berries and the shrub will grow to only about 4 or 5 feet tall, but the branches will glow as orange as the sunset next winter. The only time I've seen coppicing harm a twig dogwood (actually, it killed it) was when I heavily pruned one that was growing in shade. If your plant lacks vigor, cut back no more than a third of the branches in any given year.

Splayed trees need fixing.

Q The columnar trees in my yard got hammered in a snowstorm last winter. Now they have **splayed-out branches** and they're all spread out at the top or leaning.

Do I need to tie them up where they bend out? Can I straighten the ones that are leaning over?

A Many of the upright, narrow arborvitaes, Italian cypress, and Irish yew trees take a hit during heavy snowfalls. The most common damage is splayed-out branches, especially at the top of the plant. In some cases, plants lean; in a few worst-case scenarios, they fall over. The easiest way to fix splayed-out branches is to cut them off where they bend. Most of the time, the foliage will grow back in one season. Dig up, replant, and stake or tie any tree that is leaning or has fallen over. Don't try to simply pull it back up and stake it; usually that results in serious root damage.

Protect your Tasmanian tree fern in winter.

Q While hiking in Tasmania, I was amazed to see 40-foot-tall tree ferns that grew in the rain forests. I was even more amazed to find them for sale at my local nursery. Can we really grow **Tasmanian tree ferns** in the Northwest?

A It is possible to grow Tasmanian tree ferns (*Dicksonia antarctica*) in moist, shady areas, but they are only hardy to about 20 degrees, so it's prudent to cover them during cold snaps to protect them from winter damage. Surround the stem and crown with a round wire cage and fill it with a loose, airy mulch material such as conifer foliage or oak leaves. Avoid leaves that tend to decompose rapidly and turn to muck that could rot the trunk. Cover the top of the crown at least 6 inches deep, but leave the fronds sticking out of the top. If it gets very cold, the fronds will freeze, but you can remove them in spring without harming the plant. If the fronds survive, they'll produce energy that will encourage stronger new growth in spring. If the fronds die, be prepared for a long wait before they finally grow back in mid- to late summer. Tree ferns actually do best if you leave them uncovered during mild winter weather, so you might want to set up the wire framework, but wait to fill it with leaves until unusually cold weather is forecast. Keep in mind, however, the unpredictability of weather. A friend lost several spectacular tree ferns when overnight temperatures unexpectedly dropped from the 40s to 12 degrees.

Don't let timber bamboo get you into trouble.

Q I know I'm asking for trouble, but I can't resist planting a spectacular **timber bamboo** in my garden. The one I'm looking at is called *Phyllostachys vivax*. It's a green timber bamboo that reaches 70 feet tall and has gray-green culms with a white band at the node. I'm aware that timber bamboo can run, and I don't want all of my neighbors to hate me. Is there a way to make sure the timber bamboo won't get into any of my neighbors' gardens?

A Just mention that you're going to plant timber bamboo and watch your neighbors run screaming in terror. Yes, timber bamboo loves to run, but who can possibly resist a plant that features spectacularly colorful culms (stems) that can emerge from the ground in spring to reach over 70 feet tall and 5 inches in diameter in one season? You can keep majestic bamboos within the confines of your garden, but before you plant, take the steps necessary to keep them contained. If you don't, you not only risk making lifelong enemies of your neighbors, but you also may get sued! Most folks choose to put in a bamboo barrier. It's expensive and hard to install, and it must be patrolled regularly. And bamboo roots have a bad habit of escaping over the top of the barrier. Edge pruning is a cheaper and just-as-effective method: Dig a trench 1 foot deep by 18 inches wide and leave it open or fill it with loose gravel. Then in late summer, and again in early fall, use a special, very heavy bamboo spade (available at bamboo nurseries) to slice through and remove rhizomes trying to cross the trench. It's easy to do—but don't neglect this task or the bamboo will inevitably escape; then you'll be making regular visits to the wine shop to buy peace offerings for your neighbors.

Stop the practice of topping trees.

Q **There's a 120-foot Douglas fir growing right behind my home. It bends right over the house in a strong wind and scares the daylights out of me and my family. Will topping the tree make it safer?**

A I once warned a neighbor against topping her giant fir tree. She had it topped anyway. Years later, one of the competing leaders crashed down on her house from about 60 feet above. I'll never forget how fast that eighty-two-year-old woman sprinted out the door. If you're worried about the safety of your tree, it's a better idea to have a certified arborist thin it than top it. Light thinning of the branches will reduce the sail effect by allowing wind to blow through it, making the tree less likely to come down in a storm. A thinned tree is not only safer but much more attractive than one that has been beheaded.

Move those trees and shrubs before it is too late.

Q **I've been told that the best time to transplant trees is in winter, when the trees are dormant. I have numerous trees and shrubs to move, but I'm feeling a bit dormant myself. Do I really have to go out there in the middle of winter to dig and move these trees? How large a root system should I dig to make sure the trees survive?**

 Hey buddy, you'd best break out of dormancy this winter and move those trees and shrubs before they wake up and begin to grow. The general rule is to allow 10 inches of root ball for every inch of trunk diameter. Dig a wide but shallow planting hole. It's better to work compost over a large area than to simply mix it into the backfill. Plant the tree or shrub at the same depth that it came out of the ground, mulch it, and keep the plant well watered next summer. If you have trouble motivating yourself to do it, eat a brussels sprout casserole for energy. For many folks, just the thought of having to eat one of those things is enough to break them out of their dormancy!

Stewartia is a tree for all seasons.

Q I'm looking for a **tree** that blooms, has great fall color, looks good in winter, and will survive in shade. Does a tree like that exist?

A *Stewartia* may be the perfect tree for your shady garden. There are several varieties that reach different heights. These slow-growing, narrow trees bloom with attractive camellia-like flowers in June, have attractive bare branching patterns in winter, and put on a great fall display with spectacular color. Stewartias thrive and bloom in full shade. They are tolerant of full sunshine as long as they receive adequate moisture. *S. monadelpha* (tall stewartia) rarely exceeds 25 feet. It has delicate white flowers, and in winter the bright orange bark can brighten even the rainiest Northwest day. The leaves turn brilliant red in fall. *Stewartia pseudocamellia* (Japanese stewartia) can reach 40 feet. Among its attributes are attractive exfoliating patches on its bark, fantastic fall color, and profuse 2 ½-inch-wide flowers. For the small garden, *S. ovata* 'Grandiflora' is a gem. It reaches only 15 feet and is decorated with 4-inch white flowers with lavender anthers. Think about where you want your stewartias before you plant them; they're almost impossible to move once they become established.

Weigelas are making a comeback.

Q When I was a child, we had a **weigela** in our garden. I loved the pretty flowers, the beautiful fall color, and the amazing attraction it held for hummingbirds. How come I never see those shrubs when I attend garden tours or visit friends' gardens? I recall that it was a low-maintenance plant which required only a little pruning to keep it looking good. Are these old-fashioned plants available at nurseries anymore?

A Despite the fact that they are magnets for hummingbirds, weigelas were rarely planted in Northwest gardens in the last decade. They are becoming popular again, however, and nurseries are beginning to carry some interesting varieties. New hybrids sport colorful foliage and reach only about 6 feet tall. *Weigela looymansii* 'Wine and Roses' is a standout with deep purple leaves and bright pink flowers in spring. The leaves mature to a purplish green, then turn dark purple again in the fall. *Weigela looymansii* 'Aurea' has shiny yellow leaves in spring, becoming soft yellow with a red rim during the summer. The flowers are pastel pink. *Weigela florida* 'Variegata' is decorated with yellow, white, and green foliage highlighted by rosy red tubular flowers. Weigelas bloom on last year's growth and need annual pruning soon after the flowers fade to keep them floriferous and attractive. Remove the shoots that have flowered back to a main branch, and cut a few of the oldest branches right to the ground. Oh, la, la! Who can resist these new hybrid weigelas, with their bright foliage and beautiful flowers that attract both hummingbirds and garden visitors?

Brighten up your shady winter garden.

Q I'm looking for something to brighten up a dry, shady area right next to our main entrance. The area receives some light during the summer, but during winter it resembles a cave. I can't seem to grow anything there for long. I'm probably dreaming, but I'd love to grow a **winter-flowering shrub** with fragrant flowers in that location. I tried a *Camellia sasanqua* that was supposed to bloom with fragrant blossoms in winter, but evidently the spot was too dark, because it never bloomed. Is there anything that will survive, let alone bloom, in dark, dry shade during winter?

A Have I got the perfect plant for you! The winter-flowering *Viburnum* × *bodnantense* 'Dawn' is one of the few shrubs that will thrive and bloom profusely in deep, dry shade. All winter long, the bare branches are covered with clusters of pink, wonderfully fragrant flowers. This is not a shrub for the lazy gardener, though: Left to its own devices, *V.* × *bodnantense* 'Dawn' will quickly become an impenetrable, 10-foot-tall tangle of suckers and crossing branches. However, if suckers are removed regularly, and the shrub is thinned to resemble a small tree, 'Dawn' can easily be one of the most attractive specimens in your garden, even in summer, and a real showpiece when it's covered with fragrant blossoms in winter.

Bewitchingly beautiful trees are in bloom.

Q I'm considering planting a **winter-flowering witch hazel**. Do they come in different colors? The only one they had at the nursery had orange flowers. The tag said it should be planted in shade. Will it die if I plant it in a sunny location? By the way, why is it called witch hazel?

A No one is sure how the spectacular, winter-blooming tree in the *Hamamelis* genus became known as witch hazel. One explanation is that the earliest settlers to North America used branches from native *Hamamelis virginiana* to make divining rods and believed the tree had supernatural powers to help them find water. The real reason might be the enchanting effect created by the fragrant, spiderlike flowers that bloom on bare branches in midwinter. There are a wide variety of species and hybrids to choose from. Flower colors include dark yellow ('Arnold's Promise'), red ('Diane'), and copper-orange ('Jelena'), just to mention a few. As an added attraction, the leaves of most witch hazels color up spectacularly in autumn. Books generally recommend planting witch hazel in shade, but most varieties thrive in full sun and are as drought tolerant as a rock once established. Buy them while they are in bloom to get the color and fragrance you desire. But beware: If you fall under their spell, you might come home with a truckload of these magical plants.

Give your yucca a manicure.

Q I like the look of **yucca plants**, and I'm especially excited about trying some of the new varieties with colorful foliage. I'm worried that the pointy leaves might endanger the eyes of my kids and pets, however. Yet I've seen them in public gardens in Arizona. How do they get away with planting them where kids play?

A Yuccas are gaining popularity. These surprisingly hardy desert plants don't require much water, and the evergreen, swordlike foliage lends a Southwest look to the mixed border. Newly available varieties such as *Yucca filamentosa* 'Bright Edge', with yellow-striped leaves, and 'Color Guard', with white and cream stripes, add lively color in all seasons. Unfortunately, you're right that the sharply pointed leaves are a definite eye hazard. Don't plant yucca in places frequented by kids or pets. Wear protective glasses anytime you work near one, and take it from one who knows: Don't back into one while you're weeding! If your yucca is in a hazardous location and you don't want to move it, do what they do in Arizona: Use nail clippers to cut off the end of every leaf. It's a bit of work, but you won't have to worry about putting anyone's eye out, and you won't have to keep an eye out behind you while you're weeding. Finally, be sure that you want your yucca forever. They're nearly impossible to get rid of once established.

CHAPTER FOUR

Container Gardens and Houseplants

Keep your African violets blooming in winter.

Q I keep my **African violets** in an east window. They bloom in summer, but in winter all I get are green leaves. It's an embarrassment when my gardener friends come over. How can I get my African violets to bloom in the off-season?

A The trick to getting African violets to bloom reliably in winter is to give them as much light as possible. Place your plants in a bright, sunny window. If that's not possible, put them under fluorescent lights (one warm and one cool) placed about 6 inches above the foliage, fourteen hours a day. Fertilize with a soluble houseplant fertilizer such as Miracle-Gro, and make sure the soil remains moist at all times. Bring them out for display when company comes. Your houseplant-loving friends will be green with envy trying to figure out how you're able to keep your African violets blooming all winter long.

Save leggy African violets.

Q I've noticed that my **African violets** occasionally thin out. The stems get tall and bent, and all the leaves are right at the top. Once this happens, can I make the plant busy again, or is it best just to throw it out and start over?

A African violets become leggy over time. The bottom leaves die off, leaving a rosette of leaves at the top of a bent stem, which gives the plant an unsightly top-heavy look. The problem is easy to solve if you catch it when the stem is only about an inch long. Remove any damaged lower leaves and repot the African violet, burying stem and roots so that the existing whorl of leaves is flush with the top of the pot. New roots usually will form on the buried stem. If the exposed stem is more than an inch high, either cut it off and root it using rooting hormone, or visit your local nursery and buy five or six of the spectacular new hybrids as replacements.

Decorate your home with sea creatures.

Q While visiting the nursery the other day, I saw some totally weird houseplants called **air plants**. They looked like little octopuses. The tag said they don't need any soil and that you can just grow them in the air. Is that possible?

A Tillandsias look like deep-sea creatures. Known as air plants, these odd-shaped epiphytic bromeliad relatives come in a wide variety of shapes, sizes, and colors. Although these houseplants are usually grown for their alien-looking foliage, tillandsias also boast showy, long-lasting flowers ranging from sparkling white to blazing orange and brilliant purple. Tillandsias don't require soil to live. They add an exotic touch situated in the cleft of a decorative stone or nestled in a piece of driftwood. Grow them in bright, indirect light. Soak or mist them heavily one to three times a week (less often in winter), but let them dry completely between waterings. Spring through summer, fertilize twice a month by spraying the plant with one-quarter-strength, high-phosphorus, soluble houseplant food. Then don your snorkel and mask. You'll feel like you're starring in a Jacques Cousteau special every time you enter your home.

Don't toss that amaryllis.

Q Someone gave me an **amaryllis bulb** for Christmas. It bloomed beautifully, but now the bloom is over and only the flower stalk and some leaves remain. Is this a throwaway, or is it worth keeping on as a houseplant? Will it ever bloom again?

A Amaryllis bulbs (*Hippeastrum*) are giant bulbs from Central and South America. The big, showy flowers that can be forced to bloom right on time for the holidays make them popular Christmas gifts. Although most are thrown away after the bloom fades, they make interesting houseplants and, if given proper care, can be persuaded to bloom again year after year, although the blooms usually occur after the holiday season, in March. The first step is to cut off the spent flower stalk. That will prevent the plant from wasting energy making seed. Place the plant in a sunny window, and water whenever the soil surface feels dry. The key to getting them to rebloom is to keep them growing well during summer and allow them to go dormant in fall. Beginning in March, fertilize every two weeks with a good soluble houseplant fertilizer such as Miracle-Gro. In mid-August, stop watering to force the bulb into dormancy. Place the pot in a dark, dry area and allow the plant to dry out completely. Amaryllis won't bloom again unless they experience eight weeks of total dormancy. After the dormant period, bring the pot into bright light and remove the bulb. Remove offsets by breaking them off during the transplanting process. That will encourage a large, single bulb, more likely to bloom. (You can plant the offsets, but it can take a few years before they become large enough to bloom.) Replant the bulb in the same pot, making sure that a third of the bulb is planted above soil level. Water lightly until growth begins. If only leaves appear, it's back to the drawing board; your bulb didn't store enough energy to produce a flower. Don't give up: Feed and water well, and maybe it will bloom next year. If you see a flower bud appear, however, you win the Green Thumb Award! A spectacular flower will soon follow.

Sprout an avocado seed.

Q When I was a kid, my mom showed me how to sprout an **avocado seed**. I was going to do it with my grandkids, but I must be turning into a geezer because I can't remember how to do it. Hopefully you're still young enough to remember so you can remind me how to go about it.

A I admit to a geezerly moment from time to time myself, but fortunately I recently sprouted an avocado stone, so I remember the procedure. It's easy to do. Push three toothpicks into the side of the seed at equal intervals, about two-thirds of the way down from the top. The toothpicks will support the seed as it sits on top of a vase or cup of water with only its blunt end submerged. Keep the seed warm, at least 65 degrees, in a bright location out of direct sunlight, and make sure the bottom third stays under water at all times until you're ready to transplant. Be patient: It takes a while for roots to form, and even longer for a shoot to appear. When a shoot finally begins to grow, it's time to pot up your avocado. Begin with a 4-inch container, but plan to transplant into a slightly bigger pot in about a month. Keep the avocado in a south window until it's warm enough outside to move it out to a sunny location for the summer. During the growing season feed regularly with soluble houseplant fertilizer and pinch the growing tips now and then to keep your avocado tree bushy. It's not hot enough here to produce an edible avocado, and eventually your plant will grow so big you'll have to buy a mansion to keep it in the house during winter, but your avocado tree will be an attractive houseplant that the kids will be proud to know they grew from scratch with their own hands.

Inspect your houseplants for nasty bugs.

Q How do I know if my houseplants have **bugs**? What should I look for, and what should I do if I find bugs on my plants?

A The best defense is a good offense when it comes to bugs on houseplants. Inspect your plants often. If you catch the critters early, you might be able to control them before they spread to other plants and become an epidemic. Look for white cottony spots (mealy bugs), brownish bumps (scale), or miniature dune buggies (aphids). All of these insects suck the juice out of the plants and leave a telltale trail of sticky honeydew. Infested plants should be sent immediately to the quarantine ward. Slight infestations can be treated weekly with a Q-tip dipped in rubbing alcohol. Severe infestations are best treated with a quick trip to the grand dumpster in the sky.

Grow your own "Little Shop of Horrors."

Q I guess I'm a little weird, but I just love those **bug-eating plants**. I want to try growing them, but haven't the faintest idea how. Will they grow outdoors in the Northwest? They don't eat people or pets, do they?

A What could be more fun than watching a cobra lily devour a big, juicy fly? Fortunately, many of the most attractive and interesting carnivorous plants are hardy and will thrive outside year-round if planted in a large container. To make a bog garden suitable for growing carnivorous plants, begin by choosing a good-sized pot with no hole in the bottom. Ask the nursery to drill a hole in the side, about a quarter of the way down from the top. Fill the container with a 50-50 mix of peat moss and perlite. Sink a smaller houseplant pot (with drain holes in the bottom) into the planting mix. The top of the smaller pot should be level with the surface of the planting mix. Plant your carnivorous beauties in the mix around the small pot, and make sure that the small pot remains three-quarters full of distilled water (or rainwater) at all times. Chlorine and fluoride are both deadly to these plants, so avoid using tap water. Never fertilize: The plants will catch their own dinner. Place the container in full sun, and for extra fun, place it where your dinner guests can enjoy watching your plants chomping flies. By the way, I wouldn't get too close to this container. . . .

Marry a Canadian for a floriferous Christmas.

Q What is the trick to making **Christmas cactus** bloom at Christmas? Mine seems to bloom at all times of the year except on the holiday.

A Many garden books advise you to put your Christmas cactus in total darkness for fourteen hours every night, starting in September, to get it to bloom by Christmas. Not true! Just keep it on the dry side and give it cold nights starting in October, and your Christmas cactus almost always will set blooms for the holidays. It's easy if you marry a Canadian, like I did; evidently it's a Canadian trait not only to sleep with the windows wide open in the middle of winter, but to have a fan blowing on you as well! My Christmas cactus has bloomed right on schedule every year since we got married. The amazing thing is that I've survived my wife's Popsicle toes to see it bloom.

Create exotic fruit on your Christmas cactus.

Q Is it true that **Christmas cactus** will grow fruit? How do you make that happen?

A It's fun and easy to prolong your holiday plant display by creating colorful fruit on your Christmas cactus. You need at least two plants with different colored flowers in bloom at the same time. Remove a flower from one plant and rub the pollen-laden stamens on the pistil (the flower part that sticks out the farthest) of another. The stamens of one flower usually can pollinate the pistils of five others. If all goes well, an ornamental inch-long fruit will develop at the base of the pollinated flowers as they fade. You never know exactly what the fruit will look like, but generally they're quite colorful and will remain decorative for at least a year. When the fruit begins to soften, harvest and sow the seed within. You'll be surprised when you see the exotic colored flowers the seedlings produce.

Epiphyllums are the orchids of the cacti world.

Q I recently saw a plant that resembled a **Christmas cactus**, but the blooms were much bigger. It was spectacular, and I must have one! What is it, and are they difficult to grow?

A The plant you saw is called an epiphyllum, or orchid cactus. These plants are not easy to find, but they show up from time to time in quality nurseries. They are cacti that live on the branches of trees in the forests of Mexico and Central and South America. They remind me of Christmas cacti on steroids. The flowers are spectacular and vary in size from 3 to 10 inches across. I have an intense orange one, but colors include white, yellow, pink, lavender, and scarlet. These tropical plants are easy to grow, requiring only rich, well-drained potting soil, bright light out of sunshine, and a shot of high-phosphorus fertilizer every other week. Keep the soil moist during the growing season, but allow it to dry out between watering in winter. These cacti are not hardy, so overwinter them in a protected but cool, bright spot, such as an unheated garage near a window. To make new plants, take 4-inch cuttings in the summer, allow them to dry for a day or two, and pot them up. They'll root within a matter of weeks.

Practice crowd control.

 My container looked just beautiful when I planted it full of annuals and perennials in spring, but now some of the plants are getting too big and suffocating the other plants. Can I **cut the offending plants back** without killing them?

 We tend to cram plants into containers for instant effect, but just as an overachiever can wreak havoc in the border, an overly rambunctious annual or perennial in a pot can snuff out neighbors, or throw off the balance and symmetry of your design. Cut back bullies that are taking over too much space, getting out of proportion, or suffocating neighboring plants. Don't worry if your efforts leave the offending plant looking ugly and hacked back. The nurseries are well stocked with attractive, better-behaved replacements that will keep your container looking great.

Ya gotta love cyclamen.

 A special friend gave me a **cyclamen** as a holiday present, and I don't want to kill it. I have anything but a green thumb. What do I need to do to keep it alive?

 Pay attention to the person who gave you the florist cyclamen (*Cyclamen persicum*). According to folklore, its leaves can be added to an herbal concoction that makes anyone who eats it fall madly in love. Although eating florist cyclamen (which I don't recommend, by the way) may make you fall madly in love, trying to grow one of these picky plants could simply drive you mad. They need special conditions to prolong their inevitable journey to the compost bin. Place your cyclamen in a cool (50 to 60 degrees), brightly lit spot, out of direct sunlight. A north-facing windowsill is ideal. Keep the soil moist at all times, but take care to avoid wetting the central tuber to prevent it from rotting. High humidity is a must, so stand the pot on a pebble tray and mist often. In spring, the plant will begin to drop leaves and go dormant. Most folks throw them away, but for fun, try planting the tubers a foot or more deep in a well-drained area of the shade garden. It's a long shot, but if you're not off on a honeymoon, you might be surprised to see the flowers reappear in fall.

Desert combinations are hot.

Q I'm a big-time cactus lover. I move much of my collection outdoors during the summer, but I'm wondering if there's a way to combine them in a large container that would look attractive. Any suggestions for a cool **desert plant combination?**

A Planting succulents together in a container looks great and adds a desert ambience to your garden. For a dramatic centerpiece, try *Agave americana* 'Marginata', with fleshy, lance-shaped gray-green leaves margined in yellow, or the similarly shaped *Furcraea gigantea* 'Striata', with bright, glossy, swordlike green leaves with white stripes. Surround the spiky centerpiece with the rounded rosettes of the black-purple *Aeonium arboreum* 'Zwartkop' and a few similarly shaped multicolored echeverias. Reflect the vertical effect of the centerpiece by adding a few sharply upright aloes, and complete the composition with some brightly flowering annual portulaca to weep over the edge of the pot. Voilà, you've got a scene out of a John Wayne western on your front porch. By the way, you'll get to enjoy this desert scene inside during the winter months, because the container needs to be brought into a warm, brightly lit room to survive the cold weather.

Plant an award-winning container garden.

Q My local nursery is having a container garden contest, and although I'm something of a novice, I've decided to enter. Any tips you can give me to help me **design an award-winning container?**

A A number of my local nurseries hold container gardening and hanging basket contests. Some of the prizes are pretty cool. Having been a judge, I can say that the biggest problem is that folks don't always follow the directions, so my first tip is to make sure you understand what the rules are! Here are a few other helpful hints: The height of the plantings should be in proportion to the size of the container. I find plantings most appealing if they have plenty of contrasting texture and colored foliage, so take some chances: Mix perennials with annuals, and maybe even a little tree and a tropical plant or two. Adding an unusual plant sparks interest. Finally, don't forget to make sure that the combination of plants gets adequate water, fertilizer, and bug control; even the most artistic planting will lose if the plants look as though a flame-thrower hit them.

Add a spring surprise in your winter container.

Q I often plant up container gardens in fall. I begin by planting a small evergreen shrub or perennial as a centerpiece, then fill in with evergreen grasses and winter-blooming flowers such as pansies, violets, and cyclamen. The containers look great throughout the winter, but I'd like to **extend the display** by planting spring-blooming bulbs in the containers to come up through the plants to bloom in spring. Will my idea work?

A It's easy and fun to extend the blooming period by planting spring-blooming bulbs in winter containers. Begin with a frostproof pot that is at least 9 inches deep. Place the bulbs on a 3-inch base of soil after mixing in the appropriate amount of bulb food. Cram in as many bulbs as possible, but don't allow them to touch each other or the side of the pot. Some bulbs, such as tulips, have one side that's flatter than the other. Plant the flat side toward the side of the pot to cause the foliage to grow outward rather than crowding the center. Cover the bulbs with soil and fill in with evergreen perennials, colorful grasses, and winter-flowering annuals. Make sure there is space between the root balls and along the side of the container to allow the tulips to slip through. Then, next spring, enjoy the added touch of elegance that spring-blooming bulbs will bring to your winter container.

Make gardening fun for kids by giving them their own container to plant; they can achieve a fabulous composition in a limited space, without having to weed or do lots of difficult maintenance. The only problem is that it's a bit embarrassing when your four-year-old's container looks way better than yours!

Don't make houseplants chubby.

Q I've been bitten by the bug! My boyfriend made the mistake of giving me a lovely African violet for my birthday. That was about six months ago, and now my house is full of tropical houseplants. I can't get enough of them, and my boyfriend is threatening to move out if I don't stop buying them. My actual question, though, is about **fertilizing**. I know you're supposed to fertilize houseplants only when they're actively growing. When should I stop feeding for the winter, and when should I begin again? Will my plants get chubby if I feed them too much?

 You're the woman of my dreams! My wife has threatened to leave several times if I buy one more houseplant. As it is, visitors to our house have to take malaria pills. Stop feeding your houseplants by the end of August unless you're growing them under lights. There isn't enough light in winter to promote growth, and most plants go into a dormant or semidormant state. Your plants won't get chubby if you feed them in winter, but salts may build up in the soil that could eventually harm the roots. If a white or gray salt deposit forms on top of the soil, scrape it off with a spoon. It's OK if you expose the roots, but don't tear into them. Then cover with a fresh layer of planting soil. To prevent the buildup of excess salts, immerse the entire pot in warm water until it stops bubbling. Then lift the pot and let the excess water drain out. This can be done every month during the growing period, and at least once during the winter months. Begin fertilizing houseplants again when growth begins in March. By the way, your boyfriend should be grateful that you're going to so much work and expense to make sure there's adequate oxygen in the house!

Rid houseplants of salt buildup.

 What's the best way to get rid of that ugly white crusty stuff on the soil of my potted houseplants? It looks a bit like fertilizer. I feed monthly year round. Am I **fertilizing too much**?

 Most houseplants should be fertilized only when they are actively growing in spring and summer, or if they are located under grow lights. The only exceptions are houseplants that bloom or set fruit in winter. Overfertilization can result in a harmful salt buildup that shows up as white to gray crusty deposits on the soil surface. Rid your plant of this harmful menace by using a spoon to scoop off the crusty soil. Remove just enough to clear off the salt buildup. It's OK to expose the roots, but avoid tearing into them. Replace the scraped-away soil with a layer of fresh potting mix. To prevent recurrence, fertilize only when the plant is actively growing and, from time to time, leach out excess salts by plunging the entire pot into a tub of water and allowing the excess to drain out.

Outwit fungus gnats.

Q **Fruit flies** are embarrassing the tweetle out of me! I'm positive that I've rid the house of every bit of fruit, yet the little devils still manage to come out in droves every time I have company. Other than moving, is there anything that will solve this annoying and humiliating problem?

A If you have rid your house of fruit and still find yourself being embarrassed by annoying little critters that resemble fruit flies, you've got a different pest at work: fungus gnats. These are little flies that lay their eggs in houseplant soil. The maggots hatch and feed on compost before emerging as adults that lay more eggs to start new generations. Happily, it's easy to outwit this annoying pest. Go to your local garden store and purchase a few small bags of washed sand. Use it to cover the soil about one-eighth inch deep in every houseplant container in your home. This trick fools the female fly into thinking that the compost-rich houseplant soil is a sandy beach, far too lean to raise a family. The fly flitters about for a few days in search of appropriate soil to start a new brood, becomes exhausted, and never lays her eggs. Be sure you apply sand to every container in the house, and within a week or two, you'll be rid of these embarrassing little gnats for good. That is, until you bring home another infested houseplant.

Gardenias like to shower with you.

Q My mother-in-law gave me a spectacular **gardenia** for a gift, but I'm afraid I'm killing it. I've placed it in a bright, sunny spot, but the leaves keep turning brown and falling off. It's not going to go over well if I murder my mother-in-law's gift. Help me save this plant before I get into big trouble!

A Gardenias forced into bloom for the holidays are popular gift plants. The porcelain flowers are attractive, but there's no doubt that the sublime fragrance is the raison d'etre of this shrub. A gardenia is not the ideal present to get from a mother-in-law. They are difficult to keep alive in the house during winter. Gardenias require direct sunlight, warm days, cool nights, and pleasant conversation, or they'll drop their buds. Worst of all, gardenias despise the dry conditions that exist in our homes. Most efforts to raise humidity fail, and unless you control the spider mites that inevitably follow, all of the leaves soon drop off. Make good friends with your gardenia, because the only way to control the mites is to shower with the plant at least once a week during the winter months. Be sure to wash under the leaves. If you can keep it alive until spring, move it outside to a sunny patio for the season. If you regularly water and fertilize it, your gardenia will thrive and bloom nonstop all summer long. By the way, if I were you, I'd find out where your mother-in-law bought the gardenia and ask them to put another one just like it to the side. Something tells me you'll need it.

Get those fuchsias and geraniums growing.

Q I overwintered some **geraniums and hanging fuchsias** in my garage. When should I bring them back out to encourage them to begin growing? I left them in the pots they lived in last summer. Do I need to transplant them? How far back should I cut them?

A When to begin the process of bringing nonhardy geraniums (pelargoniums) and fuchsias out of dormancy depends on the weather. It's usually time to repot in fresh soil and begin placing your plants outside on nice days in mid-March. If the weather is especially cold, however, wait to begin the process until early April. When transplanting, gently tease the roots out of the root ball in a tub of warm water, and replant into the same container, or into one an inch bigger. Cut back the branches to 6 inches from the pot. When you take the plants outside on nice days, place your fuchsias in shade. Geraniums need full sun, but before putting them in a hot, sunny location, acclimatize them by locating them in morning sun and giving them progressively more sun each day for about a week. Don't forget to bring the plants back into the garage on cold nights until around Mother's Day, when you can safely leave them outdoors for the rest of the season.

Give that special someone a lucky plant.

Q I want to give my new boyfriend a plant to breathe some life into his apartment. There isn't much light, and he has a black thumb and has either drowned or forgotten to water every plant he's ever owned. Other than plastic, is there any tough **houseplant** that has a fighting chance of surviving under these conditions?

A The only plant that could possibly survive in your boyfriend's apartment is lucky bamboo, and it might even bring him luck. For centuries the Chinese have given lucky bamboo as a New Year's present to bring good fortune and prosperity to the recipient for the following year. Feng shui masters give lucky bamboo high marks for increasing *chi* and *qi* in the home. Interestingly, lucky bamboo isn't bamboo at all. It's actually *Dracaena sanderiana*. Known as ribbon plant, lucky bamboo does not grow as an aquatic plant in its native Cameroon, yet for some unknown reason it can live for years with its roots in a half-inch to 2 inches of water. For an attractive gift, put it in a beautiful handmade vase filled with decorative stones or marbles. Lucky bamboo is a tough plant: It thrives in very low light and makes a long-lasting kitchen or bathroom decoration. The only care required is (for you to come over) to change the water every couple of months. It's lucky they are hard to kill because if a person murders a lucky bamboo, it will bring the person who gave it to them twenty-nine years of bad luck (only kidding)!

Choose safe houseplants around babies and toddlers.

Q I recently had my first baby, and it struck me that some of my **houseplants might be poisonous** if eaten. I don't know how likely it is that a toddler would eat the leaves of a plant, but just in case, is there a way to find out which ones are safe?

A The number-one reason people call poison control centers nationwide is because a child under 5 has eaten the foliage of a houseplant. The easiest way to safely enjoy houseplants is to choose only those known to be nontoxic. Several websites offer lists of nonpoisonous houseplants; for instance, here's one from the University of Illinois Extension: African violet, aluminum plant (*Pilea*), bloodleaf (*Iresine*), coleus, corn plant (*Dracaena*), dusty miller (*Senecio*), devil's walking stick (*Aralia*), gardenia, hibiscus, jade plant, palm, peperomia, pocketbook plant (*Calceolaria*), pregnant plant (*Kalanchoe*), prayer plant (*Maranta*), primrose (*Primula*), purple passion plant (*Gynura*), spider plant (*Chlorophytum*), Swedish ivy (*Plectranthus*), umbrella plant (*Schefflera*), and wandering jew (*Tradescantia*).

The best way to rid your houseplants of spider mites is to bring them in the shower to blast the mites off the back of the leaves. Be prepared to visit the relationship counselor if your partner catches you showering with the houseplants.

Give your jade plant a rest.

Q My **jade plant** was healthy and happy all summer long, but now that winter is here, it is looking droopy. It's growing in a south window, I water it once a week, and I fertilize only in spring and summer. What am I doing wrong?

A It's almost impossible, but you should try to resist watering your jade plant from October until March. You can always tell when a jade plant has been overwatered: The branches hang down like an umbrella and then swoop back up. This is an early indication of root rot and often ends in tragedy. Try to resist watering until at least half of the leaves have shriveled and fallen off. It may look like the end of the road, but even if all the leaves fall off, they will usually grow right back as soon as the plant receives a little water. Wait to water again until March at the earliest. As soon as spring growth appears, resume your normal watering and fertilizing schedule.

Jerusalem cherries are no good around kids either.

Q My husband came home with a **Jerusalem cherry plant** as a holiday decoration. The woman at the store didn't think the cherries were poisonous, but she wasn't sure. The plant's tomato-like fruit is attractive, but my young grandchildren will be visiting for the holidays. Is this plant safe to keep around?

A Jerusalem cherries are a familiar sight during the holidays. The little shrubs make nice decorations because they're covered with masses of berries that look just like cherry tomatoes. But you'd best get rid of them: The berries are poison and are tempting to kids. Christmas peppers are a better choice. These plants are covered with attractive peppers that turn from green to yellow to red and are not poisonous. They are bred from chile and cayenne peppers, however, and are so hot that if you eat one, the smoke will singe your geezer hairs on the way out of your ears! Christmas pepper plants will last a long time in your house as long as you give them bright light, keep the soil moist, and provide extra humidity by misting frequently. Keep a fire extinguisher handy too, just in case someone tries eating one. They'll only try it once!

Houseplants need a good turn.

Q My houseplants start out nice and straight, but before long they end up **leaning toward the window**. How can I keep them growing straight? What makes that happen any way?

A Many folks wonder why their houseplants lean toward the light. Believe it or not, the leaves and stems on the plant's shady side grow faster than those receiving more light. A physiological process called phototropism causes growth hormones to accumulate in the cells on the shaded side. As a result, the leaves and stems facing the light remain stocky and short, while the stems on the side that receive less light grow leggy and tall. The taller, weaker stems bend over the shorter, sturdier ones, causing the plant to lean toward the sunny window. The best way to promote attractive symmetrical growth is to rotate your houseplants a quarter turn every week.

Spider mites don't like to shower.

 Several of my houseplants have **leaves that dry up and fall off** prematurely. What's making this happen, and is there a safe way to control it? I don't want to spray chemical poisons in my home.

If the leaves of your houseplants take on a gray- or yellow-stippled appearance, develop a bronze cast, or dry up, turn brown, and fall prematurely, it's a sure sign that your plants are being attacked by spider mites, a common houseplant pest. To check, shake a few of the affected leaves over a white piece of paper. If the dust particles that fall on the paper move, you've got a problem. Spider mites love the dry air that is common in our homes during the colder months. The first order of battle is to quarantine any infested plant before it infects all of its buddies. To raise humidity, place plants on saucers filled with decorative pebbles that are kept wet at all times. Never let the water level get higher than the top of the stones. One of the best ways to prevent spider mite infestation is to get into the regular habit of cleaning off the leaves with a moistened cloth. That will remove dust that encourages mites, and it will also put *el kabatski* on any that have come to visit before they can settle in and start a new colony. If the problem persists, try showering with your infested plants, using the water to blast the mites off the bottom of the leaves. Caution: You'll have some explaining to do if your partner catches you showering with your houseplants!

Keep your containers looking good.

My gardening space is limited, so I plant mostly in containers. I cut my annuals back in July and deadhead steadily until fall, yet every September the plants begin going downhill and the blooming slows. Is there anything I can do to keep them **looking good and blooming longer** into the fall season?

A When you feel fall in the air, it's way too early to give up on your container plants. Give them a wee bit of attention in September; and perennials, fuchsias, and even annuals will bounce back with great blooms until late fall. Deadhead perennials, and lightly trim back annuals and fuchsias. Give them a shot of soluble houseplant fertilizer every two weeks, and keep them well watered. Your plants will be so grateful, they'll knock themselves out to put on a great blooming display right up until November.

Go Tropicana for Mother's Day.

Q OK already! Every year I follow your advice and plant up a container for **Mom on Mother's Day**. This year I want to surprise her with a totally new design. What combination will knock her socks off?

A If you want to impress the living tweetle out of Mom, plant up a tropical design. Start with a good-sized pot in a sunny location protected from the wind. For a tropical centerpiece, nothing can match red-leaved banana (*Ensete ventricosum* 'Maurelii'). The red-veined leaves will reach 4 feet long and 2 feet wide, so be sure to plant it in the back of the pot to leave room for other plants. Next, add an exotic touch by including a multicolored variegated pineapple (*Ananas* 'Tricolor'). Now add a Polynesian touch with *Hibiscus rosa-sinensis* (tropical hibiscus) decorated with brilliant red, orange, or yellow 6-inch flowers. Then create sizzling contrast with brightly colored gerbera daisies with 5-inch flowers and 10-inch tropical-looking leaves. Add spiky color and attract hummingbirds to your composition by squeezing in a flaming scarlet *Salvia coccinea* 'Forest Fire'. Finally, cram in a few orange-blooming nasturtiums to creep over the side. Don't forget to buy mom a pair of shades to go with this *caliente* display.

Keep your monkey-face orchid grinning like a chimpanzee.

Q Last year at the Northwest Flower and Garden Show, I bought a **monkey-face orchid**. It bloomed for months, but now the last flower on the stalk is fading. The plant looks healthy. Is there anything I can do to make it bloom again?

A I love monkey-face (Phalaenopsis) orchids. They're easy to grow, and the flowers are long-lasting and really do resemble little smiling monkeys. Here are a few tips to keep your monkey-face orchid blooming practically non-stop. Keep it warm (impossible if you're married to a Canadian, like my wife, who insists on sleeping with the windows wide open in winter). Phalaenopsis will stop blooming if temperatures dip below 60 degrees. Place it in a location that's as bright as possible but out of direct sunshine. Water as necessary to make sure that the growing medium never dries out, and keep the humidity up by misting often and placing it on a tray of moistened pebbles. The growing medium does not hold nutrients, so fertilize weekly with a quarter- to half-strength solution of orchid food. Trade off weekly between using bloom and grow fertilizers. With a little luck, you'll have monkey-face blooms grinning at you all year round.

You can't kill it with kindness.

Q I'm obviously too nice to my houseplants. I kill them with kindness by **overwatering** them. I don't think I'll ever change my ways. Is there a houseplant that I can't kill by drowning it?

A Benign neglect rarely kills houseplants. More often, we love them to death by watering them at every sign of distress until we drown them. But there are perfect houseplants for those of us who love our plants a little too much. *Cyperus alternifolius* (umbrella plant) is a close relative of the much taller *C. papyrus*, the source of our earliest form of paper. *Cyperus alternifolius* is a highly ornamental 3-foot-tall plant featuring narrow, spreading leaves that radiate out similar to ribs on an umbrella. The golden rule is to keep the roots constantly wet. Place the plant in a saucer that is constantly filled with water. Then, as long as temperatures remain above 50 degrees and your umbrella plant is located in a bright spot out of direct sunlight, it is practically impossible to love this plant to death. Look for unusual varieties such as the dwarf *C. alternifolius* 'Nanus', reaching only 1½ feet tall, or *C. albostriatus* 'Variegatus', featuring white-striped leaves. In summer, submerge your umbrella plant in your backyard pond to add an airy tropical effect.

Japanese maples make great container plants.

Q I recently moved from a home with a big yard to a condo where I can garden only in containers on my deck. The change hasn't bothered me too much, but the one thing I really miss is my **red laceleaf Japanese maple**. Is it possible to grow one of these elegant trees in a container?

A Few trees can match the refined elegance of a red laceleaf Japanese maple (*Acer palmatum* 'Dissectum'), yet they are surprisingly easy to grow in containers. Choose carefully when you buy one. Some get bigger than others, and the leaves of several supposedly red varieties turn green in summer. Of the varieties that hold their red color all season long, 'Garnet' is the fastest growing and can quickly reach 6 feet or taller. It's covered in rich red-orange leaves throughout the summer, then lights up the fall garden as it turns bright scarlet. 'Garnet' needs full sun to develop its best color. For years 'Crimson Queen' has been the standard-bearer of red laceleaf maples. This sturdy, graceful tree stays blood-red all season, changing to beautiful scarlet in autumn. It holds its color in sun or partial shade. A slow grower, 'Crimson Queen' can eventually reach over 6 feet tall. My personal favorite is 'Red Dragon'. In spring the leaves emerge bright scarlet, then darken to deep burgundy, before changing to brilliant crimson in autumn. 'Red Dragon' is the slowest growing of red laceleaf maples and can take years to reach 5 feet in a container. Any of these varieties will thrive as long as the container is at least as large as a whiskey barrel and has adequate holes for drainage. Plant in quality houseplant potting soil, water and fertilize regularly, and enjoy a spectacular tree that will add elegant charm and fiery color to your deck or patio for years to come.

Annuals need tough love.

Q The annual displays in my containers, which looked so attractive earlier in summer, are beginning to peter out. The blooms are few and far between, and the flowers occur only at the end of long stems. It's only midsummer, and I was hoping these displays would look great well into fall. What can I do to **rejuvenate my potted annuals**?

A Tropical heat-loving annuals, from hanging fuchsias to petunias, benefit from warm summer weather and bloom as if there was no tomorrow. Unfortunately, if you don't cut the stems back around mid-July, there may be no tomorrow as far as the blooms are concerned. Warm weather spawns rapid growth and heavy flowering, but in many cases the stems eventually become leggy, and most of the flowering occurs on the end of long, thin branches. Even if it is later than mid-July, it's worth a try. Cut the stems back by two-thirds, water as often as necessary, and fertilize regularly with a high-phosphorus, soluble houseplant fertilizer such as Miracle-Gro. You'll feel as if you are murdering your plants, but within two or three weeks you'll notice hundreds of buds that will soon burst into flower. Best of all, the display should last until late October.

Holiday plants can hurt pets and kids.

Q I have a bunch of grandchildren coming to visit for the holidays, and I have a number of houseplants. Are they **safe around kids and pets**?

A On one of my recent visits to the vet, one patient was a seriously ill cat that had eaten part of a lily given to his owner as a holiday gift. Houseplants beautify the home, clean the air, and add oxygen, but many are poisonous if eaten. The list is extensive, but a few of the most popular houseplants that are poisonous are the philodendron, pothos, calla lily, anthurium, and peace lily. They can all cause kidney damage to humans and pets that consume any part of the plant. Dieffenbachia is known as "dumb cane" because it causes swelling to the mouth and throat, making it impossible to speak, but it can also seriously interfere with breathing. Even the berries of popular holiday decorations such as holly and mistletoe are toxic if eaten. As you enjoy the holiday season, be aware of the possible toxicity of the houseplants and decorations you buy, and find locations to display these items that will prevent contact with pets and kids.

Give your containers a shot in the arm.

Q I planted several large pots with showy perennials and annuals on Mother's Day. I mixed in a **slow-release fertilizer** as directed on the label and have been watering regularly to keep the soil moist. The containers are located in full sun. So why is nothing happening? The plants are hardly growing, and there hasn't been a bloom. The plants have been out there almost a month. The slow-release fertilizer is supposed to last for two and a half months, but it doesn't seem to be kicking in. What's wrong?

A Even when you mix in a slow-release fertilizer such as Osmocote, plants growing in containers need a shot of quick-release fertilizer in May. Most slow-release fertilizers rely on temperature to release nutrients, and they don't kick in until warmer weather heats up the soil in late June or early July. A shot of a good soluble houseplant fertilizer, such as Miracle-Gro, applied early in the season will encourage sustained growth and flowering until the slow-release fertilizer becomes active.

Collect rainwater for houseplants.

Q Is it true that the chlorine in **tap water** is harmful to houseplants? Does it harm all houseplants? Is it better to give plants distilled water?

A It's true that a few houseplants are harmed by tap water. Despite the common belief that chlorine is at fault, it's actually fluoride that does the damage. The most common symptom, browning of leaf tips, which occurs on dracaenas and spider plants, is mostly aesthetic. Fluoride, however, can maim or even kill insect-eating plants and some types of orchids. Using distilled water will solve the problem, but why pay for it when Mama Nature gives out buckets of fluoride-free water for free? Leave out one or two clean plastic garbage cans where the winter rain will fill them. To fill them more quickly, run your rain gutter downspouts into them. Store the overflow in plastic milk containers to use in summer when Mama Nature isn't as generous with rainwater.

It's time to bring in houseplants.

Q Most of my houseplants spend the summer outside. How do I know when it's **time to bring them back into the house**? And how likely is it that harmful bugs could come into the house on the plants?

A It's risky to leave your houseplants out when temperatures begin to drop in the fall. To be safe, bring them in by the end of September. But before you bring them in, clean the pots and inspect the plants closely for insect infestation. Make sure any problems are solved before the summer plants move indoors to live alongside your other plants. Don't forget to look for slugs and snails hiding in the foliage or under the pot. A slug can do an amazing amount of damage when introduced to a bunch of plants in your house. It also might cost you a visit to the marriage counselor if your partner finds slug slime all over the new couch!

Transplant root-bound houseplants.

 How do I know when my houseplant needs to be transplanted into a bigger pot? How do you do it?

Houseplants should be transplanted only if they are root-bound, and then it should be done in spring, when the plant is actively growing. Before taking on the project, ask yourself a number of questions: Does the water run right into the saucer when you give your houseplant a drink? Does the stem and leaf growth seem to have slowed down, even if you fertilize? Does the soil dry out quickly, requiring ever more frequent watering, and/or are roots growing through the drainage hole? If the answer is yes to any of the above questions, remove the plant from the pot. If the root ball consists of matted roots with little soil visible, your plant is root-bound and needs a transplant. Gently wash the soil off the roots by soaking the plant in warm water, and repot in a container one inch bigger than the last one. Don't put pebbles and broken crockery in the bottom of the pot to improve drainage; it does the opposite. Water well and leave the plant in partial shade for a few days before sticking it back in that bright window.

Give your root-bound houseplant a bath in winter.

Q I suspect that my houseplant is rootbound. Can I **transplant it in winter,** or is it better to wait to transplant until spring? I'm worried that it will die of thirst if I wait too long.

A Unfortunately, winter is the worst time to transplant because most houseplants are dormant and will not recover from transplanting under those conditions. To keep your plant alive until the appropriate time to transplant (mid-March), occasionally soak the entire pot in a container of warm water. Leave it in until the bubbles stop. That will moisten the entire root zone. As an added bonus, when you take the plant out of the container and allow the excess moisture to run out of the pot, this will help leach out excess fertilizer salts. When you transplant, follow the procedure described in the answer above.

Grow a tropical display in a shade pot.

Q I lust for the tropical look, but I only have room to garden in pots in a shady area. Is there anything **tropical** that I can plant in a shady container?

A Don't dismay: Many of the coolest tropical plants live in the dark understory of jungle forests. Start with a good-sized pot. For your centerpiece, begin with a shade-loving, light and airy 3- to 4-foot-tall clump of *Fargesia murielae* or *F. nitida* bamboo in the back of the container. Then, to find the perfect midsized plant, search the houseplant section of your local nursery for a shrub begonia. Shrub begonias feature heavily textured elephant ear–shaped leaves and a feltlike coating. One of the best, *Begonia* 'Ramirez', features dark green fuzzy leaves, underleafed in velvet red. It flowers all summer long with white blooms covered with a mist of scarlet hairs that contrast surprisingly well with hot colors. Then create an explosion of color by filling in with magnificent, large-flowering tuberous begonias. Use mostly upright types, but add a few weeping varieties to spill over the side of the pot. Now add height and float tropical fragrance on the breeze by squeezing in of a couple of sweetly scented purple-flowering heliotrope. Then sit back, fix yourself a piña colada, put on a Jimmy Buffett CD, and chill out in your own tropical paradise.

Combine summer-blooming vines to make incredible container designs.

Q Do **vines** grow well in pots? I was thinking about combining a few to create an unusual design in one of my summer containers.

A Many types of flowering vines thrive in containers, and combining them can create a stunning vertical accent. All you need is a container about the size of a whiskey barrel and some kind of structure on which to tie the vines to help them climb. Most nurseries carry a variety of potted annual vines that bloom all summer long. Combine at least two varieties to create colorful combinations. For a knockout display, pair *Mina lobata* (sunset vine)—cloaked in sprays of scarlet-orange and yellow flowers—with the dark purple, violet-streaked blooms of the annual morning glory *Ipomoea* 'Star of Yalta'. (Don't worry: This morning glory is noninvasive.) If you want to attract wildlife, replace the sunset vine with Chilean glory vine (*Eccremocarpus scaber*), featuring hot orange flowers that are absolutely irresistible to hummingbirds. Another great combination includes *Thunbergia alata* (black-eyed Susan vine)—which has orange, yellow, or white flowers—paired with *Rhodochiton atrosanguineus* (purple bell vine). Grow these vines in full sun and keep them well fertilized. They will thank you by providing a spectacular, nonstop vertical display all summer long.

Add interest to your garden (or deck) with water plants.

Q I live in an apartment and garden only in pots on a sunny deck. I miss the lily pads and other **water plants** that grew in the pond near my house when I was a kid. Is it possible to grow water plants in a container?

A Even if you don't have a pond in your garden, you can still grow some incredible ornamental water plants in a container. All that's required is a good waterproof ceramic pot in which to submerge pots of lily pads, water hyacinths, water lettuce, elephant ears, and many other interesting water plants. I have a 3-foot-wide by 1-foot-deep pot in my driveway in which I'm growing a stand of spectacular variegated cattails adorned with green-and-white-striped foliage, topped with the classic brown cattail flowers. Regularly fertilize your water plants so they'll grow strong and bloom. Good nurseries sell slow-release aquatic tabs formulated for moderate growth and strong blooming without algae growth. Most of these tabs will provide all the nutrition needed for thirty to forty-five days, depending on the kind of plant and growth conditions. Add some little goldfish to draw interest and to prevent mosquitoes from using your ornamental water plant display as a breeding ground.

Plant up some winter cheer.

Q Getting through the cold, wet winter is depressing enough, but looking out at pots filled with dead plants left over from summer displays is a real bummer. What **winter plants** can I plant in those containers to make them look good and cheer me up?

A Only one thing bums me out more than seeing a pot sitting empty all winter long, and that's a pot sitting full of dead plants. Visit your local nursery. You'll find plenty of colorful evergreen shrubs, perennials, and flowers to create a cheery winter planting. Don't worry about choosing plants that require sun or shade. In a winter pot, the sun isn't hot enough to make much difference. Begin your design with a colorful evergreen centerpiece such as a *Chamaecyparis obtusa* 'Nana Lutea' (dwarf golden Hinoki cypress), *Phormium* (New Zealand flax), *Mahonia* × *media* 'Charity' (winter-blooming mahonia), *Camellia sasanqua* (winter-blooming camellia), or *Nandina domestica* (heavenly bamboo). Just make sure whatever you choose is in proportion to pot size. Fill in with intermediate-sized plants, such as golden *Helleborus foetidus* (stinking hellebore), white-marbled *Helleborus argutifolius* 'Janet Starnes', dusty miller, heuchera, or variegated *Hebe speciosa*. To add bold texture and color, fill in around the bottom with *Bergenia* 'Appleblossom', featuring large leaves that turn red in winter. Counterpoint with the finely textured, bright yellow leaves of *Acorus gramineus* 'Ogon' (Japanese sweet flag) or shimmering silver-blue *Festuca glauca* (blue fescue grass). Pack in a few pansies for a floriferous display and finish off with a few trailers, such as variegated ivy or creeping wire vine (*Muehlenbeckia complexa*). When you see how cheery and attractive your winter container planting looks, you'll feel like it's the first day of summer.

CHAPTER FIVE

Garden and Lawn Care

Control aggressive vines.

Q I planted an **akebia** on an arbor. I like this vine, but it's beginning to take over the garden. Can I cut it back?

A Not only *can* you cut it back, you'd better do it right away! Beautiful as it is, I rue the day I planted an *Akebia quinata* (fireleaf akebia) on my wood fence. It has entangled itself with several valuable trees and shrubs. It will take me hours to remove it without breaking the delicate branches of my *Hydrangea aspera*. My honeysuckle is beginning to look like a bully, and dealing with my wisteria has taught me several unusual wrestling moves. Vines play a key role in the garden—hiding ugly fences, producing colorful flowers, and even attracting hummingbirds—but some are aggressive and can cause serious damage to plants and structures if allowed to get out of control. Monitor your vines regularly, and cut them back hard before they work their way into your prize plants or under the roof of your garage. If they've already worked their way under your neighbors' roof, move before they find out!

237

Get a local weather report.

Q How accurate are the weather reports when they tell us the **amount of rain** that fell in the vicinity? It seems that where I live, we often don't get as much rain as the report claims. Could there be that much variation between neighborhoods?

A Rain reports are generalized, and in the Pacific Northwest the amount of rainfall varies significantly from place to place. Even my buddy Meeghan Black can't tell you exactly how much fell in your particular neighborhood. You need to entice your mom to send you a rain gauge. I've been good (well, not as bad as usual), so my mom sent me one, and it's even better than a brussels sprout casserole. It's a work of art and an attractive addition to the garden in its own right, but its real value is that it informs me of exactly how much rain fell right at my house over a given period of time. The gauge makes it easier to decide when and how much to water. If you've been bad, buy your own and put it right outside a window so that you don't forget to look at it every day. Or else behave, and maybe your mom will send you a cool rain gauge too.

Soil preparation is the key to growing great annuals.

Q Are there any tips you can give me to help me grow better **annual flowers**? Mine have been looking a bit wimpy over the last couple of years.

A Choose a sunny, well-drained location and work plenty of dolomite lime, compost, and high-phosphorus fertilizer into the soil before planting. (Consider using 14-14-14 Osmocote fertilizer when planting containers; then you won't have to fertilize again for about four months.) Don't forget to pinch out the growing tips of the young pelargoniums (geraniums), petunias, marigolds, and many other varieties of annual flowers to force lots of side branches.

Control bamboo mites safely.

Q The normally green leaves of my **bamboo** are streaked with ugly whitish-yellow lines, making them look variegated. Any idea what is causing this?

A Turn over the leaves and you'll see flat sheets of webbing filled with bamboo mites. These spider relatives won't kill your bamboo, but the damage is unattractive. Chemical miticides are often recommended, but these products can be toxic to humans and pets, and the mites often build up resistance over time. Fortunately, Phil Davidson, owner of Jade Mountain Bamboo Nursery in Tacoma, Washington, offers this safe, biodegradable alternative: In a one-gallon container, put two teaspoons of liquid dishwashing soap and two tablespoons of any vegetable oil, and then fill the remainder of the container with water. Place a golf ball inside your hose-end sprayer to act as an agitator and then fill the sprayer with the solution and set the sprayer for 2.5 ounces per gallon. Spray the leaves thoroughly, making sure to soak the undersides of the leaves where the mites laid their webbing. Every few seconds, shake the sprayer to keep the soap, oil, and water in solution. Phil says that for difficult cases, he applies up to 4 ounces per gallon with no burning or other ill effects on the leaves, but he recommends starting with a lower dosage and working up, if needed. The mites cannot build up resistance because the oil smothers them. Repeat every two to three weeks as necessary.

Mow down blackberry.

 I'm drowning in a sea of **blackberry**. Nothing seems to get rid of this stuff. I've tried all sorts of poisons,

but it just keeps coming back. Do I have to (heaven forbid) dig it all up?

A When I was the manager of grounds at Seattle University, I once called the city to give them the address of a vacant lot that was completely covered with blackberry vines, so they would contact whoever owned it and make them clean it up. Two days later, my boss called me into his office. He said that someone had squealed on us to the city about a vacant lot we owned, and told me to get out there and clean it up! I cut and removed most of the canes, but I left the crowns, planning to paint the cuts with Roundup before the new growth returned. I didn't get around to using Roundup, so I asked a gardener to mow the blackberries with an old lawn mower to cut off the new growth to give me time. I never got around to spraying, so the gardener kept mowing the lot every two weeks. By the end of summer every trace of blackberry was gone, replaced with a mix of grasses and weeds that naturalized in hot, dry conditions and could take mowing. The "lawn" didn't look too bad and even stayed green without watering. As long as you mow every two weeks, this method works equally well to rid your landscape of ivy.

Check for broken branches if you want a long life.

Q Several big conifers very near our house suffered damage in a recent windstorm. Do we need to hire someone to climb up there and repair the **broken branches**?

A There's a reason that broken branches high in trees are called "widow makers." After a snow or ice storm, go out with a pair of binoculars and inspect the trees on your property. If you see hung branches, hire a certified arborist to remove them and to repair damaged limbs by cutting them off cleanly at the proper location. This may reward both you and your trees with a longer life.

Butterfly bush is a noxious weed.

Q I'm a big fan of **butterfly bushes**, but a neighbor told me that they are considered an invasive species. Can we still plant them, and are there varieties that don't cause problems?

A To the consternation of gardeners who desire to attract butterflies and hummingbirds, the weed control programs in several Northwest states have labeled the butterfly bush (*Buddleja*) a Class C noxious weed (the least serious of the three classifications). Despite the noxious weed designation, homeowners are not required to rid their gardens of buddleja, and, in fact, nurseries are still allowed to sell all varieties. The problem is that the seeds are capable of traveling a long way and can potentially take the place of native plants where they come up in large numbers. Consider replacing your butterfly bush with a hybrid such as *Buddleja* 'Orchid Beauty' or 'Summer Rose'. These hybrids form almost no seed and therefore are not invasive. If you decide to keep your existing buddleja, deadhead the blooms as soon as they fade to prevent them from seeding and becoming a problem in native lands.

Don't be a lazy dog.

Q I try to follow your gardening advice, but you're making me work too hard. Now that it's midsummer, **can I finally just lie in the hammock** guilt-free and enjoy the garden for a change?

A Sorry, no rest for the wicked. The dog days of summer are a key time to get out there and weed. The shotweed and red-leaved oxalis are maturing in your garden as you laze about in your hammock. Before you even realize it, those nasty little weeds will be shooting their seeds all over the garden, and in no time you'll have hundreds of their offspring to deal with. So put down that cup of coffee (after you finish watching my TV show, of course), grab your weeding tool, and start doing some serious weeding!

A digging spade is a must-have.

Q I noticed that you always hand Meeghan a special **chrome shovel** when you make her do all the work on your TV show. What kind of shovel is that, and why do you use that kind in particular? Where can I buy one? By the way, how do you get her to do all of the work?

A A top-quality digging spade is a beautiful thing, and a gardening necessity. I use mine for everything from planting to dividing perennials. (It's great for slicing and dicing slugs, too.) There are a number of really good brands to choose from, but my favorite is the Holland stainless steel spade with the oak handle. I bought mine at a local nursery several years ago, and I've abused the tweetle out of it by leaving it out in the rain and using it to pry huge root balls. I even ran over it with a backhoe! It still looks great, holds a sharp edge, and doesn't have a spot of rust on it. In regard to your last question, Meeghan has the easy job. You should see how hard it is to supervise her!

Caffeine is good for your garden (but not your pup).

Q I'm a wired gardener. I can't exist, let alone garden, if I don't have my cup of espresso every morning. I've been throwing away the grounds, but the thought hit me that they might be good for the garden. Do **coffee grounds** have any qualities that could be beneficial to my plants?

A If you listen to my radio show or see me on TV, you undoubtedly know that I'm a wired gardener, too. I also brew my own espresso, and I definitely use the grounds in my garden. If you aren't a big coffee drinker, you can get some grounds from Starbucks—they give away bags of them on a first come, first served basis. The best use of grounds is to put them in your compost pile. Coffee grounds are a good source of nitrogen and, when combined with leaves and straw, they'll get the compost pile cooking. The grounds contain about 1.5 percent nitrogen, in addition to magnesium and calcium. Grounds are slightly acid, which will help your compost maintain a neutral pH balance. You can avoid the problem of fungus buildup by applying a thin layer of grounds and working them into the soil. They can also be applied as a light top dressing directly over the roots of most plants in the garden, but don't apply them more than once per month. Although very little caffeine is left in the grounds after you make a cup of coffee, caffeine is harmful to dogs, so forgo using the grounds in the garden if you have a puppy that might like to get a buzz.

Protect columbine from ravaging worms.

Q What is eating my **columbine**? I planted them to attract hummingbirds, but all I seem to be attracting are bugs that feast on the plants.

A The colorful blossoms of *Aquilegia* (columbine) are highly attractive to hummingbirds. Unfortunately, columbines are also a favorite snack for cutworms and sawflies, and if you fail to take steps to control them you may never get to enjoy the beautiful flowers. Cutworms are the worst. I recently dug a columbine to move it and found several caterpillars hiding in the soil around the plant. Had I not found them, these cutworms would have ganged up and devoured the entire plant during the night. Sawflies don't eat the entire plant, but the small black-and-reddish beelike adults lay oodles of eggs under the leaves. If you don't catch the pale green worms soon after they hatch, the veins will be all that remains of the leaves. In either case, the plant will usually survive, but it won't produce many, if any, flowers. Protect columbine from nighttime cutworm attack by applying the sharp crystals of diatomaceous earth around the plant. This treatment won't work against the sawfly larvae, but luckily, they're active during the day and therefore prime candidates for on-the-spot pest control. Don't forget to yell "El kabatski!" as you squish.

Till your vegetable garden in the fall.

Q **The soil in my vegetable garden contains a lot of clay, and it stays wet until late spring. I want to till in compost to improve the soil, but I'm worried that if I till when the soil is wet, I'll damage it. What do you recommend?**

A Digging or rototilling in wet soil will do more harm than good. It destroys the soil structure and can turn your soil into clumpy, concretelike gradoo that stays wet and drains poorly in wet conditions. In dry conditions it turns the soil to dust, making it difficult to moisten. It's a good idea to work compost into the soil, but do it in fall, during dry weather, when you can control the amount of moisture in the soil. Add moisture a few days before you till. The ideal conditions are for the soil to be about as moist as a squeezed sponge. The goal is to add enough compost so that a third of the soil is organic. To achieve this, add 4 inches of compost and work it in 12 inches deep.

It's fun to make your own compost.

Q **I recently moved into a new house with a big yard. For the first time, I have room for a compost pile. I'm eager to try making my own, but I don't know how to get started. Please advise: I want to do it right so I don't end up with a stinky mess.**

A Great compost is the key to a great garden. Making it is an art, but that doesn't mean it has to be difficult. Actually, it's a lot of fun, especially when you get the reward of sticking your hands into rich, earthy-smelling compost that you made yourself. Your compost bin should measure at least 3 feet tall and 3 feet wide. It should also be well ventilated and made of a nonrotting material. It's helpful if it opens on one side for easy access. To create fast, hot compost, you need to mix carbon-rich brown materials with nitrogen-rich green ones. The goal is to have a 30:1 ratio of carbon to nitrogen. It sounds difficult, but all you really need to do is make a 50-50 mix of leaves, straw, or finely chopped wood chips with green herbaceous plants, weeds, or grass clippings. The books tell you to add these materials in layers, but I find it works just as well to dump them in at random and then mix them together. It's important to keep the mix moist, so add water as necessary, until it's about as moist as a wrung-out sponge. It's a good idea to add some soil or active compost to the mix now and then, and also mix in a little organic fertilizer from time to time to keep the pile active. Turn it over as often as you can; the more you turn, the faster the compost will break down. A well-tended pile can break down in two to three months, but one that's never turned can take a year or more to produce high-quality compost. Never add meat, dairy products, or carnivorous-animal waste to your pile. They don't break down well, tend to smell bad, and may attract rodents. Avoid invasive weeds, as the seeds might survive the composting process. You'll know you did it right if your compost is dark, crumbly, and earthy-smelling. Try not to show it off to all of your fellow gardeners, though. It's fun to make them jealous, but if you overdo it, you'll have to install an alarm system to keep envious gardeners from pilfering your black gold in the middle of the night.

Get the heap cooking again.

 Q My **compost pile** smells like the local garbage dump, and that's putting it politely. What am I doing wrong?

I thought compost broke down rapidly in the heat of summer, but mine is only sitting there stinking to high heaven. What can I do before my neighbors send a vigilante committee after me?

A In the heat of summer, compost piles cool down or, worse, become rather pungent. It's time to activate that pile before your neighbors begin throwing their old tennis shoes into your yard for revenge. Wet down the pile by adding water until the compost is as moist as a squeezed sponge. Don't overdo this; if you drown the microorganisms, it'll really get stinky! Turn the pile to allow air in. If it smells like rotten eggs, you probably have too much green stuff, such as weeds and grass, and not enough brown materials, such as leaves or straw. While you are turning it, throw in a couple of hand-fuls of high-nitrogen lawn fertilizer (never Weed and Feed) to get things really cooking. Finally, cover the pile with an old rug to keep it from drying out too fast. Soon you'll be proud of your compost, and you won't have to dodge flying tennis shoes while you garden.

Compost food scraps without attracting rats.

Q Do you recommend burying vegetable food scraps in the compost pile? I've been doing it, but the other night I noticed what might have been a rat near my compost pile. Is there a better way to **compost vegetable scraps**?

A I used to bury my vegetable scraps in my compost pile, but I ended that practice the day I stuck my pitchfork into the pile and a humongous rat came charging out, sending both my pup Kokie and me running for our lives! Green Cone food-waste compost bins, available at garden centers and occasionally through public utilities, are a much better system. As long as you set them up correctly and never put meat or dairy products in them, the cones remain completely odorless and rodent-proof. You need at least two Green Cones for the system to work, because once they're full, it takes months for the food wastes to break down into compost. Another fun way to compost vegetable scraps is to do worm composting (see "Try worm composting," page 287).

Corn gluten (might) give you weed control.

 I'm looking for something to help me keep weeds out of my lawn and garden beds, but I don't want to use chemical weed killers. I saw something called **corn gluten** at my local nursery that's supposed to prevent weeds. This sounds like just what I'm looking for. Does it really work, and how do you use it?

Corn gluten is becoming popular as an alternative to chemical herbicides. Researchers at Iowa State University accidentally discovered that corn gluten prevents many kinds of weed seeds from germinating. It is a preemergent herbicide, meaning that it must be put down before the seeds germinate. It's important to remove existing weeds before you apply corn gluten. This product does absolutely no harm to existing weeds and will actually fertilize them and make them grow better. Unfortunately, research also shows that, for it to be effective, you need two weeks of dry weather after application. Good luck in the Pacific Northwest! Corn gluten contains 10 percent nitrogen and must be put down at a rate of 20 pounds per 1,000 square feet to be effective against weed seeds. If you try it, aim for dry weather, but even if it rains, existing plants (and weeds) will be well fertilized.

Don't spray for crane fly.

My lawn has numerous dead spots. The nursery person told me that it's **crane fly** damage. Can I spray to kill the crane flies so that I can have an attractive lawn again?

A Crane fly is that entertaining insect that resembles a big mosquito. It's amusing because it causes your partner to make cute screams when it tickles their face in the middle of the night. Homeowners spend millions on pesticides to control crane flies, and, as a result, these pesticides are showing up in waterways and drinking water sources. Recent studies have shown that crane fly infestations are uncommon and that the vast majority of lawn problems attributed to them have other causes, such as thatch buildup, poorly drained soil, or improper lawn care. If your lawn is looking sickly, monitor to see if you have a problem before you spray. Cut three sides of a 6-inch by 6-inch chunk of lawn that's 3 inches deep and fold back the sod. Cut into the sample to look for tubular, grublike worms. Multiply the number you find by four to figure out the number of larvae per square foot. If the number of larvae is less than fifty per square foot, all you need to do is fertilize and take good care of your lawn and it will recover without requiring the use of pesticides. If the number is higher than fifty, the area where your lawn is located holds too much moisture and will always have problems. Replace your lawn with an attractive mixed border filled with plants well suited to wet soil conditions.

Trap earwigs.

Q Last night my **dahlia flowers** were huge and beautiful. This morning they look like National League baseballs. Something chewed the petals right off the flowers! Not only that, there are holes in the leaves of many of my favorite perennials. I've looked for caterpillars or other bugs, but I can't find a thing. What is doing this damage, and how can I stop it from happening? Baseballs don't look that great in bouquets.

A If you go out at night with a flashlight, you'll spot the troublemakers at work. Earwigs come out at night and, yes, they often chew the petals right off dahlia flowers. They've been known to tatter the living tweetle out of rose blooms, and they also chew ugly holes in *Brugmansia* leaves as well as the foliage of other perennials. They move too fast to use the *el kabatski* method. Instead, catch them with my guaranteed-or-your-money-back earwig trap. You'll need an empty 12-ounce plastic water bottle (without lid), tape, a wee bit of yarn, scissors, and some canned tuna-fish cat food. Cut off the top third of the bottle. Place a blop (half a teaspoon) of cat food in the bottom of the bottle. Take the piece that you cut off, flip it so that it is inverted, and stick it into the top of the bottle. Note that the part you drink out of is now facing downward toward the cat food at the bottom. Tape the inverted top to secure it to the bottle. Finally, tape the yarn on the bottle to form a loop so that you can hang the trap on your plant. The little devils can't resist tuna-fish cat food and will enter the trap during the night, only to find that they can't find the way out in the morning. You'll have to figure out what to do with all the earwigs you catch. You'll also be busy shooing away all of the neighbors' cats!

Yank those dandelions.

Q I keep my lawn thick and healthy, but I can't escape an occasional **dandelion** coming up in the grass. I don't believe in using poisons and prefer to dig them out. I've seen a number of tools made to pull dandelions. Do these things work? Is there one kind that works the best?

A One good way to rid your lawn of dandelions is to yank them. I've tested several tools made for this purpose. Most of them don't work very well. Unfortunately, the best dandelion puller ever made isn't made anymore, but you may be able to find it at a garage sale or a secondhand store. It says "patented in 1918" on the metal part at the bottom. The jaws are longer and stronger, and will never break or bend. This tool works best when used right after watering or a heavy rain. I can't tell you the satisfaction you'll feel when you get the whole root. There is a downside, though: You get two for every one when you break the root.

An alternative for a weed-free lawn.

Q Is there a nonchemical way to rid your lawn of **dandelions**? I tried using a dandelion puller, but the weeds came back.

A Try spraying the dandelions with straight white vinegar from the grocery store. Apply the vinegar on a hot, sunny day. Use a sprayer to apply undiluted vinegar, and liberally soak the weed. Be warned: Vinegar will kill any plant it hits. If you use it to rid your lawn of dandelions, it will kill the grass surrounding the weed, and you'll end up with dead spots in your lawn. Wait a week, then reseed. Rough up the dead spots, or punch holes if thatch or dead sod covers the soil surface. Stomp the seed into the top layer of the soil or rake it into the holes. Sprinkle on a bit of starter fertilizer and keep the area moist. Newly germinated grass will appear in a week or two, but the dandelion you squirted with vinegar will be long gone.

Don't worry, be happy.

Q It's mid-December, and I'm totally **depressed by all of the rain and darkness**. How do you stay so cheery when it's so dreary?

A Anyone can get a wee bit depressed in winter. The best cure is to follow the lead of ancient societies. They believed that they had to hold big festivals on the winter solstice to persuade the goddess of the sun to bring back the long days. They probably didn't believe it either, but it's a good excuse to throw a fun party. Eat, drink, and rejoice in the knowledge that the days are getting longer. Soon you will actually be able to see when you garden after 4 in the afternoon.

Go on a night patrol.

Q Something is **eating a number of my plants**. I've checked for bugs, but found nothing. I thought it might be slugs, but there are no slime trails. Whatever is doing it has a voracious appetite, though; if I don't do something quickly, I fear my primrose collection will disappear! What's the cause of this destruction, and is there anything I can do to stop it before it's too late?

A I suspect that the culprits chowing down on your plants are cutworms. Cutworms are fat, greasy caterpillars that hide during the day and come out to do evil deeds during the night. They come in a variety of colors and sizes, and I've seen some that were almost 2 inches long! They cause damage similar to that of slugs, but slug bait won't touch them. You need to take action right away, because cutworms can decimate a plant. They often hang out in gangs of ten or more, and newly planted primroses, as well as many other types of plants, disappear without a trace during the night. The best control is my patented *el kabatski* method: Go out with a flashlight and look for caterpillars on your plants. Wear rubber gloves. Yell "El kabatski!" as you squish. Stand sufficiently far from the cutworm as you squeeze; cutworms make an impressive *splat.*

A foolproof way to reduce garden maintenance.

Q I hate gardening, but I have a huge yard. How can I **eliminate the maintenance** so I can enjoy my yard without doing any work?

A new study done by a local garden expert (aka Ciscoe) has revealed that adopting a new puppy will drastically reduce garden maintenance. Among the findings are that puppies make outstanding rototillers. Just tell the puppy where not to dig, and the entire area will be tilled instantly, including the peas that were 2 feet high, saving you the work of tending and harvesting them. The biggest labor savings are in weeding and general maintenance. In no time your puppy will find his way into your mixed border, and you can kick back and watch him rip out the weeds for you. Of course, he'll also rip out all of those fussy, expensive, high-maintenance plants as well. You'll be able to take the summer off, because you won't have any plants left to care for at all. If you don't like dogs, consider moving into a condo.

The best fertilizer for flowering plants is alfalfa meal (horse food). It's not high in phosphorus, the nutrient usually associated with making plants blossom, but it's loaded with micronutrients and hormones that tell your plant, "Bloom, you fool, bloom!"

Don't feed your lawn too early in spring.

Q When is the best time to **fertilize** my lawn?

A Apply an organic lawn food in late April or early May. That's when the grass is just beginning to slow down from the growth spurt that began in early spring. The addition of an organic fertilizer at this time will promote steady growth that's thick enough to compete with weeds and moss. If you water your lawn during summer, apply an organic lawn fertilizer in mid-June, early

September, and mid-October. (If you prefer using synthetic lawn food, skip the October feeding and apply synthetic, slow-release fall and winter fertilizer in mid-November.) If you don't water your lawn during summer, apply only in spring and fall, and make sure you use an organic fertilizer.

Non-dormant lawns need fertilizing in summer.

Q I'm not sure if I'm going to water my lawn this summer or let it go dormant. If I water, when should I **fertilize**? Should I avoid fertilizing if I don't water?

A If you intend to water your lawn during summer, June is a good time to feed with an organic lawn food. Feeding at this time will promote steady, even growth thick enough to outcompete dandelions and other weeds. But if you don't plan to irrigate and intend to allow the grass to go dormant, applying fertilizer in June, or anytime the grass is receiving water, is the worst thing you can do. The added nutrition will encourage active growth. In the event of drought, actively growing grass is highly susceptible to damage and could be killed. Of course, if the grass dies, it could be a wonderful opportunity to start over and add soil improvements before planting a new lawn in fall. If you don't want to work that hard, however, hold off fertilizing until the soil becomes moist again, in mid- to late September.

Fertilize in fall for deep roots next spring.

Q I admit I'm not the best at caring for my lawn. It doesn't look great, but I can live with it as long as it doesn't become too unsightly. If I **fertilize** only once per year, when is the best time to do it?

A If you fertilize only once per year, fall is the time to do it. That's because in late November, grass goes through a metabolic change. Instead of producing top growth, food manufactured in the leaves is stored as carbohydrates in a deep root system. If you use organic fertilizers, do the fall feeding in mid-October; in cool weather it may take up to six weeks for soil microbes to break down organic fertilizer, and you want your lawn to have nutrients available in late November and early December, when they're needed to develop a deep root system. Synthetic fall and winter slow-release fertilizer is best applied between mid-November and mid-December. Two important caveats, however: Never apply fertilizer to frozen ground, and don't exceed the amount recommended on the label. Some organic lawn food and most fall and winter fertilizers contain iron. If you overdo it, you will burn the living tweetle out of your lawn and turn it black. Then not only will your lawn fail to develop a deep root system, but the fertilizer may actually burn the roots and reduce the ability of the grass to withstand drought next summer.

Don't fertilize most shrubs and perennials after July.

Q I **fertilize** most of my shrubs and perennials to keep them blooming and healthy, but I'm never sure when to stop feeding them. Is there a hard-and-fast rule regarding when to stop fertilizing?

A Shrubs and perennials need to calm down, stop growing, and harden off for winter. Fertilizing after the end of July can cause them to keep growing, with catastrophic results if we get an early freeze. The only exception, as far as I'm concerned, is the rose. I give my roses a last shot of alfalfa meal in late August or even the first week of September. That's because we often get the best blooms in September and October. Yes, you could lose your rose to an early freeze. But oh, la, la, you'll finally have space for a new plant!

Some plants are big eaters.

 How often should I fertilize repeat-blooming plants such as roses and delphiniums, and what's the best fertilizer to use?

Roses, delphiniums, dahlias, *Scabiosa*, and any other plants that bloom all summer long need a constant supply of nutrients. My favorite fertilizer for roses and perennials is alfalfa meal, but any organic fertilizer high in phosphorus (the second number on the fertilizer bag) will do. Remember to fertilize every six weeks, and make sure you keep the soil adequately moist. Remove spent flowers before they go to seed, and you'll be cutting bouquets all summer long.

Go on the amazing gardening diet.

It's probably because I hate brussels sprouts and love doughnuts, but I need to lose a pound or two. The Atkins diet helped, but my doc tells me I need to exercise more. If I do more gardening, will it give me a good workout, or am I better off going to the gym?

You might find it interesting to learn that during the height of the Atkins diet craze, the sales of bread and pasta plummeted while doughnut sales rose to new highs. Hey, do more gardening and you can have your doughnut and stay in shape too. Thirty minutes of weeding uses up 180 calories, while a half hour of mowing burns 240 calories. If you really want to get buff, turn the compost pile and melt off an additional 250 calories. So get out there and work in the garden. Then you can eat a whole box of Krispy Kremes guilt-free!

Stop grass in its tracks.

Q I planted grass in a walking path between my mixed borders. The path looks great and takes foot traffic well, but the grass invades my planting beds. It's hard to pull out, especially if it entangles in the roots of my prized perennials. How can I keep the **grass from taking over my gardens**?

A Grass makes a great walking path because it doesn't mind foot traffic and it contrasts beautifully with perennials and shrubs. Unfortunately, nothing is more irritating than weeding it out of your planting beds, especially when it's entangled into the root system of your favorite perennial or shrub. Grass spreads through underground stems, and the easiest way to stop it from creeping into your planting beds is to install edging to bar its path. Metal and plastic barriers are effective, but for a more natural look, install a double row of cobblestones, available at rock and stone outlets. Place good-sized stones at least 6 inches deep to prevent roots from snaking underneath. Offset the rows in a checkerboard pattern to ensure that roots do not have a straight path into the garden. The stones in the second row will block grass that finds its way through the first line of defense. Kill any grass that comes up between the rows by spraying it with straight white vinegar on a hot, sunny day. You'll smell like a real pickle lover, but that's better than weeding grass out of the plants in your garden bed.

Trees hate grass.

Q Is it true that it's harmful to a tree to grow **grass right up to the trunk**? My partner and I have a high-stakes bet riding on this: a chocolate chip cookie! She is convinced that grass should be kept away from the trunk. She also thinks I'm harming the tree by using a power string trimmer around it. I think grass around a tree looks natural, and string trimming carefully does no harm. Who's right?

A   I don't know if it's true that opposites attract, but you've got yourself one smart partner. Grass roots emit a substance that is harmful to tree roots, and studies have shown improved root establishment and increased vigor in trees where grass is kept at least 6 inches away from the trunk. She's also right that you're harming the tree when you use a power string trimmer around its base. No matter how careful you are, you can't avoid making little cuts that will lead to long-term decay problems. If you don't believe it, allow your partner to use a weed eater to trim around your bare ankles! Use a flat digging spade to slice off the grass within at least a foot from the trunk. Avoid slicing into roots and use a sharp pruner to cut off any that are damaged in the process. Mulch thickly to prevent weeds and grass from growing back, but don't allow too much to build up around the trunk. Start mulching at the trunk with a thin layer and increase the depth of the mulch as you work your way out toward the lawn. By the way, I don't recommend raising the stakes on future bets you make with that partner of yours.

Be ready for powdery mildew.

Q   The leaves of a variety of plants in my garden are covered with **gray stuff**. It looks almost like powdered sugar, and it's especially bad in fall. It's on my zucchini, lilac tree, deciduous azalea, and several rosebushes. Is this a bad thing, and if it is, what can I do to rid my plants of it?

A   Powdery mildew is a common problem, especially in fall. Odd as it seems, the easiest way to prevent this fungus is to water adequately. Underwatered plants are highly susceptible. Generally, powdery mildew is not a problem, especially if it appears only in fall. If it attacks early, however, it can weaken the plant by reducing its ability to produce food in the heavily coated leaves. It looks unsightly as well. If you start early, it's generally easy to control. Powdery mildew is the only fungus that lives on the outside of the leaves. That's important to know, because unlike other fungus diseases, it can be easily controlled if a spray is applied at the first sign of the powdery symptom. (It's too late once leaves are covered.) Many environmentally friendly products, such as Rose Defense (made from vegetable oil) and sprays containing baking soda, are effective. It also helps to rake up infected leaves that might otherwise serve as inoculators of powdery mildew next spring. Unless you are an expert, don't compost infected leaves; send them to a compost facility equipped to handle them.

Cover the hose bibs and wrestle the snake.

Q I don't know if it's global warming, but the winters just don't seem as cold as they used to be. Is it still necessary to go to the hassle of putting those **hose bib covers** over the faucet? I'd rather just leave my hose attached all winter long.

A I used to think that it was a waste of time to cover hose bibs. That changed some years ago when a neighbor called me at work to tell me that I had a skating rink in my backyard! Even during an *El Niño*, you never know if a cold front might unexpectedly blow in from the north. It's easier to put on a Styrofoam cover in late fall than in freezing cold winter weather, and it's certainly a lot less hassle than repairing an exploded hose bib. Freezing and thawing will ruin your hose as well. Bring it in while it's in a thawed-out state. Coiling a frozen hose is like wrestling with an anaconda: The anaconda always wins.

Don't toss out dead-looking plants.

Q After some of our cold winters, I never know **how long to wait before ripping out dead-looking plants**. Is there a way to tell whether they are still alive?

How long should one typically wait before giving up and composting them?

A After ice-cold weather, many of our plants resemble crispy critters. At the same time, some that don't look too bad may be goners. In spring it's difficult to tell which plants are fatally damaged and which will come back. Often, even if the top is killed, the plant may grow back from the roots. When it comes to cold-injured plants, patience is usually the best policy. Cut off obviously dead foliage, but if it's a valued plant, wait until at least mid-June to dig it out.

Turn off irrigation systems.

Q Are there any special preparations I need to make to my **irrigation system** to ready it for winter? I'm embarrassed to admit that I forgot to turn it off last year, and it ran all winter long. After paying the water bill, I won't make that mistake again, but is shutting it off all I need to worry about?

A Don't you feel like a noodle-head for forgetting to turn your irrigation system off? You're not alone. Last winter, while out for a late-night walk with my pup Fred, I slipped and almost landed on my kazutski. Someone's irrigation system had been running, and the sidewalk was a block of ice. Don't feel too bad, though. It's easy to forget to turn off the irrigation system, especially if it's set to go off in the middle of the night. Usually all that's required is to turn off the switch, but if you live where there are hard freezes, prevent pipes from breaking by hiring an irrigation specialist to blow out the lines. While you're at it, bring those hoses into the garage for the winter. Nothing destroys a hose faster than freezing and thawing through the winter. By the way, there's a trick to winding up the hose: Twist it as you pull, to make it form loops.

Water to try to prevent dieback on Japanese maples.

 Last summer a few branches on our prized **Japanese laceleaf maple** died, and the same thing happened again this year. A nursery person told us it has a fatal disease and we will have to remove it. Is there any way to be sure it really has the disease before taking such a drastic measure?

 Branch dieback on a Japanese maple can be a sign that it is under attack by a serious soil-borne fungus called verticillium wilt. The symptoms include one or more dying branches with leaves that turn yellowish or brown and hang on for long periods. There is no cure for this disease, and maples suffering the symptoms are usually removed. But don't be in too much of a hurry to send your maple off to the dumpster. Drought or underwatering can cause similar symptoms. Cut off all of the dead wood and give your maple an inch of water a week via soaker hose. To find out how long to run the soaker, place a few plant saucers under the hose and time how long it takes to fill the saucers 1 inch full, and run the water for that amount of time each week. If drought was the cause, you will notice a marked reduction in branch dieback. If, on the other hand, dieback continues, think about replacing your Japanese maple with a tree that is immune to the disease, such as dogwood, birch, or any conifer.

Apply lime to your vegetable garden.

 I've heard it's important to add **lime** to one's vegetable garden from time to time. Why is it important? Does it matter what kind of lime? How much should I apply, and when should I do it?

 Vegetable gardens need a yearly application of lime to prevent calcium deficiency. It takes time for limestone to break down, so add lime in the fall so that the calcium will be active and available when plants need it for spring growth. Adding lime will also help keep the pH range close to neutral, which is best for most vegetables (except potatoes). Agricultural lime works great, but every fourth year, apply dolomite lime to add magnesium. Work in 10 pounds of lime per 100 square feet. Wait for a dry period before tilling in the lime: If you turn over wet ground, your soil might end up the equivalent of concrete.

Deter moles with Mint Mole Blaster.

Q I've tried everything from expensive vibrating machines to Juicy Fruit gum to rid my garden of moles, but nothing seems to work. I've heard traps are the best method, but I don't want to kill the moles, I just want them to go away. Do you have any suggestions for a **mole repellent** that really works?

A Gardeners are constantly searching for effective ways to rid their gardens of pesky moles. Most folk remedies fail to pass muster when tested by Washington State University scientists; but having said that, an increasing number of home gardeners tell me they've successfully repelled moles by using mint. I'm not guaranteeing anything, but you might as well give Mint Mole Blaster a try. Begin by running a couple of big handfuls of mint stems and leaves through the blender with just enough water to make slurry. Then mix the blended concoction into a large soup pot full of water and simmer for about thirty minutes. This will make a concentrate that can be diluted to make about six gallons of mole blaster. Whenever you detect mole activity, pour the diluted mixture into mole holes and around the surrounding area. Irrigate lightly after application if the soil is dry. The key to success seems to be persistence. The moles evidently hate the smell of mint—and if all goes well, the varmints will pack their bags and set up shop in your neighbors' gardens.

Encourage moss to grow in your lawn.

Q How do I get rid of the **moss** in my lawn? I have a shady lawn, and even though I use moss killer, the moss seems to come back faster than I can get rid of it.

A Grass hates shade and will thin out no matter what you do. Moss is opportunistic and colonizes where grass is thin. Can't beat it? Learn to love it. In the shade, moss is pretty, soft, and nice to lie on. To create more moss, when your partner is away, fill the blender one-third full with buttermilk. Add a handful of moss, fill to the top with water, and blend well. Pour the mixture where moss is desired. Keep the area moist, and in no time you'll enjoy a thick bed of moss. If your partner's eyes bug out after sipping their next milkshake, run!

Sharpen mower blades.

Q How often do you need to sharpen **mower blades**? I've noticed the top of the grass is turning brown. Is this something I can do myself, or should I take it to a mower shop?

A Dull mower blades tend to tear the grass rather than cut it cleanly, resulting in ugly brown-topped grass blades that are susceptible to disease. If you're a do-it-yourselfer, remove the blade and sharpen the beveled edge with a relatively coarse single-directional file. If you're mechanically challenged (like me), take the mower, or at least the blades, into a mower shop to have a pro do it. Always remove and secure the spark plug wire before you do anything under a mower: Turning the blade has the same effect as pulling the starter cord.

Shop until your mail carrier drops.

 What's the advantage of ordering plants by mail or online? I've never done it before.

A January has been proclaimed National Mail-order Gardening Month. According to the latest statistics, Americans are expected to spend $2.2 billion on mail-order plants, bulbs, seeds, tools, and other garden supplies this year. (Is that all? I spent at least half that on mail-order plants last year, and I spent the other half at the Northwest Flower and Garden Show!) Mail-order and online shopping is the only way to get some incredibly rare plants, so quit drooling over the catalogs and order as soon as they arrive, while an excellent selection is still available.

Mulch your garden.

Q I keep hearing that **organic mulch** is good for my garden. Why is it so important, and what kind do you recommend?

A A layer of mulch does much good in the garden. The soil surface will be 15 degrees cooler on a 90-degree day if it's covered with an inch of mulch. That means much slower evaporation and less-frequent watering. Mulch can also help keep weeds down, improve soil structure, and protect plants from winter cold. Which mulch is best depends on where you use it. Wood chips (available free from tree service companies) make great mulch. Chips don't tend to pack down or repel water, as do other, more uniform mulches. Wood chips have been found to greatly increase the numbers of soil mycorrhizae. These are fungi that play a key role by taking nutrients out of the soil and making them available to woody plants. Wood chips break down relatively quickly to form rich topsoil. The one problem with wood chips (or any raw organic substance), however, is that they must not be worked into or mixed with soil, or a serious nutrient deficiency will result. Therefore, compost is a better choice in any garden where plants are frequently moved or replaced. Digging and mixing in compost improves soil structure by increasing organic matter and boosting moisture and nutrient-holding capacities. Compost also helps aggregate fine soils, improving drainage. Hence, wood chips are the best choice in tree and shrub beds, while compost is usually a better choice for the perennial border or vegetable garden.

Give your plants some air.

Q **Every winter I move a number of semitender plants into my garage for the cold-weather season. But this year the leaves on many of my plants became moldy, and a few rotted. What caused a fungus to attack my overwintering plants?**

A If you overwinter evergreen plants in an unheated garage, a greenhouse, or even a sunroom, it's important to provide air circulation to prevent fungus diseases that thrive in moist, stagnant air. Use a fan to circulate the air through the foliage and to bring a fresh supply of carbon dioxide to the leaves. Another advantage of using a fan is that in an unheated space it helps keep temperatures stable by pulling warm air off the ceiling and distributing it evenly throughout the space. Make sure to use a big enough fan to move air throughout the entire area where your plants are spending the winter, but locate it far enough from the plants so that it won't blast the leaves off. Inexpensive, soft-wing fans, available online at www.charleysgreenhouse.com, are safe and quiet, yet can move air up to 30 feet. They come equipped with a clamp for easy attachment.

Use care when choosing materials for pathways.

Q My garden lacks structure. I'm thinking about adding a few **pathways** to break it into sections and to make it more accessible and interesting. What materials are the best to use for pathways?

A Constructing pathways adds structure by giving you something to plant around. Pathways enable you to enter the garden, to see and smell the plants up close, and to interact with the bugs and the birds. Pathways also add interest because they break the garden into sections, and you can give each section its own artistic composition. Choose pathway material carefully. Stepping-stones look great, especially if you fill the spaces between them with a spectacular array of low-growing treasures. They can become unsightly weed patches, however, if you don't keep open spaces filled with plants. Crushed rock is less attractive, and weeds thrive in it. Grass makes a good path, but it can invade and become like a weed in the garden, and it must have at least a half day of sun to remain thick and lush enough to take traffic and resist weeds. Hazelnut husks look great and pack down so hard that weeds rarely grow in them, but make sure the husks are packed down or surrounded by edging deep enough to prevent them from being kicked into the garden. If they build up in the garden, you'll soon find that you can't get a spade through the ground, and you'll end up with a dead zone where nothing will grow around the sides of the path.

Take steps in fall to reduce fungus problems next spring.

Q This spring some of the flowers on my **peony** never opened, and others that did open turned brown. During summer the leaves developed brown, dried-up-looking

spots. I tried watering more, but the problem only seemed to get worse. Is this a disease?

A It's highly likely that your peony has botrytis, a fungus disease that attacks a wide variety of perennials. Peonies are highly susceptible to the disease, which shows up in summer as dark brown, crispy spots on the leaves. In spring, if conditions are wet and rainy, infected flower buds turn black and never open; or if they do, the flowers turn brown. In the worst-case scenario, shoots rot at the base soon after they come up. Usually a dense, velvety gray mold covers the rotting portions. The fungus overwinters in plant debris. Remove all leaves and stems when the plant dies back in fall. Unless you are the world's best composter, send the foliage to a recycling facility equipped to deal with fungus. If the problem persists, you may need to move your peony to a location where there is more sun or better air circulation.

Don't despair if your partner is a lazy bum and won't help you garden. My wife is a great gardener, and we argued so much over what to plant, we finally had to divide the garden down the middle. When we have a visitor, we stand shoulder to shoulder and demand: "Which side's the best?" (And I'm positive that she's bribing them!)

Give aphids a bath.

Q I followed your advice and used one of the commercially available **pesticidal soaps** to kill aphids on my rose. It didn't work: I came back a week later, and the aphid population had doubled. Does pesticidal soap not work, or did I do something wrong?

A Pesticidal soap is a safe and environmentally friendly way to rid your plants of aphids. That fat little aphid on your plant already has a cluster of live young in her, however, and those have live young in them! Every baby that pops out of mama is capable of giving birth to clusters of live young within a week of being born if conditions are right. Pesticidal soap will kill only soft-bodied insects that are hit directly. Every aphid you miss will be popping out babies faster than I can eat brussels sprouts. Therefore, you need to come back and spray every two days (usually about three times) until the problem is under control. Soap can burn plants, so be sure to read the label for warnings regarding plants that should not be sprayed, and apply pesticidal soap only when the plant is not in sunshine.

Avoid planting *Photinia.*

Q Something is attacking my beautiful Photinia **hedge.** First little brown spots showed up on the leaves, and not long after that most of the leaves fell off. What is it, and how can I prevent it?

A *Photinia* × *fraseri* (Fraser photinia) is one of the most popular plants for use in evergreen hedges because it's fast growing and almost indestructible, and the 5-inch-long leaves turn a beautiful red when new growth appears in spring. Unfortunately its Achilles heel is a fungus disease called photinia leaf spot, which begins with ugly leaf spots and ends in leaf drop—resulting in a thin and unattractive plant. Although there are fungicides available to help prevent the disease, every spring several perfectly timed sprays are required to control it. So, it's better to choose a disease-resistant alternative. *Prunus lusitanica* (Portugal laurel) is rock tough; needs little water once established; and sports attractive dark green lustrous leaves, white flowers, and bright-red to dark-purple fruit. It grows equally well in sun or shade. Another good choice, although slower growing, is *Arbutus unedo* (strawberry tree). This extremely drought tolerant Mediterranean native features attractive reddish bark and interesting strawberry-like fruits that attract birds in winter. It also thrives in sun or shade. If you don't need a tall hedge for privacy, try *A. unedo* 'Compacta': It rarely exceeds 12 feet and will save you endless hours of pruning.

Plant those plants!

Q I've been to several plant sales and I've got a driveway full of **potted plants**, but the weather report is for rainy, yucky weather. How long can I wait before I plant them in the ground?

A The quickest way to murder a plant is to leave it sitting in the pot. Make a goal to have them all planted in a week. That way, at least a third will be planted by the end of summer.

Protect plants from the cold.

Q I'm new to gardening, but I'm getting into it big-time. I planted a variety of perennials and shrubs, but now I'm wondering if they will survive the winter. Will most plants survive if I leave them alone, or do I need to do something to **protect my plants during the winter**?

A In the Pacific Northwest, you never know what kind of winter we're in for. If we luck out with a normal winter, temperatures will rarely dip below 25 degrees, and most plants will sail right through. Occasionally we suffer an Arctic blast with temperatures in the low 20s or colder, however. That's capable of harming or even killing many relatively hardy plants such as ceanothus, phormium, evergreen penstemon, and most of the zone-challenged rare and expensive plants that are able to squeak by when our winters are warm. The first line of defense is to cover the roots with a heavy layer of mulch such as compost or wood chips. Many plants will survive if the roots don't freeze, even if the top is frozen. To protect top growth, put a few bamboo stakes around the plants. Then, if a killing frost is forecast, throw a sheet over the plant. Although it will raise temperatures only about 4 degrees, that's usually enough to get the plant through alive, and the stakes will prevent a heavy snowfall from flattening the plant. Pull the sheet off the minute the temperature rises above freezing; then keep your fingers crossed. You won't know for sure if it worked until next spring.

You can bring home a puppy and have your garden too (maybe).

Q It's your fault! My kids saw your puppies with you on TV, and now they demand one. I like dogs, but I'm fearful of what a puppy will do to my prize garden. How can you have a **puppy and still have a spectacular garden**?

A It's possible to bring home a new puppy and continue to have a beautiful garden, but it's important to plan ahead to prevent disaster. Before you bring your pup home, decide which areas are going to be off limits to him and then protect your prize garden by installing a fence to keep him out. I learned this the hard way: When I introduced my eleven-week-old puppy, Fred, to our garden, it took him about thirty seconds to wipe out my pea patch and dig out several newly planted (and expensive) trees. Admittedly, the fence is only a training aid, but it will give you an observable barrier to teach the little devil to stay out of the garden (at least until he sees a squirrel in the forbidden area). Also, make sure to give your puppy plenty of room to play and his own spot to dig and bury his treasures, but don't let him dig holes in your lawn. Freddy looked so cute when he dug his first hole in the grass, but now the lawn resembles a moon surface. Also, install a doggy door so that your pooch is not trapped for hours in the backyard. Lock him out and he'll soon find a way to amuse himself in your garden. Better he takes it out on the furniture. And take it from me: If you think one puppy is bad, wait until you see what happens if you adopt a sibling for your first one!

Rhody lace bugs don't like to shower.

Q Something is wrong with our **rhododendron**. The leaves are turning sickly yellow and have a stippled appearance. What would be causing this, and how we can prevent it?

A Turn over the yellow, stippled leaves and look for tarry-brown spots. If you find them, look closely and you'll see a tiny bug with lacy transparent wings, known as the rhododendron lace bug. Most recommendations call for chemical pesticide applications in late spring when the nymphs (baby bugs) are present. Well-timed, powerful blasts of water, however, work just as well. Cup each leaf in your hand as you go so that you don't knock it off the plant, and blast the little troublemakers off the undersides of the leaves. It's best to start this process in May or June, but a few blasts in July or August will wipe out the present generation before they can lay eggs that overwinter on the veins under the leaves. If the problem persists, consider moving your rhododendron to a shadier location: The problem is much worse on rhododendrons growing in too much sun.

"To rototill or not to rototill" is a difficult question.

Q I'm an old-time vegetable gardener. When I moved into my home, the soil was horrible clay. Over the years I've tilled in compost, and now I have wonderful rich soil that grows spectacular vegetables. Recently I read that new research states that it's bad for your soil to **rototill**. My beautiful soil seems to disprove the theory. Which method do you recommend?

A Recent research does indeed state that you're better off avoiding the rototiller. Instead, apply a layer of compost and plant directly into it. Applying compost on the soil surface will work well if you already have good soil; the mulch cover will help conserve moisture, suppress weeds, and, over time, improve structure. In poor soil conditions, however, applying compost only on the surface has drawbacks. Compost holds too much moisture, and root problems are likely to occur in plants growing in it. Also, applying a layer of compost on the soil surface will do little to improve clay soils, and it will take years before any improvements are realized. A better solution is to fork in amendments in fall, when conditions are dryer, using a digging fork. Forking in the amendment will also make a much bigger difference in improving aggregation and soil structure. Forking in composted organic material will greatly increase the number of beneficial organisms in the soil, too. It's a lot of work, but in a few years you'll have a soil that would make even an old-time gardener proud.

Behead promiscuous plants.

Q I spent a mint for a fancy kind of mullein at a plant sale last year, and the following spring it came up everywhere. How can you tell if the plant you buy is going to seed itself all over your garden?

A You're not the only one this has happened to. Being a real sucker for the newest rare plant, one year I spent $22 for a *Euphorbia dulcis* 'Chameleon' in a 4-inch pot. It was a real show-stopper with red leaves and chartreuse flowers. Unfortunately, it also turned out to be quite a self-seeder. The next spring, I had about 8 million of the little red plants coming up all over my garden. I went back to the nursery, and the same plant cost $1.95! It's hard to know which plants are going to seed all over and cause problems, especially if you're into planting the newest and rarest plants you can find. You learned the hard way, like I did. The only real solution is to watch carefully to see which plants tend to seed too readily, and either yank them out or cut off the spent flowers before they go to seed and become a nuisance.

Turn your friends on to slime mold.

Q Help! I noticed some kind of **slimy, iridescent goober** on my lawn—and it's moving! How can I destroy this alien life force before it takes over the earth?

A Not everyone gets to experience the thrill of discovering a gooey, quivering, psychedelic blob moving across their lawn! Don't panic: That slimy, amoeba-like creature isn't an alien life form—it's slime mold! The brightly colored, pulsating, jellylike mass comes in a variety of iridescent colors ranging from orange, red, or yellow to brown, black, blue, or white. Slime mold consists of hundreds of thousands of harmless mold cells that group together to form a mass that can grow as large as 14 inches in diameter. Each cell contains tiny microfilaments that act as muscles, enabling the blob to crawl at a rate of about $\frac{1}{25}$ of an inch per hour in search of their favorite snacks, including decaying vegetation, bacteria, fungi, and other slime molds. Slime molds are perfectly harmless to humans, animals, and plants, although they can turn grass yellow by blocking out light to the blades. The blob will disappear as soon as drier weather returns, but if you need to move it, don't spray it with a hose in wet weather; that'll only spread it around. Instead, rake it up and disperse it in an out-of-the-way location. Better yet, take friends out with a flashlight and watch them run screaming when they discover the quivering alien life form.

Throw a party for the slugs.

 I heard that you can trap slugs with beer. How do I do that?

Slugs are party animals, but they don't know when to say when. Entice them to a last drink at Slimy's Saloon by putting out cottage cheese containers filled with about a half inch of beer. (I like to use German beer, or cheap beer with a German name, because it makes the slugs yodel.) The goal is to get the slugs to stop at happy hour on the way to dinner, so put three beer containers around each plant you're trying to protect. If the beer disappears unusually fast, and your puppy Fido has a silly grin on his face, cut 1-inch holes near the top of the container, and put a heavy stone on top of the lid.

Stay away from poisonous slug and snail baits.

I've heard that slug baits containing metaldehyde are unsafe to use around pets. I've raised dogs for years, and I've never had a problem. I find it hard to believe that it is really that bad. Am I really risking my pets' health by using my favorite slug bait?

Despite warnings that bait containing metaldehyde is dangerous to animals, many folks still use it to try to control slugs and snails. Metaldehyde is poisonous, and every year it kills dogs, cats, birds, and many other wild creatures. According to Todd Tams, chief medical officer for VCA Animal Hospitals, one of the biggest veterinary chains in the nation, many of their animal hospitals report treating as many as three dog slug-bait poisonings per week. My puppy Ruby was one of those statistics a while back, when she slipped her collar and ran away from us. By the time we caught her, she had eaten a few mouthfuls of metaldehyde slug bait that had been liberally applied in a neighbor's backyard. Thanks to prompt treatment at the vet's, she survived the experience. Don't risk your pets' lives: Use one of the newer, safer slug baits such as Sluggo, WorryFree, or EscarGo, which use iron phosphate as their main ingredient (see below).

Try out the newer, safer slug baits.

Q I recently moved here from the Midwest. Let me tell you, back there we had no idea what **slugs** were like. I've since learned that these slimy buggers are eating machines, and they always seem to find my most expensive plants! I read the warnings on some of the packages of slug bait, and with two young children and a dog, I'm terrified to use them. Is there anything safe that will control these monsters without endangering my kids and pet?

A The traditional slug baits are dangerous and can harm birds, pets, and children if ingested. You're wise not to use them. Try one of the newer, much safer products, such as Sluggo, WorryFree, or EscarGo, all of which contain the active ingredient iron phosphate. This stuff really works. You won't see the slugs die, but the eating will stop. It's registered for use in the vegetable garden and can be used safely around edible plants. One woman selling it at the Northwest Flower and Garden Show was actually eating it to show how safe it is! Now that I think about it, I haven't seen her since then. . . .

Safe slug bait needs moistening in dry weather.

Q I tried one of the safer **slug baits** that you recommend. It seemed to work fine in spring, but in the heat of summer it failed, and slugs devoured one of my prize hostas. What went wrong? I used the same amount and applied it the same way. If the safer kind works, I'd rather use it, but I don't want to lose any more of my plants.

A You're in luck—I know why the slug bait didn't work for you. Sluggo, WorryFree, and EscarGo, the newer and safer slug baits, need to be moistened in dry weather to make them attractive to the slugs and snails that are out doing nasty deeds in your garden during the night. Once it's moist, these marauding mollusks can't seem to resist the stuff. So wet down the bait before you go to bed, and you'll soon be saying "*Hasta la vista*, baby!" to slugs and snails.

Don't let slugs make wedding vows in your garden.

Q Is it necessary to use **slug baits** in autumn, or do slugs die in the winter?

A Adult slugs often die if the winter is cold. That doesn't really matter, however, because fall is the season for slug love. (Slugs are hermaphroditic, which means that each slug is both male and female. When they mate, both become pregnant and can lay up to a hundred eggs each.) Apply one of the safer slug baits (see opposite) in autumn to eliminate the critters; otherwise, those hundreds of eggs will overwinter and hatch to make your life miserable next spring.

Try biological snail control, and *Bon appétit*!

Q This year for the first time, I found **snails** in my garden. How did they get there, and how can I get rid of them? Is there a way to do them in without using slug bait?

A Common garden snails were brought to California in the 1850s as a source of *escargots*. Whoever introduced them should have been taken out and shot. They quickly spread to become a serious garden pest from California to British Columbia. Like slugs, garden snails are hermaphroditic. When they mate, both become pregnant and capable of laying about a hundred eggs each. It's important to deal with these potential baby factories before they build up huge populations in your garden. Use one of the newer, safer slug baits (see page 274), or try the only effective biological control: Boil for about fifteen minutes, constantly clearing off the scum that forms on the surface of the water. When the scum no longer forms, they're done! Add butter, garlic, and parsley, and serve with brussels sprouts.

Put a timer on your faucet.

Q I'm embarrassed to admit that I often forget to turn off the **sprinkler** when I'm gardening. I tried setting a timer, but if I don't turn off the water as soon as the timer rings, I get going on something else and forget. What tricks do you use to remember to turn off the hose?

A I recently talked with a friend who accidentally left a soaker hose running; he left for a weekend trip and returned to find his basement flooded 3 feet deep. Even if you run oscillating sprinklers, it's easy to forget about them. You may want to look into the new, inexpensive timers that attach to the faucet and run without batteries. You'll find them at nurseries and garden centers. They are easy to set, and you'll feel great knowing that you aren't wasting water. And believe me: It's much more enjoyable to wade at the beach than through your flooded basement.

The tent caterpillars are coming.

Q While doing a little winter gardening, I found a number of **Styrofoam-looking bands** on the twigs of several of my trees. The bands were an inch or so wide, sort of shiny grayish brown and flat, almost encircling small branches. It looks as though someone stuck their old chewing gum on the branches. Do I have to worry about these strange things?

A What you found are tent caterpillar egg cases. Each egg case contains about two hundred caterpillars, enough to possibly defoliate the average-sized tree. The caterpillars hatch around the time the leaves open, and soon weave the familiar web that covers large areas of the tree. Fortunately, now that you've discovered the egg cases, you can practice one easy technique for preventing insect infestation: Cut them out of the tree and destroy them before they hatch. Of course, if there are a great many egg cases in a large tree, cutting them out may be impossible. A commercially available biopesticide, *Bacillus thuringiensis* (Bt), is a safe, naturally occurring bacteria that is very effective at controlling tent caterpillars. For Bt to be effective, the tent caterpillars must eat leaves that have been sprayed with it. They will die within two days or so. Bt affects only caterpillars, so even if a bird eats infected larvae, it will not be harmed. Bt works best when the caterpillars are newly hatched. Sun breaks down the bacteria, so if possible, apply Bt on a cloudy day with no rain. Despite the fact that tent caterpillars often show up in huge numbers, there is no need to panic. A healthy tree can withstand the loss of a third of its foliage without suffering lasting damage, and even if a tree is defoliated, it will usually recover as long as defoliation does not happen two years in a row. Fortunately, tent caterpillar populations migrate and rarely cause serious damage for more than two years in a given area.

Garden naked to celebrate the summer solstice.

Q The **summer solstice** is my favorite day of the year. Is there anything unique you would recommend doing to celebrate this special day?

A Garden naked all day, get an even tan, and follow the ancient tradition of lighting a bonfire at sunset to thank the sun for solstice. Make a big brussels sprout casserole as an offering to the sun goddess, and to appease the police when they come to arrest you.

It takes time to establish drought tolerance.

Q I recently planted lavender and other Mediterranean plants, as well as some drought-tolerant trees, in my parking strip. I chose drought-tolerant plants because it's difficult for me to water the garden they're in, but now they're turning brown. Won't these plants grow without **supplemental watering**?

A No plant is drought tolerant until it establishes a deep, strong root system. Even plants such as lavender and rosemary must be given adequate water for the first season after they're planted. Balled-and-burlapped trees and shrubs are the most susceptible to drought damage. Once the clay in the root ball dries out, it's practically impossible to get it moist again. Mulch and use soaker hoses to water right around the trunk. Sometimes it helps to punch small holes in the root ball to make sure water will penetrate. Once a healthy root system is developed, plants known for drought tolerance will need little more to drink than Mama Nature offers. Slowly wean your herbs and Mediterranean plants off regular watering, but keep an eye on them. If they wilt, that means the roots are not sufficiently established, and you'll need to keep nurturing them a little longer before turning off the tap.

Look before you spray.

Q My trees are infested with **tent caterpillars**. Do I have to spray to keep them from harming my trees?

A Before you spray, look at the caterpillars to see if they have white tubular eggs, about one-sixteenth inch long, attached to their bodies. If so, that's good news for you. The eggs are from a beneficial insect called a tachinid fly, which looks like a housefly. When the eggs she attaches to the caterpillar hatch, the maggot will bore its way inside the caterpillar, eating the unessential organs first, then doing the caterpillar in. If you notice that about a third of the caterpillars have eggs on them, don't spray. Instead, let Mama Nature take care of the problem for you, and be happy that you aren't a caterpillar.

Do the sprinkler test.

Q I'm at a loss to know how often to **water my lawn**, and how long to let the sprinkler run. Are there some general guidelines I can use? I don't want to waste water, but I do want an attractive, green lawn.

A Lawns generally need only 1 inch of water per week, even in the hottest weather. To figure out how long to run your sprinkler, place a few equal-sized cottage cheese containers or houseplant saucers on the lawn. Use an indelible pen to mark an inch up from the bottom of the container. Time how long it takes for the majority of the containers to fill to the mark. That's how long you need to run your sprinkler each week to provide an inch of water. One application per week is best, but if you have clay soil or a sloping lawn, you might want to apply half the amount two times per week.

Let sleeping lawns lie.

Q It's the middle of summer, and my lawn looks like a desert scene from *Lawrence of Arabia*. Will **watering** turn it from brown to green again?

A I've seen water running on a lot of brown lawns in midsummer, but it's not a good idea. Once the lawn has turned brown, it's dormant. It would take at least two weeks of watering every night to bring it back to active growth and start the greening process. That would be a tremendous waste of water. It won't do any harm to let your grass remain dormant until fall. Wait to water until mid-September, and then fertilize with an organic lawn fertilizer. Apply about an inch of water a week if it isn't raining; however, chanting to the rain goddess wouldn't hurt. Your lawn will gradually green up, and you won't have to worry about wasting water or paying an incredibly high water bill.

Inspect irrigation systems.

Q I have an automatic **watering system** and water only at night, and I've done the saucer test to make sure that I'm applying 1 inch of water per week. Yet some of my plants, and a few areas of the lawn, are turning brown and don't look as if they are getting adequate water. What's wrong?

A A visit to your garden in the middle of the night, when the irrigation is running, might give you the answer. On one of my wee-hour-of-the-morning walks through the neighborhood, I noticed that a number of sprinkler heads on a neighbor's automatic irrigation system were aimed in the wrong direction and were watering the sidewalk rather than the flowerbed. Ironically, I'm certain that this problem was going unnoticed because the system ran only at night or early in the morning, in an effort to do the right thing and avoid wasting water. Fortunately, you don't have to go out and check it at night. Inspect your automatic irrigation system by firing it up in daylight at least once a month to check if there are broken or clogged heads and that everything is working correctly. Wear your swimming suit. This is a perfect excuse for running through the sprinkler while you are making repairs and adjustments.

Water new plants regularly.

Q I put in a new landscape this spring, but some of the plants are suffering. I followed the instructions and planted them during the rainy season. Do I need to **water these new additions?**

A It may seem as though the rain will never stop, but the ground warms and dries out rapidly after only a few dry days in spring. The key to healthy plants is to make sure they get adequate water until they have established a healthy, strong root system. A newly planted tree, shrub, perennial, or vegetable may be harmed, and may never fully recover, if the soil is allowed to dry out after planting.

Thirsty trees don't go dormant in summer.

Q I stopped **watering** and let my grass go dormant this summer, but now the tree growing in the brown lawn isn't looking that great. It seems to be turning fall colors early and has a lot of dead branches. I thought that big established trees don't need extra watering. What's up?

A Your lawn can go dormant in summer without lasting harm, but trees can't. When you notice your tree turning color early or, worse yet, if you see branch dieback, your tree is telling you it's in trouble. All trees, even well-established big ones, need water in a dry summer. The best way to water a tree is with a soaker hose. Wrap the hose in concentric circles, starting around the trunk and working outward toward the edge of the canopy. To find out how long to run your soaker, place a few plant saucers under the tree and time how long it takes to fill most of them 1 inch deep. That's how long you should run the soaker once per week during hot dry weather. Don't buy a soaker hose that's too long; anyone who can manage to lay out a 75-foot soaker hose without kinks is in the wrong profession, and would be much better off making a living wrestling anacondas.

Some plants are big drinkers.

Q OK, wise guy. I hear you tell us that we should locate plants together according to their **water needs**. Then I see you and Meeghan Black on TV planting a water-guzzling ligularia in an area filled with lavenders and rosemary. Don't you follow your own rules? Besides, won't providing the water that these thirsty plants need harm the drought-tolerant ones growing next to them?

A Do as I say, not as I do. I know that I've advised you to plant all of your moisture-loving plants together. However, my drought-tolerant border just wouldn't be as impressive without the spectacular foliage of a few thirsty but beautiful plants such as ornamental rhubarb (*Rheum palmatum*), *Ligularia dentata*, or the colorful leaves of an easily parched bugbane (*Cimicifuga simplex* 'Variegata'). Sometimes you just can't resist adding a moisture lover or two to the dry border. If you irrigate to provide for the drinking habits of your guzzling specimens, however, you'll not only waste valuable water but also cause root rot and other calamities among the plants that prefer dry soil. Instead, every morning, treat the big drinkers to happy hour by giving them a shot from the watering can. That will slake their thirst without giving their arid neighbors a drinking problem.

Baby, it's dry outside.

Q I know that from time to time we have water shortages in the Northwest, but I feel that I must water sometimes, or my plants might die. I use an oscillating sprinkler, but I have no idea if I'm **watering enough or too much**. How in the world does one figure that out?

A In the Pacific Northwest, it's usually feast or famine when it comes to rain. We get only about 7 inches all summer long, compared to approximately 20 inches during the same time period in Wischeescin, where I grew up. Watering is an absolute necessity, but it's important to do it right. Generally, it's better to water deeply and infrequently. Lawns and planting beds generally need only 1 inch of water per week. Put out a bunch of plant saucers or tuna cans, and mark 1 inch up from the bottom with indelible ink. Now run your sprinklers as you normally would, and time how long it takes to fill the majority of the saucers 1 inch full. That's how long you need to run your sprinklers each week to get 1 inch of water. If your lawn or beds slope, divide the time in half, and water twice per week. By the way, notice whether some of the saucers didn't get much water. Maybe that's why your plants in that area are doing poorly. You might need to move your sprinkler around more, or maybe it's time to replace that beat-up old sprinkler with a new one.

Take a few minutes to help protect the environment.

 I consider myself an environmentally conscientious gardener. I use organic fertilizers to help prevent leaching harmful chemicals into our water systems. Are there any concerns that I might not be aware of when I use these products?

 It's great to keep the environment in mind in our gardening practices. Although using organic fertilizers is much better than applying the synthetic ones, it's important to remember that any fertilizer that ends up on the sidewalk or in the street will be washed right down the storm drain and into our waterways. Once fertilizer finds its way into the water system, it can contribute to harmful algae blooms and other problems. A few minutes spent sweeping fertilizer off hard surfaces will help keep our waterways clean and clear.

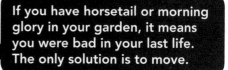

If you have horsetail or morning glory in your garden, it means you were bad in your last life. The only solution is to move.

Weeds are on the rampage.

 We had a wonderful, sunny spring, but now my garden is inundated with weeds. Is there anything I can do to make pulling them easier?

 Sunny spring weather causes perennials to grow fast and bloom earlier than usual, and it has the same effect on weeds. Fireweed, false dandelion, and many other undesirables mature at a record rate in sunny, dry conditions, and if you don't pull them before they go to seed, they will spew gazillions of seeds all over your garden. Grab your favorite weeding tool and eradicate those weeds before it's too late! It helps to water thoroughly, preferably in the morning, before you weed. Wait until the foliage dries, but do your weeding while the soil is still moist. Ideally, you'll be able to yank out the entire root without breaking it. Otherwise, you'll battle the same weed again a week or two later, when it reappears with a vengeance.

Giant hogweed is a pig.

Q A huge plant appeared out of nowhere in my garden this summer. It has enormous leaves, is about 15 feet tall, and bloomed with a big white flattened flower on top. What is this thing? It's an impressive plant, but I'm worried that it might be a **weed** that could take over my garden.

A The plant that appeared in your garden is known as giant hogweed. With compound leaves sometimes reaching 5 feet wide, and purple-blotched stems reaching as high as 15 feet, topped by huge umbels of white flowers, giant hogweed (*Heracleum mantegazzianum*) is an impressive sight in the garden. This is one plant you don't want around, however. It is listed as a Class A noxious weed (that is, a nonnative species designated for eradication) by the state noxious weed control board in every state where it has been found. Giant hogweed has sap that can cause severe burns on bare skin, particularly when the skin is exposed to sunlight. It often shows up unexpectedly in shady, moist areas, probably having escaped from gardens. Don't wait too long to get rid of it. Once those big flowers go to seed, you'll have lots more to deal with. If you think you have this weed, call your county noxious weed control program. They'll discuss safe, environmentally friendly ways to rid your garden of this menace.

Make gardening a healthy activity.

Q Lately I've been questioning the safety of using Weed and Feed and other chemical **weed killers** on my lawn and in my gardens. Are these products safe? Is there a way to get rid of them if I don't want to use them anymore?

A At an integrated pest management conference, I learned that the Canadian province of Quebec banned the use of several commonly used pesticides containing 2,4-D, including Weed & Feed, for use on home lawns. The government enacted the ban as a result of a public grassroots movement spawned by studies that linked the use of a number of pesticides to potential health problems. The citizens were especially concerned by findings that children have increased vulnerability to toxic pesticides. A recent poll found that 85 percent of the folks in Quebec are in favor of the ban. Maybe it's time for each of us to ban the use of toxic pesticides in our own gardens. Contact your city or county government to find out how to safely dispose of hazardous waste in your community.

Check trees for girdling wires.

Q Several years ago, a landscape company planted some trees around our home. The trees were staked at the time, but the **wire loops** were never removed from around the trees. Some wires are cutting into the trunks, and in a few cases the tree seems to have grown over the wire. Is this a problem? Should I try to remove the wires?

A Wires used to stake trees should always be removed after one year, or sooner if the wire is becoming tight or cutting into the tree. Left on too long, staking wires can create a girdling effect. Girdling weakens the tree in two ways. First, it blocks nutrients from reaching the roots, stunting root growth and reducing stability. Second, although the tree may grow around the wire, the girdled area often creates a weak spot where the tree could break in a windstorm or during a heavy snow. If the wires are just beginning to cut in or can be removed without severely damaging the bark, it's best to remove them. If the wire is entrenched in the trunk, however, and the tree is located where it could fall or cause damage to your house or your neighbor's house, call in a certified arborist to inspect it and to determine if it's a potential hazard.

Try worm composting.

Q I heard that it's better to use a **worm box** than to bury kitchen scraps in my compost pile. What is a worm bin? Is it something I can buy? Also, does it require special worms? If so, where do you buy them?

A Worm composting is really fun, especially if you have kids or are a gardening nerd like me. You can build your own worm composter (free instructions at www.seattletilth.org), or you can use practically any size wood or plastic container. Drill plenty of drainage holes in the bottom, and make sure there's a tight-fitting lid to keep moisture in and pests out. You'll need red worms, also available from Seattle Tilth, at local nurseries, or online at www.gardens-alive.com. Give them a nice bed of moist shredded newspaper or leaves. Every three to six weeks, move the compost to one side and add new bedding; then bury food wastes in the new bedding only. Within a month, all the worms will move into the new bedding and you'll be able to harvest the rich worm compost. The worms will eat almost any kitchen scrap. Avoid the usual suspects that you wouldn't put into an outdoor compost pile, such as meat, cheese, and carnivorous-animal wastes. You'll be amazed how fun it is to watch the worms at work, and what wonderful compost you'll get from your bin. Although you'll grow fond of them, don't worry about naming all of the worms. I tried it, and there are just too many of them!

Worm power!

Q Now I've heard everything. I understand how cow manure can improve structure and add nutrition to soil, but **worm manure**? Is this stuff as good as I've heard?

A Red wigglers are the new gardening superstars! Their castings (worm poop) are rich in plant nutrients, trace minerals, and growth enhancers, and incorporating castings into the soil significantly increases microbial life in the root zone. Now available in nurseries and garden stores, red wiggler worm castings have an NPK ratio of about 3.2-1.1-1.5. Nutrients are readily available, yet the castings are incapable of burning plants. The odorless castings have a consistency similar to peat. Work them into new plantings as you would compost to improve soil structure, and to increase moisture and nutrient-holding capacity. In existing perennial borders, in vegetable gardens, and around fruiting trees and shrubs, apply castings 1 inch deep in spring, and work them into the soil 3 inches deep. The castings will provide all of the fertilizer that most of your plants will need for the season. To help bring dried-out lawns out of dormancy, top-dress in fall, when the lawn shows signs of greening up, with a quarter-inch layer of castings. The fall rains will wash the minerals and nutrients into the root zone, and the microorganisms will help bring depleted soils back to life.

CHAPTER SIX

Birds, Bugs, and Butterflies

Plant a winter's feast for the Anna's hummingbird.

Q I recently learned that the **Anna's hummingbird** remains in the Northwest during the winter months, so there must be plants that bloom in winter and provide a food source. What can I plant to provide food and keep them in my garden during winter?

A It's true that the Anna's hummingbirds remain in the Northwest during winter. They need to eat half their weight every day to survive, so help them out while enjoying their company by planting trees and shrubs that will provide nectar in winter when they need it most. Many of the flowering plants frequented by hummingbirds in summer, such as hardy fuchsia, *Salvia* 'Black and Blue', and *Abutilon* (flowering maple) continue to flower into January and beyond if temperatures stay relatively mild. In the heart of winter, *Mahonia* × *media* (hybrid leatherleaf mahonia), *Grevillea*, witch hazel, *Lonicera fragrantissima* (winter honeysuckle), *Daphne bholua* (Himalayan daphne), *Viburnum bodnantense*, *Chimonanthus praecox* (wintersweet), and *Schizostylis coccinea* (crimson flag) serve up nectar-rich blossoms. Beginning in February, you'll find the Anna's congregating at the blossoms of *Sarcococca* (sweet box), *Daphne odora*, flowering currant, Darwin barberry, and quince. These colorful additions will not only keep your hummingbirds fat and happy but will also add color and interest to your winter garden.

Don't kill those bald-faced hornets.

Q There's a big paper nest in my rhododendron that I've been told is a **bald-faced hornets' nest**. Are these insects beneficial or dangerous?

 Bald-faced hornets are beneficial. They look like large black yellow jackets with white spots on their heads and fannies, and they build their paper wasp nests in trees and shrubs such as rhododendrons. These aren't the guys that bother your picnics; however, they pack a powerful sting, and are capable of stinging over and over again if they sense that the nest is threatened. Fortunately, they rarely sting away from the nest, and they eat many of the bugs that cause harm to plants in our gardens. For fun, watch them hover just above the lawn looking for crane flies. The crane fly hides in the grass waiting for a chance to lay her eggs. If Madame Bald-faced Hornet spots a crane fly taking off, she will swoop down and bite the crane fly's head off in midair. All you'll hear is an "Eek!" Then she'll bite the wings and legs off, and it's back to the nest for a barbecue. Put up warning signs and barricades to make sure the dog and kids can't get near the nest. Then, instead of watching nature on public TV, go out and watch the real thing in your own backyard.

Slugs are party animals. Entice them to a last drink at Slimy's Saloon by putting out cottage cheese containers filled with about a ½ inch of beer. If the beer disappears unusually fast, and Fido has a silly grin on his face, cut 1-inch holes near the top of the container and put the lid on with a heavy stone on top.

Don't tempt "eek-squish bugs" to go off the wagon.

Q I often see **big black iridescent beetles** running out of my garden when I'm working in it, and I find dead ones in the beer traps I set out for slugs. Are these beetles good or bad bugs?

A Local entomologist Sharon Collman nicknamed those shiny black inch-long ground beetles "eek-squish" bugs because that's what folks do to them when they see them run out from under cover. Eek-squish bugs have bad breath, but it's not because they don't brush their teeth. They eat slugs! Most eat slug eggs and cutworms, but you haven't lived until you go out at night to see the type of ground beetle known as the slug destroyer eat 4- or 5-inch slugs. It's more exciting than anything on the Discovery Channel! Avoid burying beer traps at ground level; the beetles will be tempted to stop in for a drink and will suffer the same fate as the slugs you're trying to get rid of. Instead, cut four 1-inch holes just below the lid of a cottage cheese container and place the traps on top of the ground. The beer-loving slugs will still crawl in for happy hour, but the beetles can't get in to join the party.

Invite your bird friends to the spa.

Q My **birdbaths** turn to ice in freezing weather. The birds seem to get agitated when this happens. Is it best to let the water freeze, or do birds need water during freezing periods?

A It's important to provide water for birds during freezing weather. During a recent cold snap, I was surprised to hear a bunch of my bird friends peeping at me through the window. I'm positive they were telling me to get off my hinder and give them a drink. Audubon and wild bird stores carry birdbath heaters that provide just enough warmth to prevent the water from freezing, or you can bring out shallow bowls of water from time to time. Keep the water flowing, and you won't have noisy birds vying for your attention.

Give the birds a safe drink.

Q I've got an embarrassing problem. I feed birds, but I've noticed that the **bird feeders are attracting rats!** My wife says I should stop feeding the birds, but I don't want my bird friends to leave. Any suggestions?

A Don't be embarrassed. Rats are a big problem. The only way to deter the rats is to stop feeding the birds. I stopped feeding birds when I discovered that it was attracting rats at my house as well. I shared your concern that all my bird friends would leave, but luckily only the rats left and my garden still resembles an aviary. What attracts birds is fresh, clean water to drink and bathe in. Birdbaths should be cleaned and refilled every day. Watching birds frolicking in the tub makes for great entertainment. Just remember to place the bath where birds of prey can't get a straight shot at it. It's hard to relax in the tub if you know a big old hawk might snatch you up at any minute.

Get over your arachnophobia.

Q I've heard experts (you in particular) say that spiders are beneficial and, at least for the most part, need not be feared. Then I hear all sorts of wild stories about people being bit by **brown recluse spiders**. Is there any way to learn if all, or any, of these scary stories are true?

A There are brown recluse spiders in Washington State; when you wake up with a bug bite, the culprit was likely a spider; daddy longlegs have a deadly bite, but their fangs are too short to pierce human skin—these are just a few of the myths and misconceptions that Burke Museum spider expert Rod Crawford debunks in his informative and entertaining Spider Myths website. (To check it out, visit www.washington.edu/burkemuseum/spidermyth.) But no matter what Rod says, I'll always believe the story about the potted cactus that exploded and shot baby tarantulas all over someone's house.

Invite bumblebees to your garden.

Q I've heard that **bumblebees** are good pollinators. Is there a way to get them to nest in my garden?

A Last spring I opened the clean-out door on my birdhouse, only to be surprised by a charge of agitated bumblebees. The fattest one bumped me on the end of my nose and hovered between my eyes, as if to say that he wouldn't hurt me if I didn't harm any of his posse. As summer progressed, my fuzzy friends and I became close friends. These gentle creatures sting only if they feel threatened. It was great fun watching them come and go from their converted bee condo, buzzing about on their endless mission to find pollen. You're wise to invite bumblebees to make a home in your garden, especially if you grow vegetables and fruit. Bumblebees are among nature's best pollinators. Make a nesting box by filling an old birdhouse or tin can with soft, non-glass insulating material, piles of grass clippings, or well-dried leaves. Place the nesting boxes in a shady, protected site. If you're lucky, a queen will decide to move in and you too will have fuzzy friends to share your garden with all summer.

Don't invite butterflies to your wedding.

Q I'm getting married soon, and I've heard that the new trend is to release **butterflies** at the end of the wedding. It sounds really cool, but I want to make sure there aren't any problems with this practice before I decide to do it.

A I'm glad you asked, because it isn't a good idea at all. It sounds spectacular: Instead of guests throwing rice, butterflies are released to create a colorful display as they fly away into the sky. Unfortunately, according to the North American Butterfly Association, this practice can spread butterfly diseases and cause inappropriate genetic mixing of different populations. Often the butterflies are released during the wrong season, condemning them to a quick death, and the high prices that folks are willing to pay for the butterflies make them targets for poachers in their natural migration stops. For an unusual ritual, consider throwing brussels sprouts at the bride and groom instead.

Keep caterpillars out of a butterfly garden.

Q I want to design a **butterfly garden**, but I'm worried that the caterpillars will destroy my ornamental plants. Can I design a garden that will attract butterflies without creating caterpillar problems?

A Most of us invite butterflies into our garden, but we don't welcome butterfly caterpillars, for fear they'll harm our ornamental plants. Only about one in a hundred butterflies make it from the egg to adulthood, so if we want to enjoy butterflies, we need to create gardens that provide for the caterpillars as well as the adults. Most butterfly caterpillars prefer native plants and will turn up their noses at your expensive ornamentals. Even if they do choose one of your favorites, the damage is almost always purely aesthetic, and your plant will recover just fine. The Brooklyn Botanic Garden's *Butterfly Gardener's Guide* is filled with fascinating information about butterflies and describes how to design attractive gardens that will entice and provide for butterflies as well as their offspring.

Plant a butterfly garden in a container.

Q Mom loves butterflies, but she lives in an apartment and can garden only in pots on her balcony. I have this crazy idea of planting a **butterfly container garden** to surprise her on Mother's Day. Can a container garden attract butterflies?

A You can definitely attract butterflies to plants in a container. You'll need a good-sized pot in a sunny spot protected from wind. Butterflies are attracted to nectar-producing flowers, but each kind of butterfly has its own preference, so plant a variety of nectar-rich plants to increase your chances of attracting many butterfly species. Here are a few good choices: *Scabiosa* (pincushion flower), *Echinacea* (coneflower), *Rudbeckia* (black-eyed Susan), *Coreopsis* (tickseed), hibiscus, rosemary, verbena, and lavender. Butterflies also like to drink out of puddles. Bury a cup up to its rim in the planter, fill it with sand, and then keep it filled with liquids. Butterfly favorites include stale beer, fruit juice, and water. Now and then stick a chunk of overripe fruit among the plants for a special treat. For an extra surprise, give mom a butterfly identification guide to go along with her butterfly container garden.

Crocosmias are hot!

Q I'm looking for plants that will attract hummingbirds, and a friend suggested *Crocosmia*. I'm not the world's greatest gardener. Is this an attractive plant that is easy to grow? It won't take over my yard, will it?

A If you plant crocosmias, you'll not only attract hummingbirds but add dazzling color to your garden as well. Although they are native to South Africa, most crocosmias are hardy in the Northwest, easy to grow, and well behaved in borders and perennial gardens. With sword-shaped leaves, crocosmias are sculptural perennials, but their raison d'être has to be the colorful blooms that come in fiery shades of orange, red, and yellow. Hummingbirds can't resist temptation once they see the flaming scarlet petals brandished by *Crocosmia* 'Lucifer'. This variety can reach 4 feet tall and often needs staking. Growing almost as tall, the newly introduced 'Star of the East', another hummingbird favorite, wins bragging rights for its enormous gold-orange flowers, which are the biggest in the genus. The most elegant *Crocosmia* hybrid is 'Solfatare'. The smoky bronze foliage acts as a gorgeous foil for the rich apricot-yellow flowers. Unlike most of the other varieties, 'Solfatare' reaches only 3 feet tall and rarely needs staking. Crocosmias generally perform best in full sun and require dividing in spring every few years if flowering diminishes. The only crocosmia to avoid is the ubiquitous orange-flowering *Crocosmia* × *crocosmiiflora*, known as montbretia. It's an over-rambunctious spreader that tends to be invasive, and it stops blooming unless it is divided at least every other year.

Got flies? Here's a beautiful way to repel them.

 I'm embarrassed to ask this, but how do you keep flies out of the house? For some reason they love coming into and flying around in my house. You can imagine how that makes me feel when company comes over. Is there anything that will repel them?

 Don't be embarrassed; you're not the first one to ask that question. On my "Gardening with Ciscoe Live" show for the Northwest Cable News station, a caller asked me the same question. Other than using window screens, I had little to provide as a solution. Then, by coincidence, the next caller happened to be an Austrian woman who offered that the real reason why Austrians plant pelargoniums (Martha Washington geraniums) in their window boxes is because they are an attractive way to repel flies. I admit I was dubious, but decided to try it. Pesky little flies used to swarm in circles between my house and garage, embarrassing the tweetle out of me whenever someone came to see my garden. After I planted the pelargoniums, the flies disappeared. Try planting a bunch of Martha Washington geraniums in your window boxes and anywhere you have fly problems, even in the house. Even if it doesn't work, maybe the visitors will notice the beautiful flowers instead of the flies.

Fountains attract sensitive birds.

I love the birds in my garden. I'm thinking about putting in a fountain. Will a fountain attract more feathery friends to my garden?

Nothing attracts birds more than water to drink and bathe in. Fountains look great, but the best feature is the sound of falling water. It's not only soothing to humans but attractive to birds as well. In my garden, the Barkman fountain is my favorite. Created by the Bainbridge Island artists Little and Lewis (www.littleandlewis.com), the Barkman is a wizened old man's face that shoots water into a basin. The hummingbirds begin drinking at Barkman's mouth and ride the water down to the basin. It's fun to watch, but don't laugh at them. I did, and Hanna whacked me in the ear with her wing as she flew by!

Attract beneficial insects.

Q I keep hearing that having **good bugs** in your garden reduces insect problems. That's all well and good, but I don't seem to have many of the good critters, and the one time I tried buying and releasing them, they just flew away. How can I attract beneficial insects to come do their good deeds in my garden?

A You're right: It rarely works to release beneficial insects in your garden. The good guys almost always fly away. But you can attract the good bugs by adding perennials known to entice them into your garden. Plants that lure beneficials offer pollen or nectar favored by the adults. Perennials that are magnets for good bugs include yarrows, angelicas, monardas, potentillas, dahlias, daisies, and asters. Beneficial insects really do significantly contribute to pest control. Some good bugs, like ladybugs, hoverflies, and lacewings eat up the bad bugs; others, like braconid wasps and tachinid flies, parasitize bad guys by laying eggs inside them. The eggs hatch and the newly hatched larvae munch their victims from the inside out! (Aren't you glad you're not a bug?) By the way, many other perennials—besides the ones listed above—attract beneficial insects. Keep an eye on your favorite plants, and if they're covered with beneficial bugs, plant more of the same and let the good guys do your pest control for you.

Keep the hummingbirds around in the winter.

Q I know you'll think I'm crazy, but I swear I saw a **hummingbird** in our garden this winter. As far as I can find out, no one in the neighborhood is feeding them, so what do they survive on? What can I plant to attract them to my winter garden?

A You saw an Anna's hummingbird. They tend to stay here during winter, and they are even more fascinating to watch in the off-season than in spring and summer. To attract them, plant shrubs and perennials that bloom with nectar-rich flowers in winter. Of the above-mentioned plants, fuchsias and flowering maples are alluring food sources that often continue to bloom until Christmas; the *Mahonia* hybrids 'Charity' and 'Winter Sun' bloom in the dead of winter. Another seductive perennial is *Schizostylis coccinea* (crimson flag). This 2-foot-tall South African native is totally hardy here, and in a mild winter the red or pink flowers may bloom all winter long. A surprising food source is witch hazel: Hummingbirds love the spidery flowers and rely on them for nourishment in midwinter. In late winter, they find sustenance in the fragrant flowers of *Sarcococca* and Darwin barberry. And if you want to hear your hummingbirds shout "Oh, la, la!," plant the Australian shrub *Grevillea* 'Canberra Gem' (I found mine at Jungle Fever Nursery in Tacoma, Washington). The dazzling red flower clusters last all winter and drive hummingbirds (and gardeners as well) into frenzies of crazed lust.

Have a personal encounter with a hummingbird.

Q I'm a bird lover with time and money on my hands. I've decided to redo one of my gardens as a **hummingbird garden**. What are some of your favorite plants that will attract these little acrobats? I have a lot of space, and I plan to use a variety of trees, shrubs, vines, perennials, and annuals.

A Great idea! Hummingbirds are so beautiful that the Mayans believed they were created from all the colorful scraps left over after making the other birds. The real fun comes, however, when you watch these fine-feathered mischief-makers doing aerial acrobatics and chasing each other around the garden in an endless mating game. In fact, you haven't lived until you've witnessed a male hummingbird doing his mating dance! A good list of the many plants that attract hummingbirds can be found in the *Sunset Western Garden Book*; below are a few of my favorites. These plants are so attractive to hummingbirds that you'll need to wear a hard hat when you walk in your garden.

Trees

Embothrium coccineum (Chilean fire bush): This tree will grow quickly to 30 feet tall, but it spreads to only about 8 feet wide. It grows fast; after four or five years, every May the entire tree will be covered with 1½-inch brilliant red tubular flowers. This plant hates pots. Do a web search, order it online, and plant it immediately in well-drained soil in a sunny location. Don't fertilize (this tree cannot tolerate added phosphorus); water as necessary to keep the soil moist, and be patient. I can almost guarantee that once it blooms, you'll be making friends with hummingbirds in your yard.

Shrubs

Abutilon (flowering maple): Native to South America, these showy members of the hibiscus family aren't reliably hardy. Plant them in containers to be moved indoors or into a bright unheated garage for the winter; or take your chances and plant them against a south wall, and leave them out over the winter. The flowers on these 6-foot-tall shrubs are bell shaped and come in a wide variety of colors. Best of all, these plants bloom all summer long, and in mild winters they sometimes continue to flower until spring. My favorite species is called *Abutilon megapotamicum*. One of the hardiest of the flowering maples, it sports red-and-yellow flowers that hummingbirds can't resist.

Buddleja (butterfly bush): These Chinese shrubs are in danger of being listed on the noxious weed list, but it's hard to find a shrub that is more attractive to hummingbirds, particularly the pink-flowering varieties. Stick with the hybrids to avoid the invasive tendencies. 'Harlequin' has attractive variegated leaves. My wife recently planted a variety with yellow leaves and purple flowers. (Sorry, she can't recall the name, but keep an eye out for it at quality nurseries.) Plant buddlejas exposed to full sun in almost any soil.

Fuchsia: There are many varieties that are hardy in the Pacific Northwest. The hardy varieties need full sun.

Grevillea victoriae and *G.* 'Canberra Gem': No one expected these southern Australia shrubs to be hardy in the Northwest, but they've not only survived but thrived in recent winters without showing the slightest damage. The gray-green conifer-like evergreen foliage on these 6-foot-tall shrubs is a delight, but the real show comes in winter. Grevillea blooms from October through April with clusters of brilliant red flowers that the overwintering Anna's hummingbirds lust after. Give these plants full sun and very well drained soil.

Lavnadula (lavender): No one believes that lavender is attractive to hummingbirds, but the fact remains that the little avian acrobats love the flowers. Lavender plants need full sun and good drainage. Don't forget to shear them back hard in spring.

Mahonia × *media*: The ones I recommend are hybrid relatives of Oregon grape, common in the Pacific Northwest. Although they look a bit like the grape, they are different in that the hybrids' foliage is more attractive and they bloom with huge yellow, fragrant flowers in the middle of winter. They are a major food source for the Anna's hummingbird, which overwinters in our region. A few of my favorite hybrids are 'Charity' and 'Arthur Menzies' (15 feet tall) as well as 'Lionel Fortescue' and 'Winter Sun' (6 feet tall). There are also two outstanding species of mahonia that are spectacular winter bloomers: *M. bealei* and *M. lomariifolia* (both 12 feet tall). Mahonias thrive in partial shade and well-drained soil.

Phygelius × *rectus* (Cape fuchsia): This South African shrub is often mistaken for a perennial. It may die back to the ground after a hard winter, but rises from the roots in spring to bloom with attractive fuchsia-like flowers that hummingbirds love. Flower color varies, but the red-flowering varieties are most attractive to hummingbirds. Look for new introductions with yellow leaves and red flowers, but don't pass up my favorite green-leaved introduction, called 'Sensation'. The magenta flowers truly are sensational. *Phygelius* prefers full sun but will grow and bloom in partial shade.

Ribes sanguineum (red flowering currant): Native to the coast from British Columbia to California, this shrub usually reaches about 6 feet tall. Hummingbirds returning after winter migration seek out its red flowers, which appear in clusters in early spring. Planted in morning sun or bright shade in well-drained soil, this low-maintenance plant is drought resistant and is rarely bothered by insects or disease.

Weigela: Give these old-time plants another try. There are incredible new varieties with fantastic flowers and colored foliage. Check out *W.* 'Wine and Roses', with dark foliage; *Weigela* 'Looymansii Aurea', with yellow and red foliage; and *W. florida* 'Variegata', with spectacular variegated leaves.

Annuals, Perennials, and Vines

Agastache (hyssop): These members of the mint family bloom all summer long with spectacular flowers that hummingbirds and gardeners can't resist. Depending on the species, they come in all sorts of colors, including pink, apricot, and blue. Full sun and great drainage are required. Hyssops are not always hardy. Look for seedlings, which often show up in spring.

Aquilegia (columbine): I know, these native plants seed around and become a pest. Hey, a pest that's a magnet for hummingbirds—that I can live with. Besides, the seedlings are easy to pull if they come up where you don't want them. Columbines perform best in semishade.

Crocosmia: These incredibly colorful and easy-to-grow perennials bloom in mid- to late summer and drive hummingbirds mad with desire. The most attractive to hummingbirds is *C.* 'Lucifer', with orange-red flowers. It gets 4 feet tall and needs staking. The coolest of all crocosmias are *C. solfatare*, with elegant bronze foliage and yellow flowers, and 'Star of the East', with orange blooms that are the biggest of all crocosmia flowers.

Delphinium: One of my favorite perennials, the delphinium blooms with flowers that are irresistible to hummingbirds. Plant in full sun and rich, moisture-holding, well-drained soil. Feed heavily, and never allow the soil to dry out.

Kniphofia (torch lily): The repeat-blooming flowers come in shades of red, orange, and yellow that are extremely attractive to hummingbirds. When the flowers fade, the seeds are an important food source for nuthatches and other songbirds. The foliage is spiky; in my opinion, the varieties with finer foliage are the most attractive. Give *Kniphofia* full sun, but make sure the soil remains moist; torch lilies are not drought tolerant.

Lobelia: These easy-to-grow, late-blooming, sun-loving annuals and perennials give hummingbirds a reason to stay longer in your garden.

Monarda (bee balm): These moisture-loving plants can be aggressive, but it's not hard to yank out unwanted ones. Their long blooming period in the middle of summer make them a great plant for rich soil in full sun. 'Jacob Cline' is a red-flowering variety that is a magnet for hummingbirds.

Salvia: Another member of the mint family that is guaranteed to attract hummingbirds. There are endless varieties to try. Some aren't reliably hardy, but all bloom the whole summer long in full sun and well-drained soil. Experiment with different species and varieties to see which work best in your garden.

Campsis (trumpet vine): These clinging vines climb quickly cover walls at astounding rates. The flowers are usually orange or red, and hummingbirds give them a lot of attention. These are drought-tolerant vines that require full sun to bloom well. Watch out: they tend to form suckers. Pull any that appear, or you'll have lots of them in no time.

You'll swear it's a hummingbird.

Q How can I attract a rare **hummingbird moth** to my garden? I've heard they look and fly just like hummingbirds.

A If you plant the right perennials and annuals, you might luck out and attract a rare hummingbird moth. Hummingbird moths are actually white-lined sphinx moths. They fly just like hummingbirds and have a 3-inch wingspan. They are attractive in flight, featuring white-streaked forewings and pink-banded hind wings. Although these hummingbird mimics are rare, I occasionally see them visit the same nectar-rich flowers that hummingbirds and butterflies love, such as columbines, delphiniums, *Abutilon*, petunias, nicotianas, and honeysuckles. By the way, if you find a 3-inch-long, bright green, dark-spotted caterpillar with a horn on its tail, give it a home in a shoebox or an aquarium. They pupate underground, so add a 3-inch-deep layer of soil. Toss in a bit of whatever they were eating, and soon you'll hatch your own hummingbird moth right in your house. Don't tell your partner. You haven't lived until you see their face when they discover a hummingbird moth flying around in the house.

Create an Audubon masterpiece for Mama.

Q Every year the kids and I plant up a container and give it to Mom for Mother's Day. This year we want to try something different, maybe a container full of **plants that attract birds**. Do you have any suggestions?

A This year for Mother's Day, surprise the living tweetle out of Mom by presenting her with a stunning container filled with plants that attract hummingbirds. Pick a good-sized container. Then begin plant selection by choosing an attractive centerpiece. Don't worry if it attracts hummingbirds; just try to find something showy that is in proportion to the size of the container. Then fill in with midsized plants known to attract the little avian acrobats. Flowering annuals such as nicotiana, pelargoniums (zonal geraniums), *Cleome*, and zinnia are hummingbird favorites that bloom all season long. To add interest, mix in a few perennials that not only attract hummers but also have colorful foliage, such as *Heuchera*, salvia, or lobelia. Finish up by cramming in some spillers, such as nasturtium, annual lobelia, or *Zauschneria*, which will tumble over the side with flowers that will drive hummingbirds crazy with desire. Won't Mom be impressed!

Throw a holiday blast for the birds.

Q I love birds and colorful fruit. I found what appears to be the perfect plant, a **pyracantha or firethorn**, at my local nursery. Do birds like the fruit, and if so, what conditions does firethorn need?

A Birds won't touch the attractive fruit of *Pyracantha* (firethorn) until the berries ferment in early winter. Then every bird from miles around will fly in to join the festivities. When I was the manager of grounds at Seattle University, the birds used to get so drunk that I actually had to stop traffic to allow my inebriated feathered friends to stagger across the road. Pyracantha needs full sun and is easy to grow in almost any kind of soil. Once established, it is as drought tolerant as a rock. Buy it when in fruit to get the perfect color for your garden. Then get ready for a raucous party.

Invite spiders into your garden.

Q I swear that half the **spiders** in the state live in my garden. Are they doing some good out there, or am I at risk by hosting so many spiders in my garden?

A Spiders play a key role in helping to control harmful insects. They eat more bad bugs than does any other creature. The more spiders you can persuade to live in your garden, the less pest control you need to worry about. Although there are health concerns related to a house spider commonly known as the hobo spider, none of the common spiders found in the garden are harmful to humans. Instead, most protect human health by eliminating disease-carrying insects such as mosquitoes and fleas. You can do several things to attract more spiders. Apply light, fluffy mulch such as grass clippings, leaves, or wood chips. Plant closely so that the leaves of plants touch, and allow grass to reach 3 inches tall before mowing it to 2 inches. Avoid using broad-spectrum pest controls; they are deadly to spiders. In short, be nice to Charlotte and she'll put her web to "terrific" use in your garden.

It's not a bug problem.

Q Something is making a uniform pattern of holes from the top to the bottom of my birch tree. Recently I saw a **woodpecker** on the tree looking for bugs. Is my tree a goner?

A Don't panic. Chances are it's not an invasion of wood-boring insects making these holes. Instead, it's a beautiful 8 ½-inch woodpecker. This bird isn't looking for bugs in your tree. Instead it pecks its way from the bottom to the top of the tree and then works its way from bottom to top again to drink the sap that fills the holes it made on the first run. The most common of these woodpeckers is the yellow-bellied sapsucker. It's a spectacular bird, with a bright yellow breast and a red crown and throat, surrounded by black bands. If you're really lucky, the bird feeding in your tree may be the rarely seen red-breasted sapsucker. This handsome guy is decked out in red plumage on its head, neck, and breast. As a general rule, the birds feed in pairs, and although the damage they inflict might look bad, it won't kill or even seriously harm most trees. For some unknown reason, however, once in a while, huge populations of the woodpeckers choose an unlucky tree for their favorite restaurant and feed so heavily they kill it. C'est la vie! Buy a replacement and think of it as a living bird feeder.

Make a housing development for wildlife.

 Sadly, one of our big old fir trees died recently. It's not located where it would do any harm if it fell down. If I leave the dead tree standing, will it attract wildlife?

A Don't be depressed because your fir tree finally gave up the ghost; your loss is another creature's gain. Assuming that the dead tree is located where it does not pose a safety hazard, you can safely leave it as a snag and it will become a condo for wildlife. Nearly seventy-five species of mammals and birds nest or den in snags, and another forty-five species forage for food in them. Your snag may attract small birds such as nuthatches, chickadees, woodpeckers, and kestrels, but if you are lucky, you might even attract hawks, eagles, and owls. So put the chainsaw away and get out the binoculars: Your dead tree is going to turn your backyard into a wildlife sanctuary.

Be persistent in your aphid control. That fat aphid on your plant is already pregnant with a cluster of live young, and each baby inside Momma already has a cluster of live young in her, and each one in her has a cluster of live young, etc. They're like Russian dolls, open one up and there's another, and another, and another, and . . .

Shoo away pesky yellow jackets.

Q We bought a home with a patio because we love entertaining and serving dinner outdoors. Well, forget it! The **yellow jackets** are getting more of the salmon than we are. We tried hanging a fish head up to keep them busy, but there were so many of them that it didn't help. The yellow jacket traps we hung up are full of dead wasps but haven't seemed to put a dent in the yellow jacket population. Is there anything that will keep these intruders away, or are we stuck eating inside for the rest of the summer?

A When yellow jackets crash the party, it's practically impossible to enjoy a salmon and brussels sprout dinner on the deck or patio. Yellow jacket traps, not to mention the old trick of hanging a salmon head over a tub of soapy water, do little to dissuade the hordes of hungry wasps determined to share your dinner. Fortunately, yellow jackets cannot stand the smell of Bounce, the antistatic strips for the dryer. Hang some in tree branches or, if the wasps are really bad, put the strips right on the picnic table. (Tell the kids not to touch them, as I have no idea what's in those things.) The number of strips you'll need depends on how heavy the yellow jacket pressure is. Unfortunately, only the scented kind works, and you may be repelled as well, but at least you'll be able to enjoy eating without worrying about getting a bite of yellow jacket along with your salmon.

CHAPTER SEVEN

Garden Shed

Turn your home into an Italian villa.

Q My wife and I recently returned from a trip to Italy, where we loved the colorful walls and stone walkways. On returning home, our cement patio and walkways seem boring, and the bare concrete wall is just plain ugly. Is there any way to **add a touch of Italy** that will make the surfaces look a little better without costing us an arm and a leg?

A According to Thomas Hobbs, author of the best-selling *Jewel Box Garden*, a few treatments to hard surfaces can turn a so-so garden into a masterpiece. Plain-looking concrete patios and walkways detract from potential beauty, and ugly walls are blank canvases waiting for you to turn them into works of art. Rent a concrete saw (or hire someone) to cut a pattern into your concrete patio and surrounding walkways to create the look of stone pavers. Then stain the patio, walkways, and any bare walls to add a patina of age. Finally, go for the "Full Monty" and paint your house in a terra-cotta shade. Presto: Your home resembles an Italian villa, the perfect backdrop for a magnificent garden. Too bad you'll be too exhausted to go out and buy new plants to match the new look!

Grow a Christmas present for Grandma and Grandpa.

Q I thought it would be fun to have my kids grow an **amaryllis bulb** as a Christmas present for their grandparents this year. How should we go about it?

A Kids will love growing an amaryllis bulb to give to Grandma and Grandpa for Christmas. The huge bulbs are native to South America and are for sale at local nurseries. Choose a decorative pot that is 2 inches wider than the bulb, and set the bulb so that the top third is above the soil. Place it in full sun, water regularly, and stand back. The giant flowers grow so fast that the flower stalk is liable to knock you over! It takes four to six weeks before the spectacular trumpet flowers open, so pot it up in early November so that it will be about to bloom when the kids present their horticultural wonder to Granny and Gramps for Christmas.

Make a jungle Christmas tree.

Q I remember seeing you make a **bromeliad Christmas tree** on TV. It looked like a fun project to do with my kids. How did you do it?

A In the jungles of Costa Rica and Ecuador, Mama Nature decorates trees with beautiful bromeliads and strange-looking tillandsias (air plants). Go to a beach and find a weathered branch with enough side limbs to support several plants. Put it in an attractive pot, and fill in with stones around the branch to hold it securely in place. Remove the bromeliads from their pots and wrap the root balls with sphagnum moss. Tightly attach the root balls to the branches with green, plastic-covered wire, making sure all the wire is covered with moss. Tillandsias need no moss and can be placed in branch unions or anywhere else you can get them to stay. Keep the cups of the bromeliad filled with water, and mist the sphagnum moss and foliage of the bromeliads and tillandsias at least a couple of times per week. You'll feel as if you are enjoying Christmas in the tropics. Don't be surprised if a howler monkey comes down the chimney instead of Santa.

Make gardening fun for kids.

Q I read that you began gardening when you were only ten years old. My kids are nearly the same age, but show little interest. Have you any suggestions for a **fun way to get them excited about gardening**?

A It's easy to make gardening fun for kids: Just give them their own container to plant. Container gardening is a great way to get kids started because they can achieve a fabulous composition in a limited space, without having to weed or do lots of difficult maintenance. Begin with a little lesson in planting and caring for the plants, and then let them loose at your favorite nursery. At first you'll probably need to help the little ones pick out the plants, but before long you can give them a budget and let them pick out their own. Kids love designing and caring for their own container gardens, and they learn fast. The only problem is that it's a bit embarrassing when the kids' containers look way better than yours!

Discover surprising ideas.

Q Where's the best place to find **garden design ideas**? I read garden books, but it's hard to visualize how some of the ideas would work in my situation. Where do you find inspiration?

Attend garden tours to discover new ideas. You'll see fantastic designs, meet all sorts of gardening fanatics, and have a chance to chat with the homeowners or garden designers. Tours are fun because you never know what surprises you'll find. For example, years ago while attending a local garden tour, I noticed something odd about a recently constructed fence. It was obviously built for privacy, yet the section by the patio, where the homeowners dined regularly, was made up of big, open squares, allowing the neighbors to watch them as they ate. When I asked about it, the homeowner told me that when they built the fence, they forgot about the neighbor's dog, who regularly visited at dinnertime. The first time they dined after the new fence went in, they heard their old buddy crying on the other side. They felt so sorry for him that they had the fence company come right back and rebuild the patio section to allow old Fido to stick his snout through for dinner treats. There's another reason to attend local garden tours: The proceeds almost always benefit good causes. Keep an eye out for tour advertisements in the newspaper or at your local nursery.

Give your partner the perfect gardening gift.

 My partner likes to garden, and I'm a total addict. Can you suggest some gardening gifts that we both would enjoy?

 You bet! Here are some unusual gifts that you will truly enjoy giving to that special someone you garden with.

Light up your partner's life

A grow-light setup will enable you (I mean your partner) to grow rare and unusual vegetables, perennials, and annuals from seed. It will also enable you (I mean your partner) to store their huge succulent collection under lights in the cool garage in order to trigger blooming next spring and summer. And you can take cuttings of cool, rare plants from your friends' gardens that will make your (I mean your partner's) side of the garden look way better than their (I mean your) side.

Fill the house with blooms

Buy a collection of orchids. Even if your mate is not into orchids, they won't be able to resist the spectacular, long-lasting, and (in some cases) fragrant flowers. Of course, you'll have to put them in all of the best windows in the house, even if you have to move a few of your partner's existing plants, but they won't mind because they'll know that you are doing this strictly for their enjoyment.

Add an artistic flair to the garden

Your spouse will swoon when they look into the garden to see a water feature created by the famous artist team of Little and Lewis (www.littleandlewis.com). Maybe water will be trickling into a pond from an elegant moss-covered column, or perhaps it will be cascading from a superbly colored giant *Tetrapanax* leaf. Of course, your sweetie may be slightly disconcerted when they see that the art is located on your side of the garden. But it isn't your fault if the only electrical outlet is located way over on your side; you can feel confident that the soothing sound of the falling water will be audible throughout the garden, and the calming effect may save you from another visit to the marriage counselor.

Bring the mountains home

Here's the ultimate gift for the gardener in your life. Imagine the surprised look on their face when they wake to see several huge boulders piled in the driveway, next to a rented backhoe! Wait until they learn that you're going to use it to install a beautiful mountain scene in one of their gardens, right next to the house! There may be a few feeble objections, if your other half recalls the time you made that minor slip and put a two-ton rock through the side of the house, but since the boulders are already in the driveway, it shouldn't be too hard to convince your doubting sweetie that there really is no alternative. Besides, you know how ecstatic they'll be once the landscape is in place and the house is still standing!

Buy dad some top-quality hand pruners for Father's Day, and see if he'll give up his hedge shears. For the first time in years, you may end up with attractive, natural-looking shrubs instead of balls and doughnuts.

A bouquet of flowers works wonders.

Q I pruned the shrubs around the house using the hedge trimmer, and now my wife is threatening to use the hedge trimmer on me. I've already offered to take her to the Northwest Flower and Garden Show. Any other ideas on how I can **get back into her good graces**?

A Though it may be hard to believe, even I get myself into a little domestic hot water now and then. One thing I've learned is that a nice bouquet can reduce the number of nights spent cuddling with Fido on the couch. Fortunately for you, the Northwest Flower and Garden Show is the perfect place to get inspiring ideas on how to make a great flower arrangement. Problems caused by minor transgressions, such as having bought several expensive orchids, can usually be solved by copying one of the artistic combinations created by talented members of the Washington State Federation of Garden Clubs. For more serious lapses in judgment (such as getting caught planting on your partner's side of the garden), you may need to master the skills on display at the ikebana exhibition. Major faux pas (such as pruning everything in the garden into the shapes of balls and doughnuts) most likely require a spectacular creation such as the ones on display in the entry foyer, which are designed by the top professional florists in the state.

Decorate your house with prickly holly.

Q **Every year around the holidays, I decorate my home with boughs of holly. Is this an ancient practice, or is decorating with holly a modern idea?**

A Sometime in the distant past, the pagans of Europe placed sprays of holly in their homes to give fairies and elves places to hide as they did their good deeds. Although I worry about my puppy Fred eating the little people, there's actually a better reason to decorate with holly than having little do-gooders about. According to English and German folklore, a sprig of prickly leaved holly is a "he," while a sprig of the nonprickly holly is a "she." The type of holly first brought into the house at Christmastime determines who will be the head of the household the following year. I'll let you know if it works: I've been decorating the house with prickly sprigs since I learned about this in July.

Koi owners, watch your fish for aggressive tendencies.

Q **I'm thinking about raising koi in my pond, but I have two dachshunds who might enter the pond, and I'm concerned that the koi might hurt them. These prize show dogs are my pride and joy. Do koi bite or have aggressive tendencies that I need to worry about?**

A Don't let your dachshunds near the pond until you watch to see if it's safe! Fears of an aggressive gene in some koi have been substantiated. Concern surfaced after a young man was attacked by a koi named Howard at the Northwest Flower and Garden Show one February. The man escaped without serious injuries but suffered mental trauma, and blames his ongoing marital problems on the attack. Rumors that he was bitten are untrue; he actually suffered a massive hickey on the left side of his neck. Howard's virility is well known, and it's feared that the aggressive gene may have been handed down to his many offspring, thousands of which have been sold to unsuspecting pond owners throughout the Pacific Northwest. There is only one known diagnostic technique at this time: Avoid and report to authorities any koi that smile.

Sorry, only kidding. Your wiener dogs have nothing to fear from koi; however, you might want to protect the koi from your wiener dogs. I understand they can be vicious.

Plant a living legacy of Christmas.

Q We are going to plant a **living Christmas tree** this year. Is there anything we need to know to make sure our tree survives to become a long-lived reminder of Christmas?

A Living Christmas trees make a wonderful, and ideally long-lasting, reminder of a special Christmas. Don't forget that the cute little Christmas tree may turn into a 60- to 100-foot monster, however; if you plant a giant under the eaves of the house, your Christmas memory may end up as firewood twenty years later. The worst thing that can happen to a living Christmas tree is for it to dry out or break dormancy while on display in the house. Keep the root ball well watered, try to keep the room cool (under 70 degrees), and keep the tree in the house for only seven to ten days. Plant your tree in a well-drained, sunny location as soon as possible after bringing it back outside. If freezing weather is forecast, store it in an unheated garage and wait to plant it until milder conditions return.

Wanted: a few good gardeners.

Q I understand that you're a WSU Master Gardener. I'm trying to decide if I should take the training and become a **Master Gardener** myself. What can you tell me about the program?

A If I were you, I'd take the plunge. I'm proud to say that I've been a King County Master Gardener for more than twenty years. Master Gardeners are a fine group of folks who give garden advice to the public using scientifically proven, environmentally sound methods. You'll get some of the best training available from Washington State University professors and others. In return, trainees are required to complete sixty hours of volunteer service by the end of their training year. After that it gets easier, and you have to volunteer only twenty-five hours per year. There's a charge for the training, but some scholarship money is available. To get an application, visit www.metrokc.gov/dchs/csd/wsu-ce/gardening/mastergardener. By the way, not only are the Master Gardeners knowledgeable, but they have a wild side too, as is evidenced by that one-of-a-kind 2006 Kitsap County Master Gardeners' Gardening Au Naturel Calendar. Just call me Mr. November!

Mistletoe is magical stuff.

Q Where does the **mistletoe** used for Christmas decorations come from? Why are you supposed to kiss anyone who stands under mistletoe?

A Decorative mistletoe is a parasitic plant that's harvested mostly from oak trees. You can order it online, and most companies that sell it guarantee it'll last about a month. It's believed that the Druids were the first to use mistletoe as a holiday decoration. They dedicated the plant to the goddess of love and hung it above their doorways to bring good fortune and romance. Be careful how you use it. According to folklore, if you kiss someone under the mistletoe, his or her chances of getting married greatly increase. And research shows that after a passionate kiss, powerful endorphins remain active in the system for up to four hours. Add a couple of glasses of wine to the mix, and the person who received the kiss might not have to wait until the new year for a marriage proposal. Kiss under mistletoe if you dare, but don't eat under it. The berries are poisonous.

Give a basket to your condo mama!

Q Any suggestions of what I could give **Mom for Mother's Day**? She loves plants, but she lives in a condo with a deck.

A Run out to the nursery and buy Mom a nice hanging basket. Wondering how much to spend? Just think back to what kind of a kid you were, and what you put your mom through. Now fork out the bucks for the really big one!

Help the kids make a Mother's Day surprise.

Q The kids and I want to do something special for **Mom on Mother's Day**. We're looking for a gardening project that will impress her but that won't be too difficult.

A Why not surprise the living tweetle out of Mom by planting up a hanging basket for her? By Mother's Day, you can generally plant annuals without worrying about their suffering cold damage. Don't worry if you aren't the greatest at designing a container. Just choose a nice hanging cedar or coconut fiber pot. Quality nurseries have folks on hand to help you choose the perfect plants. They'll give you technical advice regarding how to plant it up and how to care for it as well. The kids will love helping make Mom a hanging basket, and will learn a few gardening skills in the process. Best of all, Mom might reward you with a brussels sprout casserole. Won't the kids love that!

Give your sweetie a spring surprise.

Q **Guess what? My partner and I divide up the garden the same way you and your wife do, and we fight over gardening territory just as you do. We recently removed an old tree, opening up a new gardening space. Any negotiating tips to help me win control over that space?**

A Amaze your partner and facilitate gardening by cleaning the garage. Eliminating dirt and debris, and reorganizing the impenetrable tangle of tools and equipment, will enable you to get your semihardy plants in and out of the garage on warm spring days. You might even find all of those cool tools you forgot you bought last year. But most important, cleaning the garage may help you in your efforts to win new gardening territory. You'll gain great advantage if you negotiate while your partner remains suspended in the out-of-body state they will experience upon realizing that you undertook this project without cajoling.

Plant a holiday surprise.

Q **My husband invited his side of the family to come stay for the December holidays. I can accept that the garden always looks pretty shabby in December, but I'm embarrassed that the big planters right next to the front door inevitably are full of dead plants that froze in the winter cold. What can I plant in my winter planters that will look presentable when the relatives come?**

A Fool your holiday guests by using cut conifer and shrub branches to add interest to your winter container plantings. Begin by planting a few florist cyclamen to provide colorful flowers. Then add an appropriately sized golden or blue conifer branch as a centerpiece. Conifer branches usually remain fresh-looking for a couple of weeks. Add colorful contrast by inserting long-lasting red or yellow dogwood twigs. For special effect, stick in a few holly or beautyberry branches, but wait to cut and add them until just before the guests arrive, since these additions won't last as long. Your guests will never suspect that your container is filled mainly with cut branches. For a little extra holiday fun, confuse the living tweetle out of your guests by discreetly changing the centerpiece to one of a different color several times while they are visiting.

Don't let your poinsettia gift wilt.

Q I just bought a huge **poinsettia** to give to a very special friend this holiday season. Last year I brought one home and before I knew it, all of the leaves had fallen off. Unfortunately, I'm stuck caring for this one for several days before I give it to my friend, and I don't want that to happen again. What do I need to do?

A One holiday season a friend of mine tried to impress a woman he hardly knew by surprising her with a huge poinsettia. Unfortunately, before giving it to her, he left it out in his freezing-cold car all morning. From her initial reaction, it seemed that his grand gesture was a big success. That is, until about five minutes later, when all but four of the leaves suddenly fell from the plant! Poinsettias are from tropical Mexico. They can't stand cold temperatures for long, and dropping their leaves is how they show their displeasure. When you buy that poinsettia, especially if it's a surprise for a special someone, take it home and keep it in a warm room rather than leaving it in the car while you shop or do errands. As soon as you get it home, tear some holes in the bottom of the decorative foil and place the pot in a plant saucer. If you don't remove the foil, it will prevent water from draining out, and the plant will drown. Poinsettias also drop their leaves if they dry out. Water whenever the soil surface feels dry, but don't forget to empty out any extra water that collects in the saucer. Keep the plant in the sunniest spot you can, but avoid placing it in a cold draft or where a heater vent blows right on it. Don't worry: As long as you do all of the above, the poinsettia should look great when you give it to your new friend. Of course, if you don't follow my directions perfectly, it will drop all of its leaves five minutes after you give it to her. Maybe next time you should give her a cactus.

Don't be a dim-dim.

Q I kept my **poinsettia** from last Christmas, and now I want to make it bloom again. I followed the instructions I heard you give on your radio show: I transplanted it and cut it back to about 4 inches last spring, and I've been growing it outside in full sun for most of the summer. I even pinched the growing points regularly to make sure that it branched well, and fertilized with a soluble houseplant fertilizer every two weeks. The plant looks great. Now how do I get it to rebloom?

A If you went to the trouble of keeping your poinsettia alive all summer, early October is the time to begin the darkness treatment to encourage it to flower again. Keep your poinsettia in total darkness for fourteen hours every night from now until the buds set, usually within ten weeks. Don't forget to bring it back out into a brightly lit spot every morning to keep it growing and healthy. Remember that if your poinsettia is exposed to any light whatsoever during the darkness period, flowering will be delayed for as long as a year. Speaking from experience, I strongly advise you to put a big sign on the poinsettia-closet door that reads, "Hey, dim-dim, don't open this door!"

Preserve your holiday decorations.

Q I cut branches from all sorts of evergreen trees for holiday decorations, but the holiday cheer doesn't last long, as my decorations soon turn brittle and drop their leaves. Is there a way to **preserve my holiday decorations** so I can keep the holiday spirit going a little longer this year?

A Evergreen branches from holly, eucalyptus, cedar, and many other plants can be preserved with glycerin to make holiday decorations that won't get brittle. Glycerin is a syrupy liquid that is often mixed with rose water and sold as a skin moisturizer. Straight glycerin can be purchased in pint containers at most drugstores. Mix one part glycerin with two parts very hot water and stir vigorously to combine. Stand stem ends in a 3-inch-deep solution (refill solution whenever less than 3 inches remains) and put in a dark, cool place for about two weeks. The supple and pliant branches will be easy to use in long-lasting holiday decorations.

Start early on next year's holiday gifts.

Q I have several rhododendrons and camellias that branch low. I'd like to layer some of the branches to **propagate new plants to give to friends** for the holidays next year. How exactly should I go about it, and when is the best time?

A It's hard to believe, but as soon as the December holidays are over, it's already time to begin making next year's gifts. Choose a low branch of an azalea, camellia, daphne, evergreen huckleberry, or almost any other type of broadleaf evergreen shrub. Cut a notch one-third of the way through the branch, at a leaf node that can be buried under the ground. Without removing it from the mother plant, bend the branch down and bury the section with the notch, making sure that the growing end remains above ground. Use a heavy stone or brick to keep the branch in place.

Next fall, gently tug to feel if the branch has rooted. If it pulls out easily, wait another year; if there is resistance, cut the branch from the mother plant where it entered the soil, carefully dig out the rooted portion, and pot it up in an attractive container. Voilà, a free (but hopefully much appreciated) holiday present.

A chrome digging spade is a gardening necessity for digging plants, dividing perennials, and slicing and dicing slugs. They also provide a welcome change from the multitude of candy dishes when you give them as wedding presents.

Protect fragile art and containers.

Q I recently bought a magnificent concrete sculpture at a flower and garden show. Now I'm beginning to wonder if freezing winter weather might harm it. I also have some expensive garden containers that I'm not sure can be left outside in winter. Is there a way to **protect garden art and containers** from freezing weather?

A Decorative garden art and outdoor containers are not always cold hardy. I learned this the hard way years ago. I purchased a giant skull and some bones that made it look as if a dinosaur had died in my garden. The faux bones, made of concrete, were amazingly realistic, and I loved the way they shocked the tweetle out of visitors when they discovered the huge skull hidden among the perennials—that is, until I left it out in a very cold winter without waterproofing it. Evidently, the concrete was porous. Water penetrated and then froze. Now the skull looks like a pitted concrete block with eye sockets, and I use it for a plant stand. Many planting containers will suffer the same fate if you leave them out in winter cold without applying waterproofing. If you own art fashioned out of concrete, or have planting containers you're not sure are weatherproof, check with the artist or the store where you purchased them to find out if the items in question are frostproof and if you can protect them if they aren't. If you're not sure, move them into a protected area before rain and freezing cold turn your expensive sculpture into a pitted plant stand.

Meet your gardening neighbors.

Q I'm new to town and I've noticed that many of my neighbors have terrific gardens. Can you advise me on the best way to get to know them and get them to **share their garden secrets** with me?

A One thing I love about gardening is talking to all the neighbors who walk by. That's why it takes me four hours to complete a one-hour task. Many cities sponsor an annual event dedicated to meeting your neighbors. In Seattle the tradition is called Seattle Night Out, and it's held in the first week of August. Folks in many neighborhoods get together for a block party. If your block isn't having a party, why not plan one? Not only will you be building a friendlier neighborhood, but you may just meet some pretty good gardeners with whom to share tips and perennial divisions. Plus, perhaps Ethel down the street cooks a mean brussels sprout surprise! If your city doesn't have an organized day to meet your neighbors, it's time for a little social activism to make it happen!

Acknowledgments

I'd like to thank the following friends who, in one way or another, helped me to write this book. To the "Group" (Diane Laird, Linda Cochran, David Lewis and George Little, Dan Hinkley and Robert Jones, Sylvia Matlock and Ross Johnson, Dick and Sue Brown, and my wife Mary): Thanks for the raucous evenings together, the stories, the Mexican adventures, the garden visits, the out-of-control plant-shopping excursions, the spectacular plants you've turned me on to and shared with me, and most of all, for the great friendship. To Meeghan Black, for being a great friend and for being as cool in real life as you are on TV. To Steve Boyd, for being such a great guy to work with and for your talented camera work that actually makes it look as if I know what I'm doing. To Anne Erickson, producer extraordinaire, for your humor and *joie de vivre*: You make the show as fun to shoot as to watch. To Jane and Myra for all those incredibly fun dinners we've shared. To past tour companions who have become great friends: Karen for keeping me revved up with chocolate chip cookies, DeLona and Megan for laughing at my stories that you've heard too many times, and Michele and Omana for all of the laughter you bring. To cheery Alyce and Dan, Don and Chris who are always great fun, Jeanne, photographer extraordinaire, and the adventurous "Stephanies," and finally the notorious "back of the bus gang" whose names will be kept secret to protect the guilty.

Also, to our French buddies Françoise et Patrick for suffering through my French, and perhaps most of all to the woman who makes all of our travel possible: Patti Allen, the greatest house-dog sitter on earth. To David Smithgal, my longtime friend and the craziest boss I ever had. To my bug buddies: Sharon Collman, for teaching me to love slugs (well, not to hate them as much) and Margaret

Sandelin for showing me that fleas really are poetic. A huge thanks to my fellow *P-I* writers Marianne Binetti and Marty Wingate for kidding and cajoling me into finishing this book, and to John Engstrom, *P-I* editor, for his patience and quirky sense of humor. A special thanks to the wonderful staff members who worked with me for so many years at Seattle University: DC "Clausini" Clausen, Patty Wright, John Easley, Janice Murphy, Lorn Richey, Lynn "Scooter" Schultz, and last but not at all least, Tom "Arnold Palmer" Swanson. I received too much of the credit for the results of your creative, hard work. Also to long-ago staff members David Helgeson, for turning me on to perennials, and Patty Cummings for helping me learn to be a manager. Also to her husband, John T., for sharing the best homemade wine in Oregon (and some of the best stories) every time we come down for a visit. Thanks also to Extension agent, friend, and teacher Gorge Pinyuh for supporting me and helping me get my start on TV and radio, and for your gallant, although not always successful, efforts to keep my tips and answers based on science. You know and taught me more about gardening than anyone else I'll ever know.

Finally, thanks to all the viewers and listeners of my shows and all of you who read my newspaper columns. You're the ones who make it possible for me to enjoy this incredibly fun and exciting life that I wouldn't trade for anything.

Index

heather (*Calluna*), 162; 'Beoley Gold', 162;
'Firefly', 162; 'Robert Chapman', 162;
'Sunset', 162; trimming, 161; 'Wickwar
Flame', 162
Hebe, 50; *H. speciosa*, 236
hedges
    arborvitae, 140
    Arbutus unedo (strawberry tree), 267–68
    laurel, 166; laurel, pruning, 167
    Photinia, 267–68
    Prunus lusitanica (Portugal laurel), 267
Hedychium (flowering ginger), 30–31; *H.
coccineum* 'Tara', 30–31
heliotrope, 234
hellebores. *See Helleborus*
    Helleborus
    double Oriental, affected by aphids, 25
    H. argutifolius, 36–37; 'Janet Starnes', 142,
      236
    H. foetidus (stinking hellebore), 37, 63,
      236; 'Gold Bullion', 63; 'Red Silver', 63;
      'Wester Flisk', 63
    hybrid Oriental, 35; moving, 34–35;
      reseeders, 36–37; susceptible to
      botrytis, 35–36
    Oriental, poisonous, 47
Heracleum mantegazzianum (giant hogweed),
285
herbicides: corn gluten, 247; vinegar, 250. *See
also* pesticides
Heuchera, 236; attractive to birds, 305;
'Obsidian', 63
Hibiscus, 222, 295; *H. rosa-sinensis* (tropical
hibiscus), 226
Hippeastrum (amaryllis), 312; encouraging
reblooming, 209–10
hogweed, giant (*Heracleum mantegazzianum*),
285
holly
    folklore, 317
    Ilex aquifolium (English holly), 163;
      'Argentea', 163; 'Bacciflava', 163; 'Ferox
      Aurea', 163
    poisonous, 230
honey bush (*Melianthus major*), 164; 'Antonow's
Blue', 164; 'Purple Haze', 164
honeydew, 136, 211
honeysuckle, winter (*Lonicera fragrantissima*),
289–90
hornets, bald-faced, 290
hose bibs, covering, 258
houseplants, 207–36; avoiding overfertilization,
218–19; bringing indoors in the fall, 231–32;
dealing with phototropism, 224; fertilizing,
217–18; nonpoisonous, 222; poisonous,
223–24, 230; spider mites, 223, 225; tolerant
of overwatering, 227–28; transplanting, 232,
233; watering with distilled water or rain, 231
hoverflies, 298
huckleberry, evergreen, propagating, 324-25
hummingbird moths, 304–5
hummingbirds: Anna's, 289–90, 299; gardens
attractive to, 299–304; plants attractive to,
289–90, 299, 305; shrubs attractive to, 300–1;
trees attractive to, 300; wintering, 299

Hydrangea
    changing color of flowers, 37
    drying flowers, 38
    H. arborescens (smooth hydrangea), 39
    H. aspera (Asian hydrangea), 39
    H. macrophylla (pom-pom and lacecap),
      38–39;
    pruning, 39
    H. paniculata 'Grandiflora' (Peegee
      hydrangea), 39
    H. quercifolia (oakleaf hydrangea), 38–39
    pruning, 38–39
    See also Dichroa febrigua (evergreen
      hydrangea)
Hypericum (St. John's wort), susceptible to rust,
195
hyssop (*Agastache*), attractive to hummingbirds,
303

I

Ilex aquifolium (English holly), 163; 'Argentea', 163;
'Bacciflava', 163; 'Ferox Aurea', 163
impatiens, when to plant, 4
insects: aphids, 25, 136, 211, 266–67, 308;
    asparagus beetles, 98–99; bamboo mites, 239;
    bee mites, 113–14; beetles, 291; beneficial, 298;
    beneficial spiders, 306–7; crane flies, 247–48;
    cutworms, 243, 251; earwigs, 248–49; fatsia
    susceptible to, 30; flea beetles, 98; fruit flies,
    219; fungus gnats, 219; houseplant, 211; leaf
    miners, 85, 168; mealy bugs, 211; protecting
    lilacs from, 168; rhododendron lace bug, 270;
    root maggots, 121; sawflies, 243; scale, 211;
    spider mites, 17, 140–41, 152–53; 220, 223, 225;
    tent caterpillars, 277, 279; yellow jackets, 308–9
Ipomoea (morning glory) 'Star of Yalta', 234
Iresine (bloodleaf), 222
Iris
    bearded, dividing, 7
    I. reticulata, 60; 'Harmony', 59; 'Natasha', 59
irrigation systems, 280–81; turning off for winter,
259
Italian-style remodel, 311–12

J

jack-in-the-pulpit (*Arisaema*), 40; *A. kelunginsularis*,
40; *A. sikokianum*, 40; *A. urashima*, 40; *A. wilsonii*,
40
jade plant, 223; *222*
jasmine. *See Jasmium*; *Trachelospermum
jasminoides* (star jasmine)
Jasminum: *J. officinale* (poet's jasmine), 41, 62; *J. o.
affine*, 41; *J. polyanthum*, 41; *J.* × *stephanense*;
41 most fragrant varieties, 40–41
Jerusalem cherry plant, 223–24
junipers: *see Juniperus chinensis* Pfitzer, pruning, 174;
J. c. 'Torulosa' (Hollywood juniper), 149
Juniperus chinensis: Pfitzer, pruning, 174; 'Torulosa'
(Hollywood juniper), 149

K

Kalanchoe (pregnant plant), 222
kale, 137
kiwi

fuzzy (*Actinidia deliciosa*), hand-pollinating, 109; harvesting, 111
harvesting, 110–11
kiwi vine (*Actinidia kolomikta*), 'Arctic Beauty', 110; harvesting, 111
Knautia, 50; deadheading, 4–5
Kniphofia (torch lily or red hot poker), 50, 64–65; attractive to hummingbirds, 303; 'Bee's Sunset', 64–65; 'Primrose Beauty', 64–65; 'Sunset', 64–65
kohlrabi, 123
koi ponds, 317–8

L

lacewings, 298
ladybugs, 298
larkspur, 71
late blight, 128–29
laurel hedges, 166; pruning, 167
Lavandula (lavender), 295; attractive to hummingbirds, 301; Spanish, 50; trimming, 167–68
lavender. *See Lavandula*
lawn mowers, sharpening blades, 262
lawns: caring for, 237–88; crane flies infesting, 247–48; dormant in summer, 280; fertilizing, 252–53; fertilizing for deep roots, 253–54; moss in, 262; watering, 279–80
leaf miners, 85; on lilacs, 168
lemon trees, Meyer, 97–98
lettuce, 116, 123–24
Ligularia dentate, 282
lilac (*Syringa*): encouraging blooming, 168–69; protecting from pests, 168; *S.* × 'Bailbelle' (Tinkerbell lilac), 153; *S. meyeri* (dwarf Korean lilac), 153; *S. m.* 'Palibin', 153; *S. m.* 'Superba', 153; *S.*
lilies, 41–42; Asiatic, 41; Aurelian hybrid (trumpet lilies), 41, 42; calla lilies (*Zantedeschia aethiopica*), 10;
lilies, canna lilies, 11; feeding, 42; Oriental hybrids, 41–42; poisonous, 230; staking, 51; 'Stargazer', 42. *See also* daylilies
lime, applying to vegetable gardens, 260–61
lime chips, 36
Little and Lewis, 298, 315
Lobelia: attractive to birds, 305; attractive to hummingbirds, 304; preventing legginess, 3–4
Lonicera fragrantissima (winter honeysuckle), 289–90
lucky bamboo (*Dracaena sanderiana*), 221–22
lupine, 71

M

maggots, 121
Mahonia
M. *bealei*, attractive to hummingbirds, 302
M. *lomariifolia*, attractive to hummingbirds, 302
M. × *media* (hybrid leatherleaf mahonia), 289; attractive to hummingbirds, 301–2; 'Arthur Menzies', 302; 'Charity' (winter-blooming mahonia), 236, 299, 302; 'Lionel Fortescue', 302; 'Winter Sun', 299, 302
mail-ordering plants, 263
manure, rabbit, 121. *See also* fertilizer

maple. *See Abutilon* (flowering maple); *Acer*
Maranta (prayer plant), 222
marigolds: French, companion planting, 98; preventing legginess, 3–4; when to plant, 4
Martha Washington geraniums. *See pelargoniums*
Master Gardener program, 319
mealy bugs, 211
Melianthus major (honey bush), 164; 'Antonow's Blue', 164; 'Purple Haze', 164
Meyer lemon trees, 97–98
mildew, powdery, 52, 188–89, 192, 257–58
Mina lobata (sunset vine), 234
Mint Mole Blaster, 261
Miss Willmott's Ghost (*Eryngium giganteum*), 43–44
mistletoe, 319–20; poisonous, 230
mites: affecting orchard mason bees, 113–14; bamboo mites, 239; spider mites, 17, 140–41, 152–53, 220, 223, 225
mock orange
Choisya (Mexican mock orange), 170
Philadelphus, encouraging blooming, 169; pruning, 171
mold, slime mold, 272
moles, deterring, 261
Monarda (bee balm), attractive to hummingbirds, 304
monkshood (*Aconitum*), avoid dividing, 24
montbretia (*Crocosmia* × *crocosmiiflora*), 296
morning glory, '*Ipomoea* Star o. f Yalta', 234
moss, 262
moths: hummingbird moths, 304–5; lilacs affected by, 168
mowers, sharpening blades, 262
Muehlenbeckia complexa (creeping wire vine), 236
mulch, organic, 263–64. *See also* compost/composting
mullein, self-seeding, 271–72
Musa basjoo (hardy banana), 160
mushrooms, growing indoors, 112
mustard greens, 116, 134–35
mycorrhizal fungus, 107
Myosotis sylvatica (forget-me-not), 43

N

Nandina (heavenly bamboo), 162–63; 'Bay Breeze', 163; 'Gulf Stream', 163; *N. domestica*, 236; 'Plum Passion', 163. *See also* bamboo
narcissus, paperwhite, forcing, 47–48
Nassella tenuissima (Mexican feather grass), 169–70
nasturtiums (*Tropaeolum majus*): affected by aphids, 45–46; attractive to birds, 305
nectarines/nectarine trees, thinning, 126–27
neen oil, 189
neighbors, meeting through gardening, 326
Nepeta (catmint), 50
netting, bird, 86–87
New Zealand flax. *See Phormium*
Nicotiana (flowering tobacco), 64; attractive to birds, 305; *N. sylvestris*, 64
night-fragrant plants, 64

tropical, for container gardens, 226; tropical-looking, 66. *See also* flowering plants; shrubs; trees; *individual entries*
Platycodon (balloon flower), avoid dividing, 24
Plectranthus (Swedish ivy), 222
Plumeria (frangipani): encouraging blooms, 54; rooting, 54–55
plums/plum trees: pruning, 111–12, 117–18; thinning, 126–27
pocketbook plant. *See Calceolaria*
poinsettias, 322–23; encouraging reblooming, 323
poisonous plants, 230; hellebore, 47; Jerusalem cherry plant, 223–24. *See also* nonpoisonous plants
poisons. *See* pesticides; slug bait
pollinating: with bees, 124, 293–94; fuzzy kiwis, 109
poppy, California, 71
potatoes: companion planting, 98; growing in a garbage can, 117; late blight, 128–29
pothos, poisonous, 230
potted plants, planting, 268
powdery mildew, 52, 188–89, 192, 257–58
prayer plant (*Maranta*), 222
pregnant plant. *See Kalanchoe*
primrose. *See Primula*
Primula (primrose): nonpoisonous, 222; *P. florindae* (cowslip), 55–56; *P. japonica*, 55–56; *P. vialii*, 55–56; protecting from slugs, 55–56
propagating: azaleas, 324–25; bromeliads, 9; camellias, 324–25; daphne, 324–25; deciduous plants, 178–79; evergreen huckleberry, 324–25; from hardwood cuttings, 159; rhododendrons, 324–25; roses, 178–79; shrubs, 324–25
pruning: bamboo roots, 200–1; barberry, 141; bare-root fruit trees, 82–83; *Buddleja* (butterfly bush), 143; camellias, 143; cherry trees, 94–95; *Cistus* (rockrose), 183; clematis, 13–14; elderberry, 155; everbearing raspberries, 100–1; fig trees, 101–2; forsythia, 157–58; fruit trees, 111–12, 117–18; hand pruners, 316; *Hydrangea macrophylla* (pom-pom and lacecap), 39; hydrangeas, 38–39; laurel and photinia hedges, 167; Pfitzer junipers, 174; *Philadelphus* (mock orange), 171; *Pieris*, 177; pines, 180; red twig dogwood, 198; rhododendrons, 182; *Rosa rugosa*, 184; roses, 184–85; roses, climbing, 187; sprouts created by, 146; trees and shrubs, 149–50; wisteria, 73–74
Prunus: P. lusitanica (Portugal laurel), 267; *P. maackii* (Manchurian cherry), 145; *P. serrula* (Tibetan cherry), 145
Pulsatilla (pasque flower), avoid dividing, 24
pumpkins, harvesting and storing, 119–20
purple passion plant. *See Gynura*
Pyracantha (firethorn), attractive to birds, 306
pyramidalis. *See Thuja occidentalis*

Q
quince, 290

R
rabbit manure, 121
radishes, avoiding root maggots, 121
rain: avoiding depression, 250–51; rain gauges, 238

Raintree Nursery, 80, 94, 109
raspberries: everbearing, pruning, 100–1; fertilizing, 120–21; thinning, 119–20; Tulameen, 120
rats, 246–47, 292
recipes, Brussels Sprouts with Caramelized Onions and Pecans, 91–92
red hot poker. *See Kniphofia*
redbud, *Cercis canadensis* 'Forest Pansy', 157
Rheum palmatum (ornamental rhubarb), 282
Rhodochiton atrosanguineus (purple bell vine), 234
rhododendron lace bug, 270
rhododendrons: deadheading, 180–81; fertilizing, 181; propagating, 324–25; pruning, 182; rhododendron lace bug, 270; *Rhododendron luteum* (yellow-flowering deciduous azalea), 75; transplanting, 182–83
rhubarb: fertilizing, 120–21; ornamental (*Rheum palmatum*), 282
ribbon plant. *See Dracaena sanderiana*
Ribes sanguineum (red flowering currant), attractive to hummingbirds, 302
ripening
    grapes, 106
    pears, 116
    tomatoes: green, 130–31; on the vine, 130
rockrose. *See Cistus*
root-bound plants, 173; transplanting, 232, 233
root maggots, 121
rooting. *See* cuttings
Rosa rugosa, 189; 'Fru Dagmar Hastrup', 184; 'Hanza', 184; pruning, 184; 'Scabiosa', 184
rosemary, 123, 295; folklore, 122
roses, 50; bare-root, 190; black spot, 187–88, 188–89, 192; climbing, pruning, 187; compost tea for, 192; deadheading, 186; disease-resistant, 189; Easy Elegance, 189; fertilizing, 191, 254, 255; floribunda, 186; hybrid tea, 186; increasing bloom, 190–91; 'Love and Peace', 189; orange, 171–72; 'Pat Austin', 172; powdery mildew, 188, 192; propagating, 159, 178–79; protecting from cold, 185; pruning, 184–85, 187; rose hips, 186; 'Royal Sunset', 172; rust, 188–89, 192; 'Westerland', 172
rotating vegetable crops, 122
rototilling, 244, 270–71
row covers, floating, 121
Rudbeckia (black-eyed Susan), 295
Russian sage (*Perovskia atriplicifolia*), 56
rust: blackberries, 85–86; roses, 188–89, 192; St. John's wort, 195
rutabagas, 137

S
St. John's wort (*Hypericum*), susceptible to rust, 195
salt buildup, avoiding, 218–19
Salvia: attractive to birds, 305; attractive to hummingbirds, 304; 'Black and Blue', 289; herbaceous, 50; *S. coccinea* 'Forest Fire', 226; *S. uliginosa* (bog sage), 56–57
Sambucus: S. nigra 'Eva' ('Black Lace' elderberry), 154–55, 197; 'Sutherland Gold', 197

About the Author

As the grounds manager at Seattle University for 24 years, Ciscoe Morris planted the largest organic ornamental garden in the Pacific Northwest. He is a master gardener and a certified arborist. He teaches at Seattle University, the Center for Urban Horticulture at the University of Washington, and Edmonds Community College. He makes weekly appearances in print in the Seattle Post-Intelligencer, and on the air on KIRO radio and KING5 TV in the Seattle area. Ciscoe landed his first gardening job as a lawn boy for a church in Wauwatosa, Wisconsin.